HARVARD HISTORICAL STUDIES

*Published under the direction of
the Department of History
from the income of
The Henry Warren Torrey Fund*

VOLUME LXI

RUSSIA AND THE WEST IN THE TEACHING OF THE SLAVOPHILES

A Study of Romantic Ideology

NICHOLAS V. RIASANOVSKY

State University of Iowa

HARVARD UNIVERSITY PRESS

Cambridge · Massachusetts

1952

Distributed in Great Britain by
GEOFFREY CUMBERLEGE
Oxford University Press
London

Library of Congress Catalog Card Number 52-9394
Printed in the United States of America

TO MY FATHER

ACKNOWLEDGMENTS

My study of the Slavophiles is a result of a long-standing interest in Russian history, in Russian culture, and in the intellectual development of modern Europe. I would like, therefore, to acknowledge my deep gratitude to the many devoted teachers who helped me study these subjects and especially to my parents, from whom I learned much of what I know about Russia, to Professor Gordon Wright of the University of Oregon, to Professor Michael Karpovich of Harvard University, to B. H. Sumner, the late Warden of All Souls College, and to Isaiah Berlin, formerly of New College and now of All Souls College. Mr. Sumner and Mr. Berlin were the supervisors of the original version of this study, which was written as a doctoral dissertation at Oxford University, and they gave their time and their knowledge unsparingly. In particular I must pay tribute to the kindness and courage of Mr. Sumner who, already fatally ill, maintained throughout my stay at Oxford a painstaking and helpful interest in my work. Another debt of gratitude is due to libraries and librarians: the Bodleian and the Taylorian libraries in Oxford, the British Museum Library in London, the Bibliothèque Nationale and several other libraries in Paris. The bounty of a Rhodes Scholarship enabled me to study in Oxford and travel in Europe.

My friends, Mr. George Bailey and Miss Lucile Townsend, read the entire manuscript and made many improvements. Mr. David Riede gave invaluable aid in compiling the index. The publication of this book was made possible by the generosity of two agencies: the Harvard Historical Series, and, through the courtesy of Dean Walter F. Loehwing, the Graduate College of the State University of Iowa.

N. V. R.

Iowa City, Iowa
October 2, 1952

CONTENTS

RUSSIA AND THE WEST IN THE TEACHING OF THE SLAVOPHILES

A Study of Romantic Ideology

CHAPTER I

INTRODUCTION

The perplexing question of Russia's relation to Western civilization has often conditioned and sometimes even dominated the development of Russian political and social thought. The significance of this relation was emphasized by those thinkers who regarded it not as a connection between the whole and its part, but as a contrast between two independent and usually hostile entities. The Slavophile ideology provided the most comprehensive and striking treatment of this perennial problem of Russia and the West. In doing so, it gave a fuller expression to many earlier views on the subject and also greatly affected most subsequent expositions of it.

National self-awareness and an interest in the West on the part of the Russians can be traced back to the Kievan period of Russian history, as well as to the period of the State of Moscow, which gave rise to the doctrine of Moscow as the Third Rome. The modern evolution of the problem of Russia and the West dates from the time of Peter the Great, whose momentous reforms brought Western culture to Russia. But at the same time that the eighteenth century witnessed a sweeping westernization of Russia, it also saw the growth of Russian criticism of the West.

An outstanding example of this criticism was contained in Fonvizin's able, bitter, and prejudiced letters in which that remarkable writer described his three visits to Western Europe between the years 1777 and 1787. Fonvizin's indictment of the West was comprehensive, but it shared with the other writings of the period the fundamental assumptions of the Age of Reason. Fonvizin did not postulate an impenetrable barrier between Russia and the West; on the contrary, he measured both parties by the same universal standards of excellence and concluded that Russia could better satisfy these standards.

The attitude toward the West which developed during the Age of Reason was continued by such nineteenth-century groups as Alexander's "Unofficial Committee" of advisers on the one hand, and the Decembrists on the other, but in general it was rapidly losing ground to new, romantic ideologies. The Decembrists themselves were radical reformers in the tradition of the Enlightenment and of the French Revolution, but they also represented the rising forces of nationalism and in that respect bore some resemblance to the Slavophiles.[1] A number of the Russian contemporaries of the Decembrists were already strongly influenced by such romantic doctrines as those of "complete" knowledge surpassing mere reason, organic state and society, historical dialectic and mission, both national mission and that of the chosen individual.

The Russian xenophobe nationalists of the nineteenth century were inspired by a hatred for everything alien, a feeling present to some degree in all societies and in all ages, but they were conditioned by romanticism and often expressed themselves in romantic terms. It was not so much a question of the specific influences of the French traditionalists on a Magnitskii, or of the German

---

[1] The patriotic sensitivity of the Decembrists was expressed in their poetry, notably in that of Ryleev, in the works of Pushkin and Griboedov, who were close to the Decembrist circles, in the projected Decembrist constitution which forbade the Russian monarch to leave his country for any length of time, and in the "ancient Russian," archaic terms which the Decembrists adopted to denote both the departments of their own organization and the future institutions of Russia.

Some Slavophiles knew the Decembrists well, and Khomiakov, then still in his teens, argued determinedly against the Decembrists and their ideas. It is extremely unlikely that the Decembrists made a direct contribution of any significance to the Slavophile ideology, although L. Brodskii argued in detail in favor of such a contribution. He mentioned, in addition to the points listed above, the interest in Slavdom of A. Odoevskii and of the secret Society of the United Slavs, the religious element in Ryleev and Pestel, the Christian foundation of the reforms proposed by Trubetskoi and by Steingel, and suggested that all this may have influenced Khomiakov and Slavophilism. Brodskii's unconvincing argument is characteristic of his tendency to exaggerate the liberal aspect of Slavophilism. N. Brodskii, *Rannie slavianofily*, pp. XXXII–XXXV.

romanticists on a Shevyrev, as of certain basic romantic assumptions made even by those nationalists who were strangers to any sort of philosophy and who were convinced that their views had nothing in common with Western ideas. The first assumption was that of a difference in kind, of an impassable gulf between Russia and the West. Next came the belief that this fundamental difference was produced by distinct sets of spiritual principles which lay at the foundations of the two societies and determined their histories. Finally, it was natural to conclude that the true Russian principles were bound to triumph over the false ones of the West, and that in the future Russia would dominate its opponents by its might and glory, or even reconstruct the whole of human society on new foundations. The nationalist analyses of Russia usually conformed to the romantic pattern and emphasized the particular spiritual principles of the nation, the providential meaning of its history, and the peculiar nature of its spirit as revealed in its language and institutions.

Russian nationalism was stimulated by the Napoleonic wars culminating in the great invasion of Russia in 1812, the crushing defeat of the French, the victorious advance of Russian armies in Western Europe, the final collapse of Napoleon, and the new importance which Russia attained at the Congress of Vienna and in subsequent European politics. The Russian role in world history was no longer confined to the realm of theory, but presented itself as a staggering fact to be admired and interpreted. Size had always been the mark of Russia. Power, the gigantic physical, military, political power of Russia, could no longer be questioned. Russia had faced the West, and Russia had defeated the West. While the Decembrists objected to the fact that the political might of Russia was accompanied by the misery of her natives, many conservative nationalists considered this power to be providential, a certain guarantee of a future of unparalleled splendor. The year 1812 became as great a landmark in Russian thought as it was in Russian history. The Slavophiles listed it together with 862, the calling of the Varangians; 988, the conversion of Russia to Orthodox Christianity; and 1613, the defeat of the Catholic Poles and the election of the Romanov dynasty to the throne of

Russia, as one of the splendid and significant moments in the life of Russia, an expression of her true essence.

Extreme xenophobe nationalism formed the main inspiration of *The Russian Messenger*, a monthly review which was founded by S. Glinka in 1808 and which attracted a considerable number of enthusiastic readers from the lower gentry and the middle class. Glinka had been brought up in the Gatchina Military School, where all teaching was done in French. In the army he experienced a conversion to everything Russian and simultaneously developed a blind hatred of the West. Glinka's violent, venomous attacks against Europe and his ignorant and enthusiastic admiration of the Russian past were more significant as signs of the time than for any particular ideological content. As to Glinka's technique, one may mention his love of comparison between the leaders of European and of Russian culture, a comparison in which Glinka refused to admit defeat even when E. Kostrov was matched with Homer. For instance:

We shall not call Mademoiselle Volkova a new Sappho: the Greek maiden Sappho sang the raptures of passionate and ecstatic love; the Russian maiden Volkova dedicated her pen to virtue, tsar, and fatherland.[2]

Rostopchin, the governor of Moscow in 1812, was another founder of the extreme nationalist school. As in the case of Glinka, Rostopchin's education was French, and his French remained vastly superior to the self-styled popular Russian, in which he addressed the people in various pamhlets and posters. When Slavophilism was becoming a major factor in Russian intellectual life, the extreme chauvinism of the Glinka-Rostopchin brand was clearly represented by *The Lighthouse of Contemporary Enlightenment and Education*, a magazine which came out in 1840, edited by S. Burachek and P. Korsakov.

"Archaeological" nationalism also was strikingly represented by Admiral A. Shishkov and his group. As early as 1803 Shishkov had published his "Reflections about the Old and the New Style," and in 1804 an "Addition" to the "Reflections," in which he main-

[2] Quoted from: N. Koliupanov, *Biografiia Aleksandra Ivanovicha Kosheleva*, volume one, book one, p. 255.

tained that Russian and Church Slavonic were one and the same language and condemned all deviations of the former from the latter as noxious foreign borrowing. The real Russian language was, according to Shishkov, extremely ancient and basic to all other languages, which were simply its derivations. Shishkov spent much time and effort in an attempt to restore its purity by eliminating all words of foreign origin and replacing them with true Russian stems.[3] He also engaged in a heated polemic against the Russian writers, especially Karamzin, who had been seduced by the West and were destroying their native language. Shishkov's glorification of the Russian past was united with an extremely reactionary attitude to the Russia of his own day, a combination also present in Rostopchin and in the extreme nationalist school in general. Later, as Minister of Public Instruction, Shishkov argued that literacy of the common people, and especially of the peasants, would do more harm than good. Shishkov had a small, but influential group of followers, especially in the Russian Academy of which he was a member from 1796, and his views were expressed in the press by *The Russian Messenger* and by *Democritus*. Shishkov's fantastic contribution to philology was superseded in 1820 by A. Vostokov's scholarly "Reflections about the Slavonic Language," but Shishkov's influence on political thought was more lasting.[4]

The Slavophiles scorned most extreme nationalists, but they found a few kind words for Shishkov. Their own linguistic studies presented numerous parallelisms to Shishkov's "Reflections," and their very name of *Slavophiles* had been originally applied as a gibe to the Shishkov group. Finally, there was a direct personal link: Sergei Timofeevich Aksakov, famous writer and father of two leading Slavophiles — Konstantin and Ivan, was an admirer of Shishkov and belonged to his circle.

[3] One may appreciate Shishkov's efforts by glancing at the results of a similar Anglo-Saxon "restoration." E.g., "impenetrability of matter" became "ungetthroughsomeness of stuff."

[4] In spite of their ridiculous aspects, Shishkov's linguistic studies were important as pioneer works in the field. For a recent evaluation of Shishkov's contribution to scholarship, see V. Vinogradov, "Russkaia nauka o russkom literaturnom iazyke," in *Uchenye Zapiski*, volume III, book 1, Moscow, 1946, pp. 22–147, esp. pp. 40–46.

Various domestic and foreign influences such as the new "mysticism" of the emperor, the extremely conservative policy of the Holy Alliance, and the pressure of the Russian obscurantists, combined to produce the reaction against philosophy and education which marked the last years of the reign of Alexander I. Magnitskii, one of the main promoters of the reaction, saw it as a battle against the Prince of Darkness himself, who was leading the final assault against church, state, and society. The word, the press, books were the principal weapons of evil; university professors its chief agents. The philosophy of Kant, the doctrines of Fichte, the theories of the empiricists were all found to be equally pernicious, and were all to be banned from Russia. The University of Kazan, cleansed by Magnitskii himself, suffered most, but great destruction was also wrought at the universities of St. Petersburg and Kharkov by P. Runich and Z. Karneev respectively. The pietistic and obscurantist Minister of Public Instruction, A. Golitsyn, who believed that all social sciences should be replaced by the study of the Holy Writ, also played an important role, as did such extremely severe censors as A. Krasovskii. Professors suspected of even a modicum of independent thought had either to experience a sudden "conversion," as in the case of Sreznevskii, or be dismissed, as was the fate of his colleague Solntsev. The purified University of Kazan became a peculiar species of monastic barracks; the discipline was extremely severe; the writings of the Age of Reason were purged from the library, while thousands of Bibles were purchased to edify the students; a complicated mechanism of spying was set up to buttress the new order; and a double system of chronology was instituted at the University: the regular calendar chronology and the second set dated from Magnitskii's reforms.[5]

The growth of Russian historiography was more important for the development of nationalist ideology than were Shishkov's

---

[5] Magnitskii's fall illustrates the measure of the insolence and the groundlessness of his denouncements: Magnitskii informed Alexander I against his brother Nicholas, then a Grand Duke and not generally considered as heir to the throne; when Nicholas became emperor he found the denouncement among his brother's papers and had Magnitskii summarily dismissed from service.

linguistics, Golitsyn's moods, or Magnitskii's ravings. As eighteenth-century foreshadowings of this growth, one may cite M. Shcherbatov's dissatisfaction with the corruption of the contemporary Russian society and I. Boltin's defense of Russia vis-a-vis the West in his able "Notes to Le Clerc's History of Ancient and New Russia," published in 1788. But the greatest influence on nationalist thought was exercised by N. Karamzin, a leading Russian literary figure of his age, eleven volumes of whose history of Russia were published between 1816 and 1824, and the twelfth shortly after the author's death in 1826. The *History*, which began with the formation of the ancient Russian state and ended abruptly in the Time of Troubles, acquired a great popularity overnight and affected all subsequent discussion of Russian history. One reason stands out as the explanation of Karamzin's success: in the age of nationalism and romanticism Karamzin gave Russia a past, a glorious history quite comparable to the histories of the Western nations. Karamzin affirmed the worth of Russia, of her past, of her basic principles. Of these principles he considered autocracy as the most important one, as an absolute essential for the power or even the very existence of the Russian state. His remarkable literary talent, historical erudition, and moralizing fervor were all directed towards demonstrating the successes which resulted whenever Russia followed sound principles and the perils which had occurred and were bound to occur with every deviation from them. Karamzin wrote in the capacity of official historian, and he may well be regarded as a forerunner of the scholars of the type of Pogodin and Shevyrev, who emphasized enthusiastic support of the existing regime.[6]

[6] By the great stimulus which he gave to the nationalist thought, Karamzin exercised a strong influence on the Slavophiles, among others. At least two of the Slavophiles, Konstantin Aksakov and Koshelev, read Karamzin's *History* at a very early age and were taught by it to love and admire the Russian past. The Slavophiles disagreed with Karamzin's *History* on a number of essential points; in particular they objected to its neglect of the Russian people as distinct from the state, but they retained nevertheless a considerable appreciation and even love for it.

Contemporaries, for instance Belinskii, who stated once in an article that Slavophilism began with Karamzin's idealization of the time of Ivan III, as well as most students of the subject, were well aware of Karamzin's in-

The problem of national history, to which Karamzin gave a firm foundation, was further developed by various Russian intellectuals influenced by the romantic tendencies of the age. For instance, N. Polevoi in his *History of the Russian People*, published in 1829–1833, stressed the continuous, organic nature of the development of Russia, differentiated between the "historic" and the "nonhistoric" peoples and between two types of nationality — nationality as national peculiarity and nationality as creative originality, and tried to elucidate the role of Russia in world history. N. Nadezhdin, an outstanding professor and journalist, emphasized the peculiar character of Russia, the autochthonous nature of Russian history. He was skeptical of the Russian past and critical of the present, but considered the very existence, the size, and the youth of the country as a guarantee of a splendid future. The specialist in language and literature, K. Zelenetskii, argued in the spirit of Herder and Schelling that Russia, as well as every other nation, was destined to give a full development to one particular aspect of the life of humanity.

The *History of the Russian State*, was not Karamzin's only contribution to Russian political thought. In 1795 in his "Correspondence of Meliodor with Filaret" he was the first Russian to make significant generalizations concerning the French Revolution, which he saw in relation to the entire system of European civilization, and which he condemned in terms not unlike those of Burke. Gradually Karamzin formulated his doctrine of the fundamental opposition of Russia to the West: Russia stood for the established order, for autocracy, and for Christianity, the West represented atheism and revolution. The new ideology of the once liberal Karamzin was expressed very sharply in his "Memorandum about the Old and the New Russia," which he presented to Alexander I in 1811. The "Memorandum" was meant as a warning to the emperor against the projected constitutional and liberal reforms, and it began with a brief outline of Russian

---

fluence on the Slavophiles. M. Koialovich even made the extravagant claim that the Slavophile doctrine of the primacy of the inner, moral life of man as compared to the state and its institutions had its origin in Karamzin. M. Koialovich, *Istoriia russkogo samosoznaniia po istoricheskim pamiatnikam i nauchnym sochineniiam*, p. 252.

history intended to prove that the fortunes, the very life of Russia were inseparably connected with the institution of autocracy. A criticism of all projects to limit the power of the sovereign followed: such plans were found to be inadmissible both on general grounds and especially in their application to Russia. Next there was a defense of serfdom and of all the privileges of the gentry, and an argument advocating a further strengthening of the gentry, as well as of the Holy Synod. Karamzin's views were summed up in the famous sentence which declared that Russia needed fifty good provincial governors, and not reforms. In another memorandum, "An Opinion of a Russian Citizen" about Poland, Karamzin discussed the Polish problem in the same conservative vein. Practically all component elements of subsequent Russian nationalism can be found in Karamzin's writings. A detail, especially interesting in connection with Slavophilism, is that Karamzin took in his "Memorandum" a rather negative view of Peter the Great.

The conservative ideas of Karamzin, the entire trend of conservative nationalism culminated in the reign of Nicholas I in the doctrine and the practice of so-called Official Nationality. Official Nationality was created in 1833, when S. Uvarov became the Minister of Public Instruction and proclaimed his famous triple formula of "Orthodoxy, Autocracy, and Nationality." [7] Actually autocracy dominated the entire ideology of the proponents of Official Nationality. Orthodoxy came to mean an effective control of the church by the state, for religion was an important safeguard against disorder. Nationality, the most mysterious member of the trinity, was entirely at the service of autocracy. It was interpreted to mean the affirmation and the defense of the established, national order of things, including serfdom.

The official doctrine had its journalists, its writers, and its professors, as well as censors and police. F. Bulgarin and N. Grech were the most notorious journalists of the school, and they also tried their hand in literature. The views of the govern-

[7] *Nationality* is a very inadequate translation of *narodnost.* Perhaps the Russian word as used by Uvarov can be traced back to the German *Volkstumlichkeit.* Throughout my study I shall use *nationality* for *narodnost,* and either *nation* or *people* for *narod.*

ment were also reflected by such writers as the historical novelist,
M. Zagoskin, the writer of the tales from the life of the people,
V. Dal, and the playwright, N. Kukolnik. Much greater literary
figures, Zhukovskii and Gogol, were in many ways close to
Official Nationality.

Of the professors, M. Pogodin and S. Shevyrev, both of the
University of Moscow, were especially important. Pogodin in his
Russian History and his other writings gloried in the size and
the power of Russia, in the providential guidance evident in the
Russian past, in the assured magnificence of the Russian future.
Influenced by romanticism, he attached a particular significance
to the fundamental principles on which Russia was based, to
the seed out of which it grew: these foundations were peace and
harmony, in contrast to the Western principles of conquest and
strife. Pogodin supported his scheme of history by means of
outrageous generalizations and analogies, again very much in
the spirit of the Romantic era.[8]

Shevyrev specialized in literature and literary criticism, but
he became especially well known for his panegyrics on Russia
and the Russian character, which he considered to be based on
humility, and for his violent denunciation of the West. Shevyrev
was largely responsible for the introduction of the expression
"the putrid West," and his statements on the subject included
the famous passing remark to the effect that three great Russian
rivers properly directed from Alpine heights would have been
sufficient to drown all the Italians.[9] Behind the manifold activity

[8] Pogodin's analogies were cruder than the general run. See P. Miliukov's
brief analysis of them. E.g., "In Asia there is China, in Africa Egypt corre-
sponds to it, — what should correspond to both of them in Europe?" P.
Miliukov, *Glavnye techeniia russkoi istoricheskoi mysli*, pp. 311–313, p. 312.

[9] Both Shevyrev and Pogodin were scholars of considerable merit. On
Shevyrev see especially P. Struve's little-known article in which Struve described Shevyrev's contribution to learning and analyzed Shevyrev's attitude toward the West and the sources of that attitude. Shevyrev, it seems,
never used the exact expression "the putrid West," but he did describe the
West in terms which could easily give rise to this expression. P. Struve,
"S. P. Shevyrev i zapadnye vnusheniia i istochniki teorii-aforizma o "gnilom"
ili "gniiushchem" Zapade," in *Zapiski Russkogo Nauchnogo Instituta v
Belgrade*, 1940, pp. 201–263.

of Official Nationality loomed the figure of the emperor Nicholas I himself.[10]

The Slavophiles scorned Official Nationality as a whole and denounced many of its specific doctrines. The contrast between the two ideologies was emphasized by the different positions of their respective proponents in regard to the government. Although the supporters of Official Nationality included men of education, ability, and vision, and although Uvarov himself cherished a grandiose dream of a new Russian civilization destined to combine the wisdom and the experience of the West and of the East, the very *raison d'être* of Official Nationality was its service to the government: political needs came first, everything else was subservient to them. In theory, Uvarov stressed the State which possessed the full power of control and which was always right. In practice, Official Nationality meant not only the propagation of government ideology by all possible means, but also a ban on every other form of thought. The Slavophiles were, by contrast, independent thinkers, not government apologists.

But while the Slavophiles regarded Bulgarin's type as the very essence of base flattery, they made very important qualifications in favor of Pogodin and Shevyrev. The two were both spokesmen of Official Nationality and friends of the Slavophiles, as well as teachers of some of the younger Slavophiles at the University of Moscow. The Slavophiles often resented their quasi-official views and argued sharply against them, but they also coöperated with them in several publications and showed a considerable appreciation of their work.[11] In the case of Shevyrev, the Slavophiles' praise definitely outweighed their blame. Such Slavophile con-

[10] Nicholas I, it seems, was both the main planner and the chief executive of his own system. He regarded himself as the competent and the supreme arbiter of everything in Russia, including all matters pertaining to intellectual life and culture. Many writers have strongly criticized the regime of Nicholas I. For a recent defense of the emperor see the work of L. Strakhovsky who claimed that Official Nationality as practised by Nicholas I was superior to any other contemporary doctrine: L. Strakhovsky, *L'empereur Nicholas Ier et l'esprit national russe.*

[11] Petr Kireevskii was provoked into a printed polemic only once in his life, and the man who provoked him was Pogodin. The entire polemic is to be found in the *Moskvitianin* for 1845. Miliukov, *op. cit.*, pp. 318–319, indicates the fundamental differences underlying the views of Pogodin and of

cepts as that of the peaceful origin of Russia in contrast to the role of conquest in the West; of humility as the foundation of the Russian character; and of the decline of the West, as well as some others, were developed in conjunction with Shevyrev and Pogodin, who in turn used Slavophile thought for purposes of their own.

The development of the doctrines of reactionary nationalism from Fonvizin to Pogodin exercised a considerable influence both on the general outlines and the particular aspects of Slavophilism, with which it was connected by some important similarities in the treatment of the common basic problem of Russia and the West. Extreme nationalism, however, formed only a part of the Slavophile background and not the most significant part. A greater weight may well be attached to the growth of romanticism, German idealistic philosophy in particular, and its spread in Russia.

Two related influences paved the way for German idealistic philosophy in Russia: Freemasonry and mysticism. The first Russian Masonic lodges were organized in the seventeen-thirties, and soon Freemasonry became connected with the entire intellectual development of Russia in the Age of Reason. Novikov, Schwarz, Gamaleia, and other Masons distinguished themselves as teachers, translators, and publishers, as the most active force of the Russian Enlightenment. But Freemasonry also represented a reaction against the dominant belief in reason. Following Rousseau, the English moralists, and similar contemporaries, Gamaleia, Lopukhin, and other Russian Masons were in search of more complete and satisfying forms of knowledge and of life. "The inner essence of man," "true knowledge," "the awakening of the heart" became the centers of attention and hope and gave rise to a special mood, a specific Masonic attitude toward the world.

This was the sentimental education of Russian society, the awakening of the heart. In Freemasonry the future member of the Russian intelligentsia recognizes for the first time the lacerated nature, the duality

Petr Kireevskii. See also the treatment of this episode in M. Gershenzon's essay on Petr Kireevskii in M. Gershenzon, *Istoricheskie zapiski.*

of his existence and begins to yearn for wholeness and to stretch towards it. This search, anguish, and urge are repeated later in the generation of the thirties (and the forties), in particular among the Slavophiles. From the psychological point of view Slavophilism grows precisely out of Freemasonry of the time of Catherine. . . .[12]

It may be added that the Masonic element was especially strong in the Kireevskii family, which produced two of the leading Slavophiles.

Eighteenth-century Russia had interesting mystical thinkers, notably P. Velichkovskii and G. Skovoroda, but the influence of Western mystical writers was of greater significance for the development of Russian romantic thought. Gamaleia, Labzin, and some others were its chief agents, and Freemasonry the main vehicle of its diffusion. Jacob Boehme, Jung-Stilling, Saint-Martin, and other outstanding Western mystics were all translated into Russian and all acquired an enthusiastic Russian following. Labzin's review, *The Messenger of Zion*, reflected both the Masonic background and the complex nature of Russian mysticism. This mysticism gradually disassociated itself from Freemasonry and became an independent intellectual current leading directly to German idealistic philosophy, which it foreshadowed with its metaphysics and its dialectical struggle of good and evil. It is significant that the Russians were especially affected by the more religious aspects of romantic philosophy.

When Western idealistic philosophy began to spread, education in Russia was still largely a privilege of the gentry, although the number of intellectuals from other classes was increasing all the time. The church with its seminaries and academies represented another important factor. Educated members of the gentry usually knew foreign languages well — certainly French, often German, and sometimes others too. Their constant travels gave them a firsthand opportunity to study Europe and, if they were so inclined, European philosophy and European intellectual life in general. They usually received most of their education at home, which implied numerous variations in every particular case. As a rule attention was paid to foreign languages and litera-

[12] G. Florovskii, *Puti russkogo bogosloviia*, p. 116.

tures, modern European and sometimes also classical, and to elementary instruction in Russian, religion, history, geography, and mathematics. Families especially interested in the education of their children hired university professors as private tutors. As the next stage, members of the gentry could attend special military schools or universities, particularly the latter, after Alexander I increased their number from one to six. Occasionally they also studied in foreign, especially German universities. After they were established in government service or on their land, they maintained their intellectual interest by visits to Western Europe, by building up huge and valuable private libraries, by studying and sometimes translating the works of Western masters. The stepfather of the Kireevskiis, A. Elagin, for instance, was engaged in translating Kant and Schelling. Subjects of general interest were discussed in the leading Moscow salons or at more intimate gatherings. This manorial civilization of leisure, European travel, liberal and dilettante education, private tutors, private libraries, and private circles was rapidly on the decline at the time of the rise of Slavophilism. Education was spreading among broader layers of society, a Russian intelligentsia comprising elements of various classes was in the process of formation. But the Slavophiles themselves belonged wholly to the old manorial civilization; they were its last large-scale expression in the history of Russian culture.

Moscow University, founded in 1755, was the oldest and the best in Russia. Alexander I established four more, at Vilno, Kharkov, Kazan, and St. Petersburg, and reëstablished that of Dorpat. The policies of the second half of Alexander's reign did great harm to the universities, but these continued to exist and even gain in importance as intellectual centers of Russia. The University of Moscow, protected by its enlightened curator, S. Stroganov, went through one of the most brilliant periods of its history in the course of Nicholas' reign. Philosophy was taught in Russian universities until its abolition as "the rebellious science" by a special edict in 1849. Philosophy was also taught in ecclesiastical academies, where it enjoyed a longer tradition and managed to escape the vicissitudes and the prohibitions suffered in secular schools. Such leading intellectuals of the period as the dean of Russian Schellingians D. Kavunnik-Vellanskii, and the professor and publicist Nadezhdin received some of their education in seminaries.

Kant was first introduced to the Russian students by Schwarz at the University of Moscow during the last quarter of the eighteenth century, and in the early ninetenth century ten or twelve professors paid some attention to Kant in their lectures. Herder, once a teacher in Riga, did not accomplish his youthful desire of devoting his life to Russia or even writing a monumental work on Russia, but his influence in Russia as a German philosopher was both early and significant: it was plainly visible in Radishchev's famous *Voyage from St. Petersburg to Moscow* published in 1790, and it was present, in connection with other romantic influences, especially that of Schelling, in numerous works of the Russian romanticists of the first half of the nineteenth century. Schiller and the doctrine of the "schoene Seele," Fichte and his patriotic idealism, Friedrich Schlegel and his theories on history and on art — all made important contributions to Russian romanticism. These and similar intertwined influences have not been sufficiently studied to permit their classification or their evaluation with any degree of precision. Together they represented the intellectual climate out of which grew Russian romanticism; separately no Western romantic influence stood out in sharp relief in Russia until the dissemination of Schelling's doctrines.

Schelling, in contrast to the earlier romanticists, acquired a very great personal reputation in Russia, his doctrines held almost unlimited sway over the Russian intellectuals who belong to "the generation of the twenties," and continued to have a powerful influence on the thought of their successors. Schelling's role in the romantic movement did not justify his majestic position in Russian intellectual history, for he was neither more original nor more systematic than a number of his predecessors and contemporaries. It is to be explained on the one hand by the increase in education and the growth of romanticism in Russia: the field was prepared for a Schelling where it had not been prepared for a Herder. On the other hand, it is necessary to note that the Russian background was particularly propitious for Schelling, that certain elements in native thought made Schelling the most welcome romanticist in Russia. Russian Freemasonry was a good preparation for the anthropocentric tendencies of Schelling and especially for his *Naturphilosophie*.[13] Mysticism and its doctrine of growth through the struggle of opposites had stronger affinities with the thought of Schelling than with other romantic ideologies.[14] The irrational and the poetic elements, and above all the strong emphasis on religion in Schelling's system made a powerful appeal to the Russians.[15] Later the Slavophiles regarded Schelling as the ultimate peak of philosophy precisely because of Schelling's treatment of knowledge and religion in his last system. Schelling's vision of the world, especially in its early *Naturphilosophie* form, was exceedingly seductive because it claimed to be an "organic synthesis." Everything formed a part of one glorious whole, every particle, every event, great or small, had its assigned place, and acquired a meaning and infinite connections with other components of the cosmos. Schelling offered splendid opportunities for bizarre analogies of enormous sweep. The analogies were found to be extremely valuable as a short-cut to knowledge, as an easy and systematic explanation of the universe and its mysteries: the world was not only magnificently comprehensible, but the requirements for such comprehension were fortunately not too exacting. The Russian intellectuals were also strongly attracted by the aesthetic aspect of Schelling's philosophy, his emphasis on art as a deep revelation of the spirit, by his concept of the organic nation, and his views of history.

Once the Russian thinkers turned to Schelling, he came to represent in their eyes the entire romantic movement, to stand as its

[13] Florovskii, *op. cit.*, pp. 118–119.
[14] D. Chizhevskii, *Gegel v Rossii*, pp. 9–11; Koliupanov, *op. cit.*, book I, p. 442.
[15] Sechkarev wrote: "When Schelling's turn to mysticism and religion lost him his followers in the West, that very fact brought to him the best minds in Russia, for instance, Ivan Kireevskii." V. Sechkarev, *Schellings Einfluss in der russischen Literatur der 20er und 30er Jahre des XIX Jahrhunderts*, p. 1.

symbol, its highest achievement, and its cumulative essence.
Most scholars, however, agreed that in spite of its prestige in
Russia, Schelling's philosophy in the strict sense of the term received no new development there, and Chizhevskii went further
to state that until the "generation of the forties" there was in
Russia no real understanding and appreciation of Schelling's
teaching as a comprehensive philosophic system. At the time
when Schelling's influence was at its strongest, the interest
centered not on Schelling's system as such, not on his philosophic
method, but on his use of analogies and on some particular
points of his doctrine, such as the animate character of nature,
the intrinsic value of art, and the intuitive character of knowledge.[16] Some scholars distinguish two periods of Schelling's influence in Russia: in the first his *Naturphilosophie* occupied the
central position; in the second, his aesthetic doctrines. In connection with Slavophilism special attention should also be paid to
Schelling's theory of history, nation, and national mission, although Sechkarev overstated the case when he wrote that:

It is in particular the idea of the high mission of the Russian people
in the history of the world, the idea which formed the foundation of
Slavophilism which can be always traced back to Schelling.[17]

Professor D. Kavunnik-Vellanskii was the first Russian follower
and popularizer of Schelling. Born in 1774 and educated in a
seminary, Vellanskii studied under Schelling in Germany, and
then for many years taught science at the Medical-Surgical
Academy in St. Petersburg. In his able lectures and in his books,
beginning with his *Prolegomenon to Medicine*, published in 1805,
Vellanskii repeated the basic tenets of the *Naturphilosophie* of
his master: the universe was one organic whole, man formed
a parallel to nature, physiology and physics were analogous
disciplines, efforts to understand should be directed towards the
attainment of complete knowledge, not one aspect of it.

Unlike Vellanskii, A. Galich, professor from 1814 at the Pedagogical Institute and from 1819 at the University in St. Petersburg, was an eclectic rather than a disciple of Schelling, but,

[16] Chizhevskii, *op. cit.*, p. 49.   [17] Sechkarev, *op. cit.*, pp. 2–3.

again in contrast to Vellanskii, he went beyond the *Naturphilo-sophie* and described to the Russian readers some other doctrines of Schelling and Schelling's German followers. As early as 1819 Galich devoted a special section of his *History of Philosophic Systems* to a summary exposition of Schelling's philosophy.

In Moscow three professors were particularly prominent as disseminators of Schelling's theories: I. Davydov, who taught philosophy, mathematics, and literature both at the University of Moscow and at the "University Boarding School for the Gentry" and who had the gifted romanticist, Prince V. Odoevskii, among his students; N. Nadezhdin, who introduced Schelling's aesthetic doctrines into his lectures on Russian literature at the University; and M. Pavlov, who taught physics, mineralogy, and agronomy, and who was probably the ablest Russian popularizer of Schelling. Schelling's influence also spread to such provincial centers as Kiev, Kharkov, and Odessa. It has been repeatedly noted that none of these professors who introduced German ide-alistic philosophy into Russia were powerful thinkers and that in particular their allegiance to Schelling was often superficial, dependent on Schelling's German disciples and commentators, or incongruously combined with views of different origin. But they played a very important part in spreading the ideas of Schel-ling in Russia, in laying the foundations for the subsequent de-velopment of philosophy in the country, and above all, in the great, if often intangible, task of stimulating thought in general. At their best they deserved the tribute which Herzen paid to Pavlov, when he described him as a majestic figure standing at the doorway to the department of physical and mathematical sciences of the University of Moscow and arresting the students with the following challenging words: "You want to know nature. But what is nature? And what does it mean to know?" [18]

Schelling's popularity in Russia spread beyond the academic spheres and led to the foundation of the first Russian philosophic "circle," and the first Russian philosophic review. In 1823 several young men, who had been discussing Schelling in the literary circle grouped around the poet and teacher, S. Raich, formed

[18] A. Herzen, *Sochineniia*, volume VII, p. 119.

a separate society which had the study of German idealistic philosophy as its main object. The group chose the name of "The Lovers of Wisdom," insisted on "secrecy," and came to contain up to a dozen members and associates: the prince V. Odoevskii presided, the poet D. Venevitinov served as Secretary, and A. Koshelev, I. Kireevskii, and N. Rozhalin were also very active in the Society, while those mentioned less frequently in connection with it included the future proponents of Official Nationality, Shevyrev and Pogodin, P. Kireevskii, who later became a Slavophile, and F. Khomiakov, a brother of the Slavophile.[19] The Lovers of Wisdom, some of whom served in the Moscow Archives of the Main Collegium of the Ministry of Foreign Affairs and others of whom attended the University of Moscow, belonged to the most cultured and promising Russian youth of the eighteen-twenties. "The young men of the archives," a term made famous by Pushkin, were attracted to the Ministry of Foreign Affairs by the promise of a luxurious diplomatic career, and formed there a social elite comparable, in the opinion of some, to the officers of the guard at the time of Catherine the Great.[20]

The Lovers of Wisdom reflected the romantic temper of their generation in a certain kind of poetical spiritualism which pervaded their entire outlook, in their worship of art, in their pantheistic adoration of nature, similar to that of Wordsworth, and in their disregard for the "crude" aspects of life, including politics. In an attempt to disseminate in Russia the ideas of their Western masters, Schelling in particular, they began publishing the review

[19] The Russian word for "the lovers of wisdom," *liubomudry*, comes from the Masonic and the mystical literature of the eighteenth century. "It is to be found in Novikov, Radishchev uses it already in the sense of *philosophy*. . . . Labzin gives it the meaning of *love of true wisdom* as opposed to the rationalist philosophy which pretended to possess that wisdom. . . . In the twenties the term was frequently used, by Davydov among others, in the sense of *philosophy*. . . ." A. Koyré, *La philosophie et le problème national en Russie au début du XIXe siècle*, note to p. 36. The "secrecy" of the Society, some of its external characteristics and much of its spirit remind one of Russian Freemasonry.

For a brief account of the Society by a member see: A. Koshelev, *Zapiski*, p. 12ff.

[20] Koliupanov, *op. cit.*, volume I, book II, p. 59.

Mnemosyne, which had only four issues and 157 subscribers, but marked the beginning of periodic philosophic publications in Russia. The Society of the Lovers of Wisdom was formally closed by its members following the Decembrist rebellion in 1825 in which friends and even relatives of the Lovers of Wisdom were involved. The Kireevskiis and Koshelev subsequently became very well known as Slavophiles, Shevyrev and Pogodin developed into the principal professorial expounders of Official Nationality, and only Venevitinov and Odoevskii left their mark in the history of Russian thought primarily as the leading Lovers of Wisdom.

D. Venevitinov, a very gifted poet, died in 1827 at the age of twenty-two, and bequeathed only his poetry and a few articles, such as "Sculpture, Painting, and Music," or "Morning, Noon, Evening, and Night," as a record of his view of the world. This view was thoroughly romantic: Venevitinov's favorite subjects included the aesthetic theories of the romanticists; the particular roles of the several arts and their relation to the highest art, that of poetry; man as the microcosm; analogy between man's life and human history; the golden age and the cycle of huma. history; the romantic, organic theory of nations; the return to original harmony on a new, conscious level through creative effort. Venevitinov had the highest appreciation of the West, but he was deeply perturbed by the imitative nature of Russian culture and went so far as to condemn all Russian literature as imitation. He advocated that Russia withdraw from contact with the West, and develop a true culture on the basis of a real awareness of the self and of organic creativity.

Prince V. Odoevskii, who was twenty when the Society of the Lovers of Wisdom came into existence and who died in 1869, changed his view of the world several times. His most significant contribution to Russian thought was made, however, early in his life: Odoevskii was the first Russian to give a critical philosophic appraisal of Western culture and to formulate on this basis the doctrine of Russian Messiahship. He performed this task most particularly in his *Russian Nights*, a work strongly influenced by Schelling, conceived in the twenties, written in the thirties, but published in a complete form only in 1844, in the first volume of Odoevskii's collected works.

Odoevskii could not approach the problem of Russia and the West in the rough and ready manner of the extreme nationalists: Western philosophy should not be banned; on the contrary, Odoevskii had already argued in the *Mnemosyne* that the scorn which the Russians had for philosophy was responsible for Russia's inability to pass from imitation to creative, organic culture. *The Russian Nights*, in spite of the strong element of fantasy, which it contained and which made it especially resemble the works of Hoffmann, developed a logical, comprehensive, and typically romantic argument. The West had accomplished marvellous things, but it had lost its balance, its harmony, and was in the throes of a most dangerous crisis caused by the fact that it had failed to resolve the antinomy of man and society, of the private and the public. This failure had led to the perversion of science and art, to the loss of love and faith. Still, salvation was possible. Throughout the history of the world such crises had been surmounted by the appearance of a savior, a new, fresh people destined to show again to humanity the true path from which it had deviated. For the West the savior was Russia. In the time of Napoleon Russia had already saved the body of Europe; this was a symbol of the more difficult task yet to be accomplished, the salvation of the soul of Europe. Russia had been prepared for its glorious mission by its history: before Peter the Great, Russia had been distinguished by its enormous size, gigantic strength, and versatile spirit, but it lacked organization and Western learning; Peter the Great had added the latter elements, and thus Russia had attained a harmonious development unknown in the West. Russia was an organic society which knew no struggle between people and government, preserved the principles of love and unity, and believed in the happiness of all and everyone. Russian spirit was characterized by a particular versatility, universality, and inclusiveness on which a truly harmonious life could be founded. Odoevskii's benevolent idealism, his emphasis on religion, art, and science, his desire to find a place for all in the regenerated world, his willingness to recognize the value both of prepetrine Russia and of Peter the Great's reforms, as well as various other traits of his thought, were a faithful expression of romanticism in its earlier, less exclusive, and more humane form.[21]

The Lovers of Wisdom represented only one group of Russian intellectuals influenced by Schelling. He also affected Chaadaev, and to a lesser extent such Westernizers as Stankevich and Herzen, as well as most other reflective Russians of the time, especially the professors and the poets. In addition to the poetry of Venevitinov and Odoevskii, Schelling influenced some poems of Pushkin, and possibly Baratynskii and Koltsov, certainly Tiutchev, not to mention the lesser lights. Tiutchev, who united a true poetic genius with a thoroughgoing romanticism of the mystical variety, reflected Schelling's doctrines in his poetry of the night, his treatment of nature, of man's connection with nature, and of the chaos in the human soul.[22] His political views, stated in such works as *Russia and the Revolution*, were based on the idea of a fundamental antagonism between the Orthodox and legitimist Russia, and the atheistic and revolutionary West. Together with the Slavophiles, Tiutchev regarded the Crimean War as the great battle of the two worlds, and directed his hatred

[21] V. Odoevskii, *Russkie nochi.* The standard work on Odoevskii is P. Sakulin, *Iz istorii russkogo idealisma: Kniaz V. Odoevskii.*

Koyré stressed the fact that the Lovers of Wisdom were naive dilettantes, but he added that that in itself was very much in the romantic tradition, and that in Russia where philosophy was at its inception, nothing else could be expected. Odoevskii often depended on his teacher Davydov, Venevitinov on his teacher Pavlov rather than on the German originals (Koyré, *op. cit.,* pp. 137–152). A greater appreciation of Odoevskii as a thinker was given by a number of scholars, notably by Sakulin. For a very favorable treatment of Odoevskii see also: V. Riasanovsky, *Obzor russkoi kultury,* part II, issue I, pp. 303–310. For a highly critical treatment: M. Kovalevskii, "Shellingianstvo i gegelianstvo v Rossii," in *Vestnik Evropy,* book XI, November 1915, pp. 133–170, esp. pp. 166–170. Venevitinov has long been favored by the specialists, even by the hypercritical Shpet (G. Shpet, *Ocherk razvitiia russkoi filosofii,* pp. 324–333, deals with Kroneberg, his influence on Venevitinov, and with Venevitinov).

[22] For Schelling's influence on Tiutchev see Sechkarev, *op. cit.,* pp. 99–106, and Chizhevskii, *op. cit.,* pp. 46–48.

against the revolution, France, and Catholicism.[23] Schelling continued to affect Russian thought even in the last decades of the nineteenth century, especially through his influence on Soloviev, and his doctrines retained significance for the Russian religious thinkers of the twentieth century.[24]

In literature Russian romanticism achieved its most brilliant expression in the early works of Pushkin and Lermontov and in Zhukovskii. Marlinskii and other romanticists distinguished themselves by their enthusiasm rather than by their talent, but their activity was characteristic of the spirit of the age. Zhukovskii, the dean of the Russian romantic writers, was an extremely close friend of the Kireevskii-Elagin family, and lived in that family for over a year in 1814–1815. He exercised a profound influence on Ivan Kireevskii, then an impressionable boy of eight or nine. In particular, Kireevskii's aesthetic inclination and his sentimentality were encouraged by Zhukovskii's artistic tastes and constant emphasis on the delicate feelings of the heart.[25] In political ideology Zhukovskii stood close to Official Nationality

[23] On Tiutchev and his resemblance to the Slavophiles, Khomiakov in particular, see Tiutchev's biography by his son-in-law, the Slavophile Ivan Aksakov: I. Aksakov, *Biografiia F. I. Tiutcheva.*

[24] "Schelling met Russians. Not only his auditors: the Kireevskiis and Rozhalin, but a whole series of Russians wandering in Europe. Chaadaev became acquainted with Schelling in Karlsbad in 1825 and addressed to him two letters (in 1832 and 1842) about which we shall have an occasion to speak later. Schelling was well acquainted with Tiutchev, who lived in Munich from 1822. Odoevskii visited Schelling in 1842, and they engaged in a conversation about mysticism, about Hegel, about Russia (the same evaluation as the one given by Hegel in his letter to Yxhull). In 1839 Schelling was visited in Augsburg by still another former Lover of Wisdom, N. A. Melgunov, who even published a rather inane account of his conversations with Schelling (*Otechestvennye Zapiski*, 1839, IV, 3). Schelling asked Melgunov about his Russian acquaintances: A. I. Turgenev, Chaadaev, Pogodin." Chizhevskii, *op. cit.*, p. 48 .

[25] Ivan Kireevskii remained a friend and admirer of Zhukovskii all his life. In 1832, for instance, he regarded Zhukovskii's blessing as indispensable before he could begin his career as a publicist. Gershenzon even concluded that: "Between Zhukovskii and Kireevskii there is an organic connection: what had been expectations for Zhukovskii became convictions for Kireevskii, and in this sense Slavophilism, to the extent to which it remained faithful to its basic idea, formulated precisely by Kireevskii, is flesh from the flesh of Russian romanticism." Gershenzon, *op. cit.*, p. 18.

and was particularly repelled and upset by the revolutions of 1848.

The same problem, Russia and the West, dominated Russian history, Russian literature, Russian philosophy, the entire intellectual life of Russia. Shishkov and Karamzin, Odoevskii and Pogodin, Magnitskii and Polevoi were all applying their different talents and their incommensurate efforts to one task, the task of establishing the nature of Russia, its place in the world, its relation to the West in the present, the past, and the future. Shishkov stressed language, Karamzin history. The extreme anti-Western conservatives were swinging the heavy club of power, government, state, autocracy, designed both to bludgeon the West to death and to bludgeon Russia into the state of perfect happiness. Odoevskii spoke of the messianic qualities of the Russian soul. Magnitskii made a heroic effort to ban Western thought; the Lovers of Wisdom to assimilate it. To the ancient human conviction that one is always right and one's own way is invariably the best were added all the involutions and all the evolvements of romantic thought, from the *Naturphilosophie* on down. Such basic terms as *nationality, Russian character, Rusisan history, Orthodoxy, revolution, organic growth, rationalism, egoism, tradition* were being constantly discussed, criticized, and assigned new complementary or contrasting meanings to be used for construction of various disparate systems. Slavophilism emerged from these numerous crisscrossing influences. As a prelude to Slavophilism stood the scheme of Chaadaev and the one constructed by Ivan Kireevskii before Kireevskii became a Slavophile.

P. Chaadaev (1794–1856), an aristocrat of broad education and real ability, made one of the most memorable contributions to the history of Russian political thought. Although he is often accounted the founder of the Westernizer school and although he also exercised a profound influence on the Slavophiles, Chaadaev always stood apart from the movements and the groupings of his time. He was never more alone than in 1836 after Nadezhdin published Chaadaev's "Philosophical Letter" in the *Telescope*. Chaadaev's scheme, based on the French and German romanticists, Schelling included, indicated very clearly that Russia had no past, no present, and no future. Russia never really belonged to either the West or the East. It had contributed nothing to culture. It had not the dynamic social principle of Catholicism on which the entire Western civilization was based.[26] In the historic process Russia remained an outsider and as such her value equaled zero.

I do not know what it is in our blood that resists all true progress. At the end of it all we have not lived, we do not live now except to serve as a great lesson to distant posterity which will be able to understand it; today, whatever one may say, we are a gap in the intellectual order of things.[27]

Chaadaev's letter produced a great shock. *The Telescope* was banned, Nadezhdin banished, the censor, who let the "Letter" through, dismissed, Chaadaev himself officially proclaimed deranged and compelled to receive regular visits of a doctor. Later in his "Apology of a Madman" Chaadaev modified his thesis. Through Peter the Great, Russia had acquired history, had joined civilization; her future could be glorious if she would throw her entire fresh strength into the construction of the common culture of Christendom. Chaadaev also took a more appreciative view of the Russian Orthodox Church, which he had formerly compared to the church in Abyssinia.

Chaadaev's two great contributions to Russian thought were his view of religion and culture and his outline of Russian history. Affected by the German romanticists and especially by the Roman Catholic thinkers of France, such as de Maistre and de Bonald, Chaadaev proclaimed Catholicism to be the driving force of Western civilization, its very life, the essence of the West. The Slavophiles took up the problem of religion and cul-

---

[26] Chaadaev was at his dramatic best in underlining constantly the tragedy of this existence without the past, without any real roots or attachments. "We appear to be camping in our homes, we seem strangers in our families; in our cities we have the air of nomads, more nomadic than the nomads who wander in our steppes, for they have a greater attachment to their deserts than we to our cities." P. Chaadaev, *Sochineniia i pisma*, vol. I, p. 78. The letters in their original French occupy pp. 74–142 of the volume. In vol. II they are translated into Russian.

[27] Chaadaev, *op. cit.*, vol. I, p. 85.

ture as formulated by Chaadaev: for them too the life of society depended on its religious principles, and the West meant Catholicism. Only they attacked Catholicism where Chaadaev defended it, and argued for the superiority of Russian Orthodoxy and the culture to be built on the Orthodox foundation. As to the outline of Russian history, it was Chaadaev especially, who "brought Peter the Great into relief, assigned him his role in the development of Russian thought. . . ." [28] Chaadaev's salon was one of the leading social and intellectual centers of Moscow, and the Slavophiles frequented it and often engaged in debates with Chaadaev. Especially significant was Chaadaev's relation to Ivan Kireevskii.[29]

In 1832 Ivan Kireevskii, then a young man of twenty-six and favorably inclined towards the West, wrote a remarkable article on "The Nineteenth Century" in his review, *The European*. After stressing the organic nature of Western civilization and its accelerating dialectical development, Kireevskii considered Russia in relation to the West. The enormous disparity between the two implied a difference in basic principles. Kireevskii followed Guizot in his enumeration of the basic elements of the West:

These elements may be reduced to three fundamental principles: first, the influence of the Christian religion; second, the character, education, and spirit of the barbaric peoples, who destroyed the Roman empire; third, the remnants of the ancient world. From these three principles developed the entire History of Modern Europe.[30]

[28] C. Quenet, *Tchaadaev et les Lettres philosophiques*, p. 283. See also M. Gershenzon, *Chaadaev, zhizn i tvorchestvo*. Quenet supplied an excellent bibliography published separately from his work on Chaadaev: C. Quenet, *Tchaadaev et les Lettres philosophiques: Sources et recherches*.

[29] Although the "Philosophic Letter" appeared in print only in 1836, Chaadaev had been writing his letters from 1829. His thought and that of Ivan Kireevskii were developed together, along parallel lines, and in close contact. See in particular Koyré, *op. cit.*, pp. 192–193 and the special article: A. Koyré, "P. Chaadaev and the Slavophiles," in *The Slavonic Review*, 1927, vol. V, pp. 594–608. Koyré illustrates the close relationship of the dialectical reasoning of the two thinkers even when the end results were strikingly different. Chaadaev thought in terms of a universal civilization; Ivan Kireevskii had the strongest universalist tendencies among the Slavophiles.

[30] I. K., vol. I, p. 98. The entire article occupies pp. 85–108. In referring to the six main Slavophiles (see Chapter II) I shall give merely their initials and the volume and page of their works.

Then Kireevskii continued his analysis:

Which of these principles were we lacking or what did we have in excess? Already before the tenth century we had Christian religion; we also had the barbarians, and, probably, the same who destroyed the Roman empire; but *the ancient, classical world* was lacking in our development.[31]

This tragic deficiency had prevented the church in Russia from operating as an active social and political force, and accounted for the Russian lack of foundation and tradition. Russia, however, did not have to remain an outsider. In the West itself a new dialectical step meant the negation of the old — new stages in the European society and culture, in the entire European life. Because these stages were new, Russia could participate in them. Koyré noted at least two possible rhythms: thesis — Western civilization, antithesis — the eighteenth century, synthesis — the nineteenth; and, thesis — the West, antithesis — Russia, synthesis — the future.[32] On a somewhat more restricted scale, Kireevskii spoke of the "destructive" stage culminating in the French Revolution as the thesis, the resulting stage of "unity by force" as the antithesis, and the new stage aimed at a peaceful integration of the two antagonistic principles as the synthesis.[33]

Whichever rhythm of history one chose to follow, Russia was quite prepared to play her role in the coming phase of European civilization. The nature of that role became the main preoccupation of the Slavophiles.

[31] *Ibid.*
[32] Koyré, *op. cit.*, p. 193 and the footnote to the page.
[33] I. K., vol. I, pp. 87–89.

CHAPTER II

THE SLAVOPHILES

The Slavophiles were a group of nineteenth-century Russian intellectuals who were drawn together by common beliefs, attitudes, and aspirations in such fundamental issues as religion, philosophy, and the problem of Russia and the West. The foundations of Slavophilism were laid in the thirties and in the early forties; its golden age lasted approximately from 1845 to 1860. After the passing of Khomiakov and of Konstantin Aksakov in 1860, Slavophilism continued to be represented by Samarin and by Ivan Aksakov until their deaths in 1876 and in 1886 respectively.

The Slavophiles never formed an organization, never exacted conformity from the members of their group. Their strong characters, sharply pronounced individualities, and independent outlooks add to the difficulties of determining the "membership" of the movement and the connotation of the term "Slavophile." Some scholars have listed the writer S. T. Aksakov as the first Slavophile, others have indiscriminately included in the group various nationalistically inclined thinkers of the time of Nicholas I, notably the proponents of Official Nationality, Shevyrev and Pogodin. The last stage of the movement presents the greatest difficulties. "Slavophilism" was at times stretched to cover all the Pan-Slav friends of Ivan Aksakov, all champions of Russian superiority over the West, such varied contributors to Russian culture as Danilevskii, Dostoevskii, and Leontiev. These inclusions were based on confusion, on the assumption that certain striking and often superficial resemblances to the Slavophile doctrine were sufficient to make one a Slavophile.[1] The true

[1] I refer to the writers who lump these names together under the label "Slavophiles," not to those who speak of the various phases, dialectical or otherwise, in the development of the movement. The latter problem will be

leading Slavophiles were the following: Aleksei Khomiakov, Ivan
Kireevskii, Petr Kireevskii, Konstantin Aksakov, Ivan Aksakov,
and Iurii Samarin. A. Koshelev, D. Valuev, and a score of others
also belonged to the movement, although they made a much
smaller contribution to the Slavophile ideology than the first
six and sometimes differed from them on important points.

THE COMMON BACKGROUND OF THE SLAVOPHILES

The biographies of the Slavophiles present a number of striking similarities. The Slavophiles came from old and honorable
gentry families.

In a patriarchal milieu, holding strongly to ancient customs, permeated
by the traditions and the legends of the past, in the country, in the
bosom of nature, in quiet gentry nests, all the early Slavophiles grew
up.[2]

These large families were linked by blood and by marriage and
formed a closely knit group of relatives and friends. There was
therefore a greater solidarity among the Slavophiles than among
the Westernizers and the same factor conditioned the dissemination of Slavophilism, which spread almost instantaneously in several large families and hardly at all outside of them.

Furthermore, the fact of solidarity based on the blood relationship of
the Slavophiles points to the "material cause" of their views, namely
of the important place, exaggeratedly important if you wish, which the
Slavophiles assigned in theory to the attitude of kinship, to the friendly
closeness of the members of society, at the expense of legal, compulsive norms. Hence follows their persistent struggle against a *firm
foundation* — in the church, in the state, even in thought. They were
accustomed to breathe the air of complaisance of relatives, the atmosphere of amiability of the next of kin, that soft lawlessness without
which kinship itself would be unthinkable; evidently it never entered
their heads that any social group could be formed in a different man-

---

considered in Chapter VI. Especially popular is the division into "classical
Slavophiles" and "epigones of Slavophilism." My "Slavophile" equals "classical Slavophile" of that scheme.

    [2] N. Brodskii, *Rannie slavianofily*, p. X. Brodskii's book contains complete
reproductions of some of the Slavophile writings, including several articles
of Konstantin Aksakov, which cannot be found elsewhere. In quoting from
these articles, I shall refer to: K. A., Brodskii, *op. cit.*

ner, except by an evil design. Projecting their studies, their drawing rooms, and their dining rooms over the entire world, they wished to see all the world organized along the lines of kinship, as one enormous tea party of friendly relatives gathered in the evening to discuss some good question.[3]

All Slavophiles were very closely associated with Moscow, even with a particular section of Moscow. Moscow was then more important than St. Petersburg as an intellectual center of Russia, and its university, which many of the Slavophiles attended, was the best in the country. The instinctive and deep feeling of inferiority and dislike on the part of many members of the Moscow gentry towards the official capital, with its court, its numerous foreign names, and its claims of precedence in Russia, was a potent factor in the formation of a number of nationalist ideologies; in Slavophilism it attained its most complete and most powerful theoretical expression.

The Slavophiles were very well educated and highly cultured. Some professional philosophers spoke of the amateurishness of Slavophile philosophic efforts while a number of churchmen accused Khomiakov and his friends of dilettantism in theology, but these specialist opinions were contradicted by others, equally specialist, and, in any case, they did not refer to the general cultural level of the Slavophiles. The Slavophiles received the best education available in Russia, and some of them continued their studies abroad. They had very broad interests, few financial difficulties, and much leisure. Books occupied a very prominent place in their life and in their correspondence. Some Slavophiles had excellent libraries of their own; for instance, Khomiakov, who once ordered ten-thousand-rubles-worth of foreign books in

---

[3] P. Florenskii, *Okolo Khomiakova*, pp. 42–43. Also published in *Bogoslovskii Vestnik*, 1916, nos. 7 and 8. Florenskii's appraisal is an exaggeration, but it throws interesting light on the important connection between the family background of the Slavophiles and their teaching. After the death of the leading Slavophiles, their families continued to maintain the Slavophile tradition: Dimitrii Samarin, e.g., followed in many ways in the footsteps of his brother Iurii, while Khomiakov's son, Dimitrii, who restated the Slavophile view of autocracy, was called the last Slavophile.

An appendix to Florenskii's booklet contains the genealogical table of the Slavophiles, showing the relationship of the Slavophile families.

a single year, or Petr Kireevskii, whose library contained books in sixteen languages and included a particularly valuable Slavic collection. The Slavophiles scattered their learning, and some-times they scattered it very thin; they loved vague and unfounded speculation in all fields of knowledge. These traits were, how-ever, indicative of the intellectual climate of the period rather than of any specific defects of the group.

The Slavophiles were affected by numerous currents of West-ern thought which composed the cultural climate of the Romantic Age. The period immediately preceding the development of Slavophilism was characterized in Russia by the influence of Schelling, an influence to which the Slavophiles paid their due, as members of the Society of the Lovers of Wisdom and other-wise; but the growth of Slavophilism itself corresponded with the spread of Hegelianism in Russia.[4]

The first and the most important Hegelian circle in Russia gathered around N. Stankevich in Moscow in the early thirties. Its members included the future leader of the Westernizers — Belinskii, and of the Slavophiles — Konstantin Aksakov, Hegelian professors Redkin and Kriukov, the future nationalist publicist, Katkov, and the famous future anarchist, Bakunin. Herzen also participated for a time in the activities of the circle. Similar groups were organized in St. Petersburg, Tver, Kazan, Kharkov, Kiev, and even Nezhin. A considerable number of young Rus-sians, many of them on government scholarships in preparation for teaching, attended Hegel's lectures in Berlin, as well as the lectures of various German Hegelians, and soon Hegel was better represented on the faculties of Russian universities than Schelling had ever been. Hegelianism penetrated science, literature, and art. It became the favorite subject for discussion in the salons of the educated gentry as well as at the universities. The great influence of Hegel marked both a diffusion of interest in philos-ophy in Russia and its intensification. While the Russian admirers

[4] The most important works on Hegelianism in Russia are D. Chizhevskii, *Gegel v Rossii*, and B. Iakovenko, *Geschichte des Hegelianismus in Russland*. Chizhevskii's study was originally published in German. The German version has more complete reference notes and bibliography, the Russian version has the fuller text.

of Schelling rarely went beyond some particular aspects of their master's system, Russian Hegelians were interested in Hegel's philosophy as a whole, as a complete synthesis revealing the true nature of the world. In their passionate devotion to the scarcely intelligible doctrines of Hegel, the first Russian Hegelians displayed a combative, doctrinaire spirit more akin to their positivist successors of the sixties than to their idealistic predecessors of the Society of the Lovers of Wisdom.[5]

The opponents of the Slavophiles, the Westernizers, such as Herzen and Granovskii, were strongly influenced by Hegel. The minds of the elder Slavophiles were formed before Hegelianism spread in Russia and owed more to Schelling than to Hegel, although they knew Hegelian philosophy well and showed their knowledge and ability in criticizing it, but the younger Slavophiles, Konstantin Aksakov and Samarin, passed through a period of thorough Hegelianism which proved highly significant for their intellectual development.[6]

Schelling and Hegel were only two of the numerous links which connected the Slavophiles with the West. The Slavophiles were brought up in the tradition of French liberal education, and most of them were masters of several modern languages. Khomiakov's works and correspondence were written in Russian, French, and English; Samarin's in Russian, French, and German. All the Slavophiles traveled, and some of them studied in the West. Even when they did not attend regular courses at a university, as did the Kireevskii brothers at the University of Munich, they were always interested in meeting European intellectuals and in studying European culture and life. The Slavophiles were particularly attracted by the famous German romanticists and by Slavic scholars, especially the leaders of the Czech national revival, but their wide range of interests embraced various other

[5] The most famous description of the enthusiasm of Russian Hegelians is in Herzen, *op. cit.*, pp. 121–122, where Herzen stated that every paragraph of Hegel's voluminous writings became subject for several nights of desperate argument, that friendships were broken over abstruse Hegelian definitions, and so on.

[6] The influences on Slavophile thought, including those of Schelling and Hegel, will be discussed in Chapter V.

groups as well: Samarin, for instance, made a detailed study of Prussian administration and administrators, while Khomiakov's most treasured acquaintances included Oxford and Cambridge theologians.[7] Another link was the publication in the West of some of the works of the Slavophiles, most of which could not appear in Russia owing to censorship regulations. In their writings the Slavophiles mentioned almost every contemporary Western thinker of any importance and some whose importance it is now impossible to establish. They discussed all aspects of Western cultural life: from Paganini's concerts and the Dresden Art Gallery to the latest textbook in economics. Samarin, who combined an interest in economic and administrative matters with the usual Slavophile inclinations towards philosophy, religion, history, literature, and art provides the greatest number of specific references to Western intellectuals and their works.[8]

The Slavophiles had similar background, education, and interests, and their lives resembled one another in several important aspects. The Slavophiles were landowners and lived on the income from their lands. Although several of them entered government service, and Samarin had an important part in the emancipation of the serfs and in the reforms in Poland, none of them stayed long in this service, and none of them can be classified as government officials or as representing official circles. In spite of their excellent education and strong intellectual interests, none of the leading Slavophiles took up scholarship as a career. Their works often showed, together with much erudition and ability, the absence of the professional touch, in philosophy as much as in philology, and in theology as much as in history.

The writings of the Slavophiles were rarely organized according to any general, comprehensive plan, but were usually deter-

[7] The Slavophiles left interesting accounts of their meetings with the outstanding figures of European culture. See, in particular, Ivan and Petr Kireevskii's letters from Germany: I. K., vol. I, pp. 14–58; and in *Russkii Arkhiv*, 1894, book three, pp. 207–224; 1905, book two, pp. 113–173. A. Koshelev met Goethe and described him in *Zapiski*, pp. 36–37.

[8] Samarin's evaluation of European intellectuals and of their doctrines could form the subject of an interesting special study. Samarin, for instance, was one of the first to notice the significance of Friedrich List's economic theories.

mined by the social, political, and religious problems of the day, and very often took the form of a polemic. Ivan Aksakov, who became famous as a tireless Slavophile publicist, represented the extreme of this tendency, but it was also characteristic of the other members of the group. Even Khomiakov's theology was largely determined by the exigencies of the moment: except for a very brief catechism, "The Church Is One," all Khomiakov's theological writings were polemical in nature. They included three treatises in French directed against Western Christians, Catholics in particular, a letter to the Jansenist Bishop Looss urging him to join the Orthodox Church, and a series of letters to Palmer caused by Palmer's great interest in Orthodoxy and Khomiakov's desire to promote the conversion of his English friend to the Orthodox faith.

But while the Slavophiles' education and their wide range of interests were not propitious to concentration on any one subject, they provided the Slavophiles with a number of favorite themes, especially in philosophy and religion, to which the Slavophiles periodically returned from their preoccupation with their estates or with the more pressing political and social problems. At the time of his death, Khomiakov was writing his "Philosophic Letters" to Samarin and translating the Pauline Epistles into Russian; Ivan Kireevskii was struck down by cholera while working on the second part of his treatise "On the Necessity and the Possibility of New Principles in Philosophy"; Samarin's last articles dealt with Max Mueller's studies in the history of religion.

KHOMIAKOV

If the Slavophile movement had one central figure, it was Aleksei Stepanovich Khomiakov. Born in Moscow on the first of May, 1804, in an old gentry family, Khomiakov received a good private education typical of his class. As a boy he learned the French, German, English, and Latin languages, and he was adequately prepared at home to pass in 1822 an examination at the University of Moscow for a degree in mathematical sciences. Khomiakov's mother, née Maria Alekseevna Kireevskii, a woman of strong character and rigid principles, instilled in Khomiakov, according to his own testimony, his lifelong religious and moral beliefs and exercised a dominating influence on his life.[9]

In the same year in which he took his degree, Khomiakov entered military service, a convenient outlet for the fighting spirit which Khomiakov had already demonstrated a year earlier, at seventeen, when he tried to escape from Moscow and join the Greek insurgents. At the beginning of 1825, Khomiakov left service for a time and went to western Europe, where he studied painting in Paris, and visited Switzerland, and northern Italy. He returned to Russia by way of southern Slavic lands; his interest in and his love for the southern Slavs have often been dated from that voyage. During the Russo-Turkish war of 1828–1829, Khomiakov saw action in the Danube army, and was decorated for bravery. Soon after the conclusion of the peace, he retired from the service and remained a gentleman farmer for the rest of his life, dividing his time between his estates and Moscow.

Khomiakov began writing poetry as a youth. In 1829, he produced a longer work — the lyrical drama, *Ermak*, followed in 1833 by another lyrical drama — *The False Dimitrii*. Khomiakov's poetry already reflected his concept of the great mission of Russia and of the role of Russia as the leader of Slavdom. His theoretical formulation and development of this doctrine began in the late thirties. Moscow was the center of Russian intellectual life. In the drawing rooms of Chaadaev, the Elagins, and the Sverbeevs, Khomiakov met and debated indefatigably with outstanding Russian intellectuals, most of them young men in the process of formulating their own doctrines: Chaadaev, the brothers Kireevskii, the brothers Aksakov; future leading Westernizers — Herzen, Ogarev, and Granovskii; future spokesmen of Official Nationality — Shevyrev and Pogodin. By his power of conviction, fine intelligence, and excellent ability as a debater, Khomiakov exercised a strong, perhaps the determining, influence on a number of younger men, such as Konstantin Aksakov, Samarin, Valuev, and Popov, and contributed more than any other single person to the

[9] Khomiakov's mother was probably a distant relative of the two famous Slavophiles, Ivan and Petr Kireevskii, but the relationship has not been established.

formation of the Slavophile ideology and the Slavophile circle.

In 1834 Khomiakov married Catherine Iazykov, a sister of the poet, and the happy marriage lasted until her death in 1852. They had several children.

The Slavophiles became a distinct group after they broke with the Westernizers in the middle forties, and Khomiakov remained until his death their recognized leader. In 1838 Khomiakov began to work on his greatest project — a world history, which he brought down to the Middle Ages and which remained after him in the shape of a huge collection of notes, observations, and theories, a first draft at best. While working on his *History*, Khomiakov learned Greek and Sanskrit. In the winter of 1839 he read in a private group his controversial essay about "The Old and the New." His articles on numerous and extremely diverse subjects commenced to appear in the early forties, and continued to come out, in spite of censorship difficulties, until his death.

In 1844 began Khomiakov's long acquaintance with William Palmer, Fellow of Magdalen College, Oxford, and with the Cambridge theologian, Williams. In 1847 Khomiakov traveled with his family to England, France, Germany, and the Habsburg Empire, visiting his English friends, as well as various other persons of special interest to him, notably Schelling and Neander in Berlin, and Hanka and Safarik in Prague. In 1853, 1855, and 1858 appeared Khomiakov's three theological treatises, all written in French, published abroad, entitled *Several Words of an Orthodox Christian about Western Creeds*, and signed "Ignotus." The Crimean War stimulated Khomiakov's nationalist fervor and his poetic activity; the death of Nicholas I during the war combined with the more liberal outlook of his successor, Alexander II, opened new possibilities for the Slavophile writers. In 1856 they started a review, *The Russian Conversation*, which was principally inspired by Khomiakov and begun with much hope and enthusiasm. The same year witnessed the death of Ivan Kireevskii and several months later that of his brother, Petr.

Khomiakov took an important part in the resurrection of "The Society of the Friends of Russian Letters" and was the chairman of the Society until his death. His speeches from the chair reviewing the state of Russian letters and discussing their theory and practice provide valuable additional material for the study of his doctrines. Khomiakov always reacted quickly to the needs of the day, and in 1859 he presented to a leading official a detailed plan of the abolition of serfdom. The last two years of Khomiakov's life were marked by a renewed interest in philosophy as attested by his plan of a series of letters to Samarin "On Contemporary Developments in the Domain of Philosophy" — a series of which the first and a part of the second letter were written — by several brief theological articles, by translation of Saint Paul's Epistles, and by a pretentious "Letter to the Serbs" signed by a number of the leading adherents of Khomiakov's views on the subject. Khomiakov died suddenly of cholera on the twenty-third of September, 1860.

In appearance Khomiakov was short with piercing eyes and black disheveled hair. His acquaintances remembered him principally as a tireless and extremely able conversationalist and debater, and his great opponent Herzen paid him the handsomest tribute in that connection.[10] Eight stout volumes of Khomiakov's collected works consist of a volume of theological writings, a volume of poetry and plays, two volumes of various articles and speeches, three volumes of history, and a volume of letters.

A remarkable versatility was one of Khomiakov's outstanding characteristics. In the words of Berdiaev:

This Russian landlord, practical and businesslike, a hunter and a technologist, a specialist in dogs and in homeopathy, was a most notable theologian of the Orthodox church, a philosopher, a philologist, a historian, a poet, and a publicist.[11]

One may add to this list Khomiakov's activities as playwright, painter, and architect.[12] Memoirs of contemporaries contain numerous references to Khomiakov's great reading speed, excellent memory, and surprising erudition. Khomiakov had a project for

---

[10] Herzen, *op. cit.*, pp. 297–300.

[11] N. Berdiaev, *Aleksei Stepanovich Khomiakov*, p. 39.

[12] In his monumental biography of Khomiakov, V. Zavitnevich mentions over twenty different fields of Khomiakov's activity: V. Zavitnevich, *Aleksei Stepanovich Khomiakov*.

everything: from the basic problems of church, civilization, and history, to the improvement of country roads in winter, and from land reform to the breeding of hunting dogs. His scholarship was spread over many fields, related and unrelated: it centered on such items as German idealistic philosophy, a comparative study of Russian and Sanskrit, the character of England, Catholicism, the theory of art, the Vedas, and many other subjects. His technological inventions included a steam engine "Moskovka," which Khomiakov patented and sent to an exhibition in London, agricultural machinery, and guns. In medicine Khomiakov specialized in devising treatments against cholera, which, however, proved to be the one opponent to have the last word in an argument with him.[13] Khomiakov was equally prepared to lecture to Bunsen on the subject of the latter's biblical studies or to a visitor from the Aleutians about those remote islands. Khomiakov's admirers regarded him as a universal genius. Critics, such as the historian S. Soloviev, spoke of dilettantism, and even of dishonesty and hypocrisy.[14]

In pursuing his varied interests Khomiakov never showed any confusion or slackening of concentration, but assailed everything with the same amazing confidence in himself and his views, with the same drive, and the same fighting spirit. Some stories of early incidents and influences have been preserved to illustrate or illuminate the formation of a number of Khomiakov's likes and

[13] One of Khomiakov's biographers, V. Liaskovskii, stated that his own use of Khomiakov's remedy against cholera proved to be extremely successful. V. Liaskovskii, *Aleksei Stepanovich Khomiakov: Ego zhizn i sochineniia*, note to p. 48.

[14] The charge that Khomiakov was a hypocrite without real convictions stemmed from his tactics as a debater and has no serious foundation. Koshelev's explanation appears to be correct: "Thus more than once he would even pretend to be a skeptic in argument with people devoted to religion as a matter of form or superstition; and, as the opposite of that, he expressed himself practically as a formalist or a superstitious old woman in argument with people who were inclined to deny religion. This caused some people who did not know Khomiakov well to say that he loved only the argument itself and that he had no permanent firm convictions; but those who knew him well realized that this was merely a method, not at all reprehensible, often very effective, and especially favored by Khomiakov to explain and eliminate error and to affirm that which he believed to be true." Koshelev, *op. cit.*, p. 72.

dislikes: the story of Khomiakov's great-grandfather, who inherited the estate because the peasants had selected him after they had been asked by the previous childless owner to nominate the member of the family they would most like to have as their master; the story of Khomiakov's childhood admiration for the heroic Black George of Serbia; the story of how Khomiakov and his brother on their first arrival at St. Petersburg in 1815 took it to be a horrible heathen city where they were bound to be persecuted for their faith. The remarkable thing is that Khomiakov's views on the peasant commune, on Black George and Serbia, on St. Petersburg, or on anything, for that matter, were never known to have undergone any substantial change. In the words of Khomiakov's close friend and collaborator Koshelev: "I knew Khomiakov for thirty-seven years, and his basic convictions of the year 1823 remained the same in the year 1860." [15] "He came into the world all prepared, armed and armor-plated." [16]

Khomiakov was a born fighter. He challenged Catholicism, and he defied Official Nationality. He was always ready to indulge in polemics with the Westernizers, or with the Protestant divines, or even with Ivan Kireevskii. In his spare time he tried to convert Old Believers or radical Moscow University students.[17] With determination and fighting spirit went the feeling of pride. Berdiaev listed pride as Khomiakov's basic characteristic, but he emphasized that this was pride in daily life with men, not spiritual pride directed against God.[18] Rozanov made no such qualification, and regarded pride and the resulting lack of charity

[15] A. Koshelev, "Moi vospominaniia ob A. S. Khomiakove," in *Russkii Arkhiv*, 1879, pp. 265–272, p. 269.

[16] Berdiaev, *op. cit.*, p. 73.

[17] The essay "About the Old and the New" was written by Khomiakov in 1839 to be read at a private gathering as Khomiakov's side of the debate with Ivan Kireevskii. Khomiakov presented in very sharp relief first the disadvantages and then the advantages of Old Russia. The first part of the article has often been cited as proof of Khomiakov's highly critical attitude towards the Russian past. It was contradicted by the second part, as well as by numerous other writings of Khomiakov, and represented a "dialectical excess" of its author rather than a reliable account of his views.

[18] Berdiaev, *op. cit.*, p. 42.

as particularly significant in explaining all of Khomiakov and his teaching.[19]

Although he was an exhausting disputant, although he was proud, rather parsimonious, and very doctrinaire, Khomiakov was loved or admired by a number of his contemporaries. They were especially attracted by a certain integrity in Khomiakov's character, by his confidence, and optimism. Khomiakov believed what he professed to believe, and he was never in doubt of his faith; those in doubt felt that especially strongly. Khomiakov's voluminous writings, many of them polemical in nature, contain, together with much bitterness, pettiness, and excess in argument, the exhilarating spirit of an honest, open encounter, much confidence, and courage, and even some magnanimity. "He belonged to the sons, not the stepsons, of God." [20]

IVAN KIREEVSKII

Ivan Kireevskii, "the philosopher of Slavophilism," was the only man sometimes placed on a par with Khomiakov as founder and leader of the movement. Comparable to Khomiakov in his ideology, writings, and role, both in the contemporary intellectual life of Russia and in the history of Russian thought, Kireevskii as a person was the very opposite of his friend. Khomiakov's robustness, energy, and optimism were entirely foreign to Kireevskii, who was characterized by preciosity in thought, writing, and life, by a constant state of worry, and by dark pessimism interspersed with sweeping assertions of hope and confidence. Kireevskii's snobbery, exclusiveness, and dreaminess further accentuated the difference between the two leaders of Slavophilism.[21] It was indicative of the men that, while Khomiakov had a score

[19] V. Rozanov, "Pamiati A. S. Khomiakova (1oe maia 1804–1oe maia 1904)," in *Novyi Put*, June, 1904, pp. 1–16.

[20] Berdiaev, *op. cit.*, p. 71.

[21] As a group the Slavophiles were democrats rather than snobs, but Ivan Kireevskii's snobbery comes out strongly in his correspondence. E.g., in February, 1830, he wrote from Berlin: "So far I have not become acquainted with anybody, except the local Russian students, the greater part of whom had been taken from seminaries and will return to Russia as unwashed as they had come here." I. K., vol. I, p. 25.

of devoted personal followers, Kireevskii had none, or at least none outside his family. Kireevskii, who showed himself in his youth as a talented literary critic, reflected strongly the aesthetic aspect of romanticism, and has often been called the most romantic of the Slavophiles.

Ivan Vasilievich Kireevskii was born on the 22nd of March, 1806, into an old landowning family. Both his father and his mother were distinguished by strong character, good education, and a wide range of interests. Kireevskii's father knew five languages, tried his hand at translation, and even composed a few original pieces, but he was especially attracted by natural sciences and medicine, had his own laboratory, and was constantly treating the sick. He was remembered as a man of strong tastes and queer habits: a landowner of the old type who ran his estate along strictly patriarchal lines; an extremely religious man, who hated rationalism and the Enlightenment, and used to buy Voltaire's works and burn them; a convinced Anglophile; a person of overpowering moral convictions who would not condone vice in the governor of his province any more than he would in his serfs. He died in 1812 of typhus, which he caught while managing a hospital with his usual self-sacrifice and devotion.

In a few years Kireevskii's mother was married again, to A. Elagin, a man of culture, especially interested in Kant and later, Schelling. She was a remarkable woman, a brilliant conversationalist and wit, an admirer of Racine, Rousseau, and Bernardin de Saint-Pierre, a translator of numerous German and French works, including some pieces of Hoffmann and Jean Paul Richter, a relative and very close friend of Zhukovskii, and later, when she went to Germany to educate the children of her second marriage, an acquaintance of some leading German romanticists, notably Tieck and Schelling. Her education, intelligence, and charm made her salon one of the intellectual centers of Moscow.

Ivan Kireevskii grew up very rapidly in the stimulating cultural amosphere of his home. From childhood his interests were directed towards literature. By the time he was twelve he was well acquainted with the Russian, French, and German languages and literatures, and at thirteen or fourteen he developed a passion for philosophy, namely for the ideas of Locke, Helvetius, and their followers. Later Kireevskii learned Latin, Greek, and English, took private lessons from several Moscow University professors, and attended Pavlov's public lectures in philosophy. In 1824 he passed the required examination and entered service in the Moscow Archives of the Ministry of Foreign Affairs. The friends of Kireevskii's youth, many of whom were also "young men of the archives," included the brothers Venevitinov, the prominent poets Baratynskii and Iazykov, the future representatives of Official Nationality, Shevyrev and Pogodin, and the future Slavophile, Koshelev. As a boy Kireevskii had been an admirer of the rationalist thinkers of the Enlightenment; as a young man he became an enthusiastic follower of the current romantic doctrines of the age, and took an active part in the Society of the Lovers of Wisdom. Kireevskii's first literary effort was a romantic sketch entitled *A Night in Tsaritsyn*, written in 1827 for a meeting of a literary circle. In 1828 he composed a poem in honor of the Polish poet Mickiewicz, and his first article, "Some Observations on the Nature of Pushkin's Poetry"; a year later he wrote his notable "Review of Russian Letters for the Year 1829."

In January, 1830, Kireevskii left Russia for Germany. He traveled, studied at the Universities of Berlin and Munich, planned to go to Paris, learned Italian and wanted to visit Italy, but returned suddenly in November of the same year, worried by an outbreak of cholera in Russia. In Berlin Kireevskii was especially interested in the lectures of Hegel, Ritter, and Schleiermacher. In Munich, where he lived and studied together with his brother Petr and another Lover of Wisdom, Rozhalin, and where he liked to spend evenings in Tiutchev's family, he paid particular attention to the courses of Schelling, Oken, and Schorn. Kireevskii became personally acquainted with Hegel and Schelling, as well as with some other outstanding German romanticists, and his desire to spread their ideas in Russia was thereby intensified.

After his return to Russia Kireevskii wrote some fugitive literary pieces, and in 1832 began to publish a review, *The European*, for which he had gathered a brilliant group of collaborators, and in the first issue of which he wrote a leading article on "The

Nineteenth Century." *The European*, into which the suspicious censors read a subversive meaning, was closed with the second issue, Zhukovskii's interference at the court saving Kireevskii from banishment. During several years following the failure of *The European*, Kireevskii wrote nothing except two unfinished tales, and two small articles of no significance.

After his brief period of employment in "the Archives," Kireevskii spent no more time in service, although he once applied for the chair of philosophy at the University of Moscow, but continued to live the life of a landowner on his Dolbino estate and in Moscow. In 1834 he married. Kireevskii's wife was very religious, and gradually she and her father confessor Filaret succeeded in turning Kireevskii's attention to the Orthodox Church. His brother Petr also probably exercised an important influence on his change of outlook, and directed him towards Orthodoxy and the Slavophile ideas in general. Ivan Kireevskii had been born into the Orthodox Church, but he had neglected it, and his new appreciation of the church had the force of a conversion. With the passage of years, religion acquired an ever greater influence on Kireevskii. After the death of Filaret he received spiritual guidance from Father Makarii of the famous Optino Monastery, which was located not far from Dolbino, visited the monastery often, helped the monks with the translation and the edition of the works of Eastern Doctors of the church, and sought their direction in the formulation of his own philosophy.

Kireevskii's "Answer to Khomiakov," written in 1839, but published only after the author's death, was the first clear expression of Kireevskii's new Slavophile ideology. In 1845 Kireevskii took over the periodical *The Moscovite* from Pogodin, but soon gave up once more his publicist activities, partly as a result of censorship difficulties. Of his articles in *The Moscovite*, the most important was his "Review of the Contemporary Conditions of Literature." Again Kireevskii remained silent for a number of years, his next article, "On the Nature of the European Enlightenment and Its Relation to the Russian Enlightenment," appearing in 1852, in *The Moscow Miscellany*, put out by Koshelev and Ivan Aksakov. Kireevskii's last work was begun in 1856, when intellectual life in Russia was strongly stimulated by the death of Nicholas I and the promise of the new reign and when the Slavophiles started their new periodical, *The Russian Conversation*: he undertook then to formulate the new Slavophile philosophy, and wrote the first part of his treatise "On the Necessity and the Possibility of New Principles in Philosophy." But the project was cut short by Kireevskii's death from cholera on the eleventh of June, 1856.

Ivan Kireevskii was very highly appreciated by his friends, and respected by his opponents. He has been traditionally presented as an admirable person, a noble idealist, a fine example of the glorious "men of the forties." A monk said after his death that he had been "all soul and love," and this statement has been echoed and reëchoed ever since.[22] Yet Dorn's vitriolic denunciation of Kireevskii's character was probably closer to the truth.[23] All his life Kireevskii appeared to have been struggling against a horrible handicap, against something that kept him constantly worried, bitter, and suspicious, prevented him from finishing his articles and his tales, and interfered with his scholarly projects and his plans for life in general. Time and again Kireevskii tried to fight the enemy. He ascribed the power of the enemy to the excess of sensitivity in his own upbringing, or, in a philosophic vein, to the schism created in the Russian soul by the false Western learning; he was determined to overcome the enemy by will power, by hard work, by a return to the true principles of faith.

In the end the enemy won. Kireevskii struggled through the last years of his life in the grip of an unaccountable fear, which paralyzed his actions, distorted his thoughts, and made him betray the most cherished beliefs of the Slavophiles, such as the freedom of the press, the independence of the church from the

[22] Gershenzon, *op. cit.*, p. 14.

[23] N. Dorn, *Kireevskii, opyt kharakteristiki ucheniia i lichnosti*. Dorn's book is interesting, but superficial. His analysis of Kireevskii's character was spoiled by his extreme hostility to Kireevskii. Thus, in addition to presenting Kireevskii as one driven by an obsession, he described him as a calculating hypocrite. Proceeding along such lines, Dorn could find no real difference between Slavophilism and Official Nationality, and concluded that the persecution of the Slavophiles had been caused by a misunderstanding.

state, and the emancipation of the serfs. He became convinced that at the moment any change in Russia, big or small, was bound to lead to most dreadful consequences. He was terrified by his sister's desire to free her own serfs, argued that the serfs were better off than the state peasants ruled by corrupt officials, made his brother join the argument, suggested that she was acting out of vanity, threatened her with the horrors that would follow, conceded that she could emancipate the peasants in her will, but insisted that the will was to be secret, lest the peasants acquire dangerous thoughts.[24] Kireevskii's letters to Koshelev, who favored the abolition of serfdom, were permeated by an agonizing fear of change, by bitterness against those proposing "untimely and egoistic reforms," and by horrible warnings.[25]

In a similar manner Kireevskii wrote to Pogodin in 1848 against an appeal for a relaxation of censorship regulations:

It is not a great misfortune if our literature is killed for two or three years. It will come back to life. On the other hand, the delivering of a petition at the present time would make the government assume an antagonistic or at least a suspicious attitude towards those engaged in literature, and this is much worse, for it may lead to wrong and harmful consequences. At present the government must not fear any well-intentioned person. It must be convinced that at the given moment we all are ready to sacrifice all our secondary interests for the sole purpose of saving Russia from disorders and unnecessary war. We must wish only the following: that the government would not involve us in a war through some whim or through friendship to some Swedish or . . . king; that it would not set out to crush our Slavs with the Germans; that it *would not incite the people by false rumors of freedom and would not introduce any new laws until everything quiets down and the situation in the West becomes clear, that it would not, for instance, make inventories of landlords' estates, the procedure which excites the minds with unrealizable surmises . . .*[26]

And in another letter, after a complaint that a foreign spirit ruled the government and made every effort of improvement turn into disaster:

[24] I. K., vol. II, pp. 241–245.
[25] I. K., vol. II, pp. 252–258.
[26] I. K., vol. II, p. 249. Everything italicized in quotations here and elsewhere has been italicized in the original.

Therefore in the meantime I have only one desire: that they leave us alone in the condition in which we are — be it good, or be it bad — that they do not disturb us with changes, and, what is still more important, with threats of change which create a moral perturbation worse than the physical one.[27]

PETR KIREEVSKII

The life of Ivan's brother Petr Kireevskii was strikingly blank. Two years younger than Ivan, Petr was born in February, 1808, and received the same private education as his brother, first on the Dolbino estate, then in Moscow. He knew seven languages well, moved in the same circles as Ivan, had similar literary interests. Only Petr Kireevskii limited himself entirely to translations, ranging from an article in *The Foreign Quarterly Review* to Calderon and Washington Irving, with which he was occupied sporadically throughout his life and most of which remained unpublished.

In July 1829, to complete his education he went to Germany, where he spent over a year, principally at the University of Munich, attending the lectures of Schelling, Oken, Baader, Goerres, Schorn, and other outstanding romanticists. Kireevskii came to know some of his teachers personally, and enjoyed the high opinion of Schelling. Later he undertook another voyage to Western Europe in order to restore to health the fatally ill poet Iazykov,

[27] I. K., vol. II, p. 253. The fear, so obvious in this letter, can be traced far back. As early as 1830, Ivan Kireevskii wrote to his brother Petr: "The dominant, daily feeling in our family is a sort of a tense, frightened expectation of misfortune. Happiness is incompatible with such a feeling. But where is it from? Why? How to eradicate it? How to replace it with calm and courageous dauntlessness in the face of the hurricane of fate? — that is what we must consider together in order to act with joint strength." I. K., vol. II, p. 218. See Gershenzon, *op. cit.*, for the background of refined sensitivity and nervousness in the Kireevskii family.

The tragedy of Ivan Kireevskii's last years is accentuated by the presumptuous hopes of his youth. E.g., in 1827, at the age of twenty-one he wrote to Koshelev: "We shall return its rights to the true religion, unite art and morality, replace stupid liberalism by a respect for the laws, and place the purity of life above the purity of style. But what will be there to limit our influence? Where will you put its end, saying *nec plus ultra?* Let the most daring imagination construct the pillars of Hercules, a new Columbus will discover beyond them a new world." I. K., vol. I, p. 10.

but otherwise his life was spent in Russia — on his estate, in Moscow, and wandering all over the country in search of folk songs.

After the partition of the family estates, Petr Kireevskii received land of his own, where he gathered a fine library and studied Russian history and folklore. From approximately 1830 he became particularly interested in Russian popular songs and tales, and spent the last twenty-six years of his life collecting them both by personal excursions and through friends, who included Pushkin and Gogol, as well as other prominent men. Kireevskii entered into a written polemic only once, against Pogodin in 1845, and even then he did not finish the exposition of his side of the argument. Kireevskii's huge collection of songs was mishandled after his death, and many songs were lost, but the remainder formed a valuable contribution to the study of Russian folklore. Kireevskii was important to the Slavophile movement because of this contribution, because of his very close connection with his brother Ivan, and because, together with Khomiakov, he was the first Slavophile who attracted others to him. Like Khomiakov, he seemed to have been born with all his ideas set, and he never changed them.

Petr Kireevskii did not marry, did not write, did not teach, did not show interest in agriculture or in other economic pursuits, so dear to a Khomiakov or a Koshelev. Only his songs and his notebooks, crammed with information concerning the Russian past, survived him. He impressed his contemporaries as a man of high integrity, wholeness, and noble principles, but also as one who somehow did not possess his own will, his own personality; he seemed an automaton or a shadow. The writer Ivan Turgenev described Petr Kireevskii as "a man of crystal purity and translucence." A recent biographer, Gershenzon, declared:

Reconstructing the life of Kireevskii, reading and rereading the yellow pile of his letters, it is impossible to get rid of a strange, almost eerie feeling. In Kireevskii there is something phantom-like, something frightening; behind the facts of his busy life one feels a gaping void, behind his strong will — the absence of personality.[28]

[28] Gershenzon, *op. cit.*, p. 115.

As a man, Petr Kireevskii was very clumsy, and he always felt awkward and self-conscious. His letters constantly contained such expressions as "my stupid mistake," "Cad! cad! cad!" addressed to himself, and the like. In any misunderstanding with others he automatically assumed himself to be the guilty party. His inability to be at ease with people pained him greatly, but he felt helpless to deal with this "incapacity consisting not in awkwardness, not in the French language, which somehow could be managed, but in an *uncommunicativeness*, which lies in the character, which cannot be helped by external means and the effects of which go beyond fashionable society." [29] With the passage of years the urge to be alone increased. There were references to the desire "not to see a single human face." [30] And Kireevskii did remain alone practically all the time, either on his estate or on his excursions — alone or in the company of his favorite dog. All sources testify to Kireevskii's extreme exactingness towards himself, and his resulting inability to write, to complete his work, to get beyond raw materials.

Petr Kireevskii always adored his brother Ivan. The relationship was not a happy one.

But I never loved anybody more than you; and when we were together the feeling of my inferiority was always the most oppressive thing for me; it deprived me of your confidence. [31]

As time went by, this fixation, apparently, grew. Petr spoke of the fact that he wanted no family of his own, that his brother's family was also his. He died on the 25th of October, 1856 — four and a half months after the death of his brother — of grief.

[29] "Pisma bratiev Kireevskikh," in *Russkii Arkhiv*, 1894, book three, pp. 207–224, esp. p. 219.

Complaining of the lack of seriousness and purpose in Russian society, Ivan Aksakov exclaimed on one occasion that if this dangerous situation continued even the impossible might happen and "Petr Vasilievich Kireevskii himself . . . may get into the whirl of social life and take up dancing." I. A., *Pisma*, vol. I, p. 73.

[30] "Petr Vasilievich Kireevskii, Ego pisma," in *Russkii Arkhiv*, 1905, book two, pp. 113–173, esp. p. 160.

[31] P. K., *op. cit.*, pp. 118–119.

KONSTANTIN AKSAKOV

The two Aksakov brothers, Konstantin and Ivan, played as great a role in the development of Slavophilism as did the Kireevskiis. Their father, Sergei Timofeevich Aksakov, a cultured landowner, had been from his youth deeply interested in literature, especially in the theater, but his own contributions were mediocre until he began late in life to write in a simple, narrative style about the things he knew and loved: childhood recollections, the life on a manor, hunting, fishing. Then he composed such works as *The Family Chronicle*, and *Tales and Reminiscences of a Sportsman*, which were distinguished by simplicity, spontaneity, and vividness, and by the unique excellence of their remarkably pure and unaffected language and style, and which made their author famous among his contemporaries and assured him of a permanent place in Russian literature. The Slavophiles came from a manorial background which held their affections for life and exercised a powerful influence on their doctrines: nowhere was this background stronger than in the Aksakov family, nowhere was it as enchanting as in S. T. Aksakov's tales. In political ideology, S. T. Aksakov had leanings towards the nationalist Right, was associated with the Shishkov group, and proved his rigor as a censor. Through their father the young Aksakovs became acquainted at an early age with some of the most prominent Russian writers of the time. Gogol in particular was a close friend of S. T. Aksakov and an admirer of his talent, in the development of which he had an important part. Konstantin Aksakov, in turn, began his career as a literary critic with a eulogy of Gogol.

Konstantin Sergeevich Aksakov was born on March 29th, 1817. His rapid intellectual growth was connected from the very beginning with a certain kind of heroism and nationalism, stimulated by his mother, who had a passionate, naïve, and impressionable character, preferred boys to girls, and regarded the mother of the Gracchi as her ideal. At four Konstantin Aksakov learned to read, his first book being *The History of Troy*. Soon Trojan warriors were replaced by Karamzin and native Russian heroes, in whose honor Aksakov composed poems, and whose exploits formed the unique theme of his childhood games. The Aksakovs were one of the few educated Russian families of the time who spoke only Russian at home, and Konstantin Aksakov improved on his parents by seizing notes to his mother written in French and burning them to the chant of his own incantations. From his childhood on, Konstantin Aksakov was remarkably consistent: he always defended everything Russian, and attacked everything foreign. He was the Slavophile most determined to wear a beard and the "native" Russian costume, as a result of which, according to his ironical friends, he was taken by the common people for a Persian. He quickly developed into the most extreme member of the group, and his sweeping exaggerations, great naïveté, and deadly earnestness in everything often embarrassed such men as Khomiakov and Ivan Kireevskii. In the passionate enthusiasm of his views, and in the violence of his feelings about abstract intellectual subjects, Konstantin Aksakov has often been compared to the Westernizer Belinskii.

In his childhood, and in his youth, and in his more mature years, K. Aksakov fought for one cause, prayed to one god: Russia and the Russian people — it is everything for him, everything is contained in it, outside it there is nothing.[32]

In 1826, the Aksakovs moved from the country to Moscow, where Konstantin spent the rest of his life. In 1832, he completed his schooling at home and entered the University of Moscow at the then usual age of fifteen. The University was experiencing a revival: young professors, such as Pavlov and Nadezhdin, the popularizers of Schelling; Shevyrev and Pogodin, the proponents of Official Nationality; and the skeptical historian, Kachenovskii, were attracting large audiences; philosophical circles began to be formed among the students.[33] At first Aksakov fell under the influence of Belinskii and of Stankevich, and devoted himself passionately to the study of German philosophy, Hegelianism in par-

[32] Brodskii, op. cit., p. XXIII.

[33] K. A., "Vospominaniia studenchestva." Originally published in Den, 1862, nos. 39 and 40. In these recollections of his student days, Aksakov minimized the worth of the professors, but stressed the importance of student life and associations for his development.

ticular. Later, however, he was strongly affected, together with his friend Samarin, by Khomiakov and the growing Slavophile doctrines. In contrast to Samarin, who changed his orientation with much struggle and pain, Aksakov accepted Slavophilism as a logical development of his basic beliefs in Russia and its destiny, the beliefs which had only been strengthened in him by Hegelianism and other influences. As the difference between the Slavophiles and the Westernizers was becoming more pronounced, Aksakov broke relations with his former Westernizer friends and became the ardent spokesman of extreme Slavophilism.

Aksakov began his literary career by writing poetry, by translations, especially from Schiller and Goethe, and by contributing critical reviews to the periodicals with which Belinskii was associated. In the early thirties he wrote a dramatic farce in verse *Oleg at the Gates of Constantinople*; in 1848 a drama, *The Liberation of Moscow in 1612*; and in 1856 a comedy, *Prince Lupovitskii*. Aksakov's prominence as a literary critic dated from his article about Gogol's *Dead Souls*, published in 1842. In 1847 Aksakov received the degree of Master of Letters, an equivalent of the present-day Doctor's degree, for a dissertation on *Lomonosov in the History of Russian Literature and the Russian Language*.

In addition to literature and literary criticism, Aksakov was engrossed in Russian philology and Russian history, and has even been called "the historian of Slavophilism." His twenty-seven articles on Russian history, which included four long reviews of four different volumes of Soloviev's monumental *History of Russia*, were published in 1861 as the first volume of Aksakov's collected works. His linguistic studies were collected in the second and third volumes. Like most of the Slavophiles, Aksakov had a strong interest in public affairs. In 1855 he presented to Emperor Alexander II his famous memorandum "Concerning the Internal Conditions of Russia," which gave a very sharp outline of the Slavophile views on the subject and demanded in particular the freedom of the press.

Except for two visits to Western Europe, Konstantin Aksakov spent his entire life in his paternal house in Moscow. He was devoted to his family, and above all, to his father, whom he followed like a small boy throughout his life. Aksakov was never married and no women were connected with his name. There was only the pathetic story of his futile efforts to interest a German girl, a flower seller, in Schiller and German romantic poetry. Konstantin Aksakov's death on the 7th of December, 1860, followed that of his father. "The grown-up child," left alone, could not survive. Specialists were amazed by "this giant dying from longing for his father; in fact, the entire illness consisted only in that." [34]

IVAN AKSAKOV

Ivan Sergeevich Aksakov, born in 1823, was six years younger than his brother Konstantin. After the usual education at home, he went, not to the University of Moscow, but to the recently opened School of Jurisprudence in St. Petersburg, where he studied from 1838 until his graduation in 1842. Next Ivan Aksakov entered the civil service and held various positions in Moscow, Astrakhan, and Kaluga. In September, 1844, he was assigned for special missions to the Ministry of the Interior, and sent to investigate the Old Believer movement in Bessarabia. Soon afterwards Aksakov was arrested, primarily because of some sharp criticism of the government found in his correspondence, but was quickly released and retained in the service. He was a member of the revisional commission in the Iaroslav province, and wrote an interesting account "Concerning the Runners," an extreme nonconformist sect very widespread in that area.

Aksakov had been writing poetry from the age of nineteen, when he composed a fantasy, *The Life of an Official, a Mystery in Three Acts*, and he was particularly productive as a poet between 1845 and 1855. The subject of Aksakov's poetry was almost invariably one and the same: a protest against the apathy and the ignorance of Russian society, and a longing for free, productive, and meaningful work and life. In 1852 Aksakov's poem, "A Vagabond," led him into trouble with his superiors, who pointed out that the writing of such poems was incompatible with the dignity of a government official. Aksakov resigned his position and never again entered government service.

[34] V. Smirnov, *Aksakovy, ikh zhizn i literaturnaia deiatelnost*, p. 47.

As a young man Ivan Aksakov was skeptically inclined and stood closer to the Westernizers than to the Slavophiles, but gradually the influence of Khomiakov and of his brother Konstantin prevailed, and he developed into a leading Slavophile journalist. As such he ran quickly into censorship difficulties: in 1853 Aksakov's *Moscow Miscellany* was banned, the collaborators of the review were ordered to submit their writings directly to the Central Office of censorship, which amounted to a prohibition to write, and Aksakov, in addition, was forbidden to be an editor of any future publication. In 1853 and 1854 Aksakov spent a year in the Ukraine making a study of trade at the Ukranian fairs, which he published in 1859 and which received two high awards for its merit. During the Crimean War he joined the militia, but his unit did not go beyond Bessarabia. In 1858 Aksakov became the actual editor of the Slavophile periodical, *The Russian Conversation*, while Koshelev held the post nominally. In 1859 Aksakov was allowed to be editor in his own right, and started a weekly *The Sail*, but it was proscribed after the second number, partly as a result of Aksakov's own poetry. In 1860 he went abroad, trying to restore to health his brother Konstantin, who died in December on the island of Zante in the Ionian Sea. In 1861 Aksakov began to publish *The Day* which proved to be very successful and continued to come out until 1866.

In 1866 he married the lady-in-waiting, A. F. Tiutchev, a daughter of the famous poet. Aksakov's next publication, the newspaper *Moscow*, appeared in 1867, and received nine warnings and three temporary suspensions in less than two years. During the suspension periods, *Moscow* was effectively replaced by *The Moscovite* with a different nominal editor. As a result of *Moscow* Aksakov was again forbidden to edit any publication. That time the ban lasted for twelve years: the government was not willing to allow any serious criticism of its activity, and it was especially offended by Aksakov's attacks on its policy in the western borderlands. Deprived of the rights of a journalist, Aksakov remained, nevertheless, a public figure, especially in his capacity of Secretary, and after Pogodin's death Chairman, of the Moscow Slavonic Benevolent Committee. The Committee acquired a great importance in connection with the Balkan crisis of 1875–1878, and Aksakov came to be recognized as the leader and the most powerful spokesman of the Pan-Slav sentiment. For his famous oration against the Congress of Berlin he was banished from Moscow, but soon allowed to return. In 1880 Aksakov received permission to edit a weekly, *Rus*, which continued to come out until Aksakov's sudden death from heart failure on January 27th, 1886. Aksakov was also prominent as Vice-Chairman of the Orthodox Missionary Society, as Chairman of the Society of the Friends of Russian Letters, and as member of the Moscow City Council and of the Moscow zemstvo. Like a number of other Slavophiles, he was interested in economic affairs, and he came to occupy an executive position in the Moscow Society of Mutual Credit.

Aksakov's works consist of his poetry, of a few miscellaneous pieces, such as a biography of his father-in-law, the poet Tiutchev, of three volumes of correspondence, and of seven huge volumes of articles and speeches. He was the publicist and the popularizer of Slavophilism; in nineteenth-century Russia people read Ivan Aksakov more than they did all the other Slavophiles put together. His articles, remarkably similar in spirit, although he was gradually becoming more nationalist, were full of vigor, earnestness, and conviction; they were also proof of a narrow mind, and were characterized by crude repetitiousness.

In Aksakov's hands Slavophilism was not only popularized, but also modified. Doctrines were not changed: Ivan Aksakov had a profound respect for the early Slavophiles, his brother Konstantin and Khomiakov in particular, and regarded himself merely as their faithful follower; time and again he repeated bluntly such basic Slavophile dogmas as the primacy of the religious element over the racial and the national, freedom of the press, and the condemnation of the government, of the entire ruling class as antinational. But there was a certain shift in emphasis, a certain variation in spirit. Ivan Aksakov had traveled in the West as much as the other Slavophiles, he too had been powerfully attracted by German romantic thinkers, and paid homage to such German poets as Schiller and Goethe. He remembered that all his life. To a positivist, materialist generation he defended the value of meta-physics, and advocated the reading of Schiller's poetry. Yet these were only reminiscences. In his own articles he was invariably more narrow, provincial, and crudely nationalistic than Ivan Kireevskii could be in his worst moments. Ivan Aksakov was a true Slavophile, the last one; he also served as an introduction to the extreme nationalism, Pan-Slav and otherwise, which became prominent in Russia at the end of his life and which marked a negation of the principles most cherished by the Slavophiles.

IURII SAMARIN

Iurii Fedorovich Samarin, the most important Slavophile public man and a significant theoretician of the movement, was born on April 21st, 1819, in St. Petersburg. His father, a former officer, held the position of the Master of the Horse, his mother, née Neledin-skii-Meletskii, also came from court circles. French was the domi-nant language in the family as well as in the society to which the family belonged, and Samarin paid his first visit to Paris in 1823. In 1826 Samarin's father retired to devote himself to the education of his children, and the family settled in Moscow. Samarin's teach-ers included Nadezhdin, who later became prominent as professor and publicist, and the able Frenchman, Pascault, who played a particularly important role in the development of his young pupil.[35]

In the autumn of 1834, Samarin entered the department of let-ters of the University of Moscow. His fellow students there in-cluded a number of outstanding men, notably Konstantin Aksakov, Samarin's senior by two years, who became a very close friend of Samarin and exercised for a period of time a strong influence over him. Samarin, who concentrated on history and was especially attracted by Pogodin's emphasis on the particularity, the individu-

---

[35] Nolde wrote: "Classicism according to the French pedagogical pattern, which formed the foundation of Pascault's teaching, is felt in Samarin's en-tire mental structure, in the irreproachability of his logic, and in the care-fullness and the beautiful simplicity of his style, and Iurii Fedorovich ap-preciated highly the classical education which he had received." B. Nolde, *Iurii Samarin i ego vremia*, p. 9. Nolde's excellent account of Samarin and his time is the best book on the subject.

ality of Russia, was graduated from the University at nineteen at the head of his class. In 1840, he began to write his dissertation for the Master's degree, choosing as his subject a comparative study of the two leading Russian ecclesiastics in Peter the Great's reign, Stefan Iavorskii and Feofan Prokopovich. In connection with his work, Samarin probed deeply into such fundamental problems as the nature of faith, the relation of religion to philosophy, and the relation of church to state.

Strongly influenced by Hegelian philosophy, which he studied with a real thoroughness, Samarin at first found the advantage of Orthodoxy over Catholicism and Protestantism in the fact that it had no philosophical system of its own, and he even developed the idea that Hegelianism was indispensable as the only true intellectual support of the Orthodox faith. This doctrine proved to be untenable. In 1843–1844 Samarin lived through a severe intellectual and emotional crisis, experiencing in himself a bitter struggle of Orthodoxy against Hegel. Orthodoxy won, and the decisive influence was that of Khomiakov, whom Samarin met early in 1840 and who became his friend and teacher. Khomiakov's perfect confidence of his faith, and his conviction that faith is to be affirmed as the fundamental experience of man, not deduced from metaphysical systems, finally prevailed over Samarin's doubts, and Samarin became Khomiakov's grateful disciple for the rest of his life.[36]

The disputation for the degree was held on June 4th, 1844, and Samarin acquitted himself brilliantly. He wanted to continue in the field of scholarship, but ceded to the wishes of his father, entered the civil service, and spent the eight following years at various tasks as government official. In 1846 Samarin used the opportunity provided by his work on the revisional committee in the city of Riga to write A History of the City Institutions of Riga, and Letters about the Baltic Provinces. The latter work, circulated in manuscript copies among Samarin's friends, was a determined

---

[36] The best account of Samarin's crisis and of the reorientation of his thought was provided by Dimitrii Samarin in Dannye dlia biografii Iu. F. Samarina za 1840–1845 gg., which served as one of the introductions to the fifth volume of Samarin's Collected Works. S., vol. V, pp. XXXV–XCII.

attack against the Baltic Germans and the government which did their bidding at the expense of Russian national interests and also of the downtrodden natives of the area. It led to Samarin's arrest and twelve-day imprisonment in the fortress of St. Peter and St. Paul, at the end of which period he was summoned before Emperor Nicholas I, who himself lectured Samarin on the impropriety of Samarin's behavior and then had him released and retained in the service.[37] Samarin, however, soon retired and devoted himself to the composition of his projects for the emancipation of the serfs and to his activity as a Slavophile publicist.

Samarin was one of the principal authors and a leading executor of the great emancipation reform. He did a prodigious amount of work both in the Editing Commission in St. Petersburg, in 1859–1860, and in the Samara province; in general he was more liberal than his colleagues, more conscious of the interests of the peasants. After the emancipation of the serfs in Russia proper, Samarin was appointed, together with his colleagues and friends N. Miliutin and Prince Cherkasskii, to investigate the position of peasants in Poland and outline the necessary reforms. This mission, which was a direct consequence of the Polish rebellion of 1863, united two subjects of the greatest importance to Samarin: the peasant problem and the question of the borderlands of Russia. The conclusions of the three men, among whom, according to Nolde, Samarin played by far the leading role, became the foundation of the Russian policy in Poland in the following decades.

Samarin spent the last twelve years of his life as a landlord, public figure, writer, and publicist, living on his estates and in Moscow and visiting the West almost every year. He worked indefatigably in the zemstvo of the Moscow province; continued his polemical writings on the borderlands; answered in 1865 the Russian Jesuit Martynov with five long letters on Jesuitism and the Jesuits; published in 1867 in Prague Khomiakov's collected theological works, and in his famous introduction to the volume called Khomiakov a Doctor of the Church; analyzed, in 1872–1875, Kave-

---

[37] The best account of the conversation between Nicholas I and Samarin is in Nolde, *op. cit.*, pp. 47–49.

lin's *Problems of Psychology*; and wrote in 1875, jointly with F. Dmitriev, a booklet entitled *Revolutionary Conservatism*, aimed against constitutionalism in Russia, which he regarded as an effort on the part of the gentry to acquire power for their class at the expense of the people. Samarin died on March 19th, 1876, in Berlin, of blood poisoning which followed a minor operation on the arm. Samarin was well known and much appreciated in his lifetime; in 1869 he was made an honorary member of the University of Moscow, in 1872 of the Moscow Theological Academy.

Fourteen volumes of Samarin's collected works, of which only eleven were published, center around three basic topics — reform in Russia, in particular the emancipation of the serfs, the borderlands, and religious and philosophical studies — but they include numerous other subjects as well. Samarin expounded and defended the Slavophile ideology on almost every plane: he not only championed the peasant commune, both in theory and in the practical work of emancipation, not only fought for the borderlands, but also promulgated Slavophile doctrines in philosophy, religion, psychology, economic theory, literature, and education — in short, in every aspect of life and culture.

He possessed an excellent literary style, distinguished by precision and power, and exhibited the talent of a first class polemical writer. Contemporaries were particularly impressed by Samarin's great ability for work, which was combined in him with an overbearing sense of duty. Samarin drove himself with an equal intensity in the Editing Commission for the emancipation of the serfs, in his studies of Hegel and the Orthodox Church, or in his struggle against the Baltic Germans. He was never negligent, disorderly, or confused, but this order and logic were very exacting. Samarin's friends admired his devotion to duty, but suggested that he should have a fuller private life, that, perhaps, he should marry, which Samarin never did. In 1859, under the strain of work in the Editing Commission, Samarin had a very dangerous nervous attack. Although he made a good recovery, the attack was repeated in 1864, and in general, after 1859, Samarin was not a healthy man.

As in the case of some other Slavophiles, Samarin's numerous interests and varied activities were unified by the basic beliefs, the fundamental outlook which he had acquired in his youth, in the age of romanticism. This outlook stamped him for life. Shortly before his death Samarin wrote from Berlin:

Here is an expression concerning me personally which kept coming up after conversations on all sorts of subjects: it is hardly possible to find among us such a thoroughgoing representative of our old views.[38]

[38] S., vol. VI, p. 488.

CHAPTER III

WE AND THEY

The variety and the diversity of the Slavophile writings made some scholars doubt the propriety of the very expression "Slavophile thought." For instance, Professor Zenkovskii, in his history of Russian philosophy, pointedly refused to discuss "Slavophile philosophy" and treated the Slavophile thinkers as individuals.[1] Most specialists, however, considered the Slavophile ideology to be a logical whole, while Berdiaev and many others also claimed that all Slavophile thought was organically interrelated as a living expression of Russia, or of Orthodoxy, or of both at the same time.[2] The connected and complementary nature of Slavophile writings is evident even without Berdiaev's assumptions: the Slavophiles discussed related subjects, often in a similar manner; more interesting is the fact that their approach and their inspiration were essentially one and the same. The Slavophile ideology was based on a dichotomy, and their arguments were invariably constructed around two terms. This sharply pronounced two-term pattern of the entire Slavophile thought, as well as, of course, the particular meanings attached to the two terms, were responsible for the unity of Slavophilism. The two terms may be called "We" and "They."

"WE" AND "THEY" – PSYCHOLOGICAL

In the West the Slavophiles could not relax. The West was a challenge to their thought and life, and as such it produced a strong reaction even before the Slavophile doctrine itself was formulated. In 1830 Ivan Kireevskii wrote from Germany, after a few months stay: "With Germany we are already choked up." [3] And: "No, on the entire globe there is no nation worse, more soul-

---

[1] V. Zenkovskii, *Istoriia russkoi filosofii*, volume I, p. 188.
[2] See, e.g., Berdiaev, *op. cit.*, p. 24.
[3] I. K., vol. I, p. 49.

less, dull, and vexing than the Germans. Bulgarin is a genius by comparison with them."[4] Such statements occurred in Ivan Kireevskii's correspondence next to accounts of excellent educational opportunities which he enjoyed at German universities, and of friendly receptions accorded to him by such men as Schelling and Hegel.

Little incidents gave rise to unexpected emotions. On one occasion Ivan Kireevskii communicated to his sister the following illustrated estimate of Germany:

In order to drive the Germans out of Russian dreams, send me your portrait as soon as possible. After looking at it, at brother, at Rozhalin, and at everything that came with us from Russia throughout the day, I hope to be free at least in my dreams from Germany which, by the way, I do not dislike, but hate! I hate it as a chain, as a prison, as a coffin in which people are buried alive. You can not understand from your Russia what sort of thing this Germany is. All that travelers tell about it is almost entirely nonsense. And if you want to know what it is then listen to the Germans themselves. The Germans alone tell the truth about it when they call it the land of the oaks (*das Land der Eichen*), although, barring the Germans themselves, there are practically no oaks in Germany. But then the Germans themselves are the most wooden of all the oaks. Only yesterday brother hooked one of them with his umbrella, and so awkwardly that the umbrella broke. Brother apologized in Russian with his usual: "Oh! pardon me!" The German felt the blow some twenty steps later, suddenly stopped dead, his eyes bulging, and remained silent. After he finished meditating about the incident, he finally took off his hat and answered brother: "I beg you not to worry, Baron! It is nothing!" I do not know what you will call such liveliness, as to me I have no word for it except: "German."[5]

The letters of Petr Kireevskii reflected a spirit very similar to his brother's; to both of them "German" often served as a synonym for "undesirable" or "bad," and "Russian" for "desirable" or "good." The same direct, personal hostility to the West permeated the writings of the other Slavophiles, and could be found in Khomiakov's letters from Paris in the twenties as well as in Samarin's letters from Berlin in the seventies, although it often took less crude

[4] I. K., vol. I, p. 48.　　　　　[5] I. K., vol. II, pp. 221–222.

and less clear forms than it did in the Kireevskiis' corespondence.[6] As the Slavophile ideology was developed, the Slavophile attitude towards the West appeared in the form of a dilemma: on the one hand the Slavophiles stressed the uniqueness of the true Russia, the fact that their beliefs and their ideas were so far above and beyond anything attained by the West that the West could not even understand them; on the other hand, they demanded recognition by the West.

Whether the West could understand them or not, the Slavophiles felt certain that it would not do so. The West was full of hate towards Russia, towards the East. As Khomiakov complained to his Oxford friend Palmer, ever since the separation of the Orthodox and the Roman Catholic churches,

the Western communities have nurtured a deep enmity and an incurable disdain for the unchanging East. These feelings have become traditional and, as it were, innate, to the Roman-German world, and England has all the time partaken of that spiritual life.[7]

To the Slavophiles Western hatred of the East was an axiom. This conviction affected every aspect of their doctrine, from their evaluation of Catholicism to their consideration of the Eastern question, and from their opinion on Napoleon III to their estimate of contemporary German scholars.

The Western attitude of hate was a dreadful sin, but its origins could be explained: it was a result of the guilt of the West in its relations with the East.

In the number of laws which govern the world of mind, there is one, the divine, strict truth of which allows no exception; it is the law that evil bears evil. Every undeserved insult, every injustice strikes the guilty party harder than the victim; the offended one endures, the offender becomes corrupted. . . . This law has an enormous significance in history.[8]

[6] It is interesting to note that Koshelev's descriptions of the West did not contain this hostility. Koshelev was closely associated with the Slavophiles, but he also differed from them on several points and, according to Ivan Aksakov, was connected with the movement by "external" rather than by "inner, spiritual" bonds. I. A., *Pisma*, vol. I, p. 1.

[7] *Russia and the English Church during the Last Fifty Years*, volume I, *Containing a Correspondence between Mr. William Palmer, Fellow of Magdalen College, Oxford and M. Khomiakoff in the Years 1844-1854*, pp. 8-9.

[8] Kh., vol. II, p. 97.

The West provided instances of that law both in history and on the personal plane. Samarin, for instance, deplored the fact that while the Russians, even when they realized the German danger, retained intellectual and moral integrity in their attitude towards Germany,

everywhere, where the German element dominates, the opposite is the case. As soon as Russia or a Russian is in question, minds seem to become clouded and consciences become silent. The most truthful spirits willingly accept falsehood as a weapon; men, most honorable in every other way, throw themselves wholeheartedly into calumny, and the public allows that to happen; nobody protests, nobody brings them to their senses.[9]

The particular psychological attitude of the Slavophiles was fundamental to their view of the world, and it also appeared in a striking fashion in numerous special fields of their activity. One of Khomiakov's best known lyrical pieces dealt with a young lady whose soul was as clear as flame, who understood "the tones of the heart," who could share the joy, the suffering, the noble thoughts and the pure dreams of poets, who has been marked from her birth by the angel of purity and beauty. Yet the poet would not give his love to the lady. He would not do that because Russia was foreign to her, because she preferred other lands, other skies, because she did not follow a native song, because her heart did not tremble at the words "Holy Rus."[10]

Konstantin Aksakov fought his battle even in philology. He introduced into linguistics

especially into the discussion of the noun, his personal feelings — love and disgust, sympathies and antipathies. . . . He *loved* particularly

[9] *Correspondence de G. Samarine avec la Baronne de Rhaden, 1861–1876*, p. 180.

[10] Kh., IV, pp. 21–22.

The beautiful lady was a Russian of foreign origin, the very prominent A. O. Rosset-Smirnova. See Koshelev, "Moi vospominaniia ob A. S. Khomiakove," p. 266. And: Koshelev, *Zapiski*, p. 30.

O. Miller, a leading Pan-Slav of the seventies and eighties, exulted in the fact that Khomiakov had concentrated his attention on Slavdom, and had spurned the beautiful lady who would not share his views. O. Miller, *Slavianstvo i Evropa. Stati i rechi, 1865–1877*. The article entitled "Khomiakov — poet slavianstva," pp. 114–130.

well the sound ъ, which plays such an important part in our language and which is so helpful in philological research; to the same extent he acquired a hatred of the enemy — the sound *s*, the hatred which the kindest heart can feel towards something odious. He showered this enemy with epithets such as "irksome," "importunate," "intruding wriggler," "obsequious," "servile. . . ." [11]

In his analysis of Russian grammar and of the history of the Russian language, Aksakov struggled against noxious Western influences along more conventional Slavophile lines.

Slavophile theology contained numerous illustrations of the same psychological attitude. The following long and significant account, which deals with the addition of *filioque* to the Creed in the West and the resulting split of the Western and the Eastern churches, is the best example of it:

Now let us betake ourselves to the last years of the eighth or the beginning of the ninth century, and let us imagine a wanderer who had come from the East to one of the cities in Italy or in France. Pervaded by the feeling of ancient unity, and quite confident that he is in the midst of brethren, he enters a church to sanctify the last day of the week. Full of love, he concentrates on pious thoughts, follows the service, and listens to the wonderful prayers which had gladdened his heart from early childhood. Words reach him: Let us kiss one another, that we may with one mind confess the Father, the Son, and the Holy Ghost. He is listening carefully. Now the Creed of the Christian and Catholic church is proclaimed, the Creed which every Christian must serve with his entire life, and for which, on occasion, he must sacrifice his life. He is listening carefully, — But this Creed is corrupted, it is some new, unknown creed! Is he awake, or is he in the power of an oppressive dream? He does not believe his ears, begins to doubt his senses. He wants to find out, asks explanation. An idea occurs to him: he may have walked into a gathering of dissenters cast away by the local church. . . . Alas, this is not the case! He heard the voice of the local church itself. An entire patriarchate, an entire vast world fell away from unity. . . . The shattered wanderer complains; he is comforted. — "We but added the smallest thing," they tell him, just as the Latins keep repeating it to us today — "If it is so insignificant, then why add it?" — "Oh, this is perfectly abstract matter." — "How do you know that you have understood it?" — "Well, this is our local

---

[11] From P. Bessonov's introduction to the third volume of Konstantin Aksakov's collected works, K. A., vol. III, pp. I–XXXVI, esp. p. XXVII.

tradition." — "But how could it find a place in the universal Creed, in spite of an explicit rule of an Oecumenical Council prohibiting any change in the Creed?" — "Well, this is a tradition of the universal church, the meaning of which we expressed following our local opinion." — "But we do not know of any such tradition; and in any case, how could a local opinion find a place in the universal Creed? The comprehension of divine truths, is it not given to the entire church in its totality? Or did we for some reason deserve to be excommunicated from the church? You not only did not think of turning to us for advice, but you did not even take the trouble of sending us notice. Or is it that we have fallen so low? However, no more than a century ago, the East produced the greatest Christian poet and, perhaps, the most glorious Christian theologian, John of Damascus. And now too there are among us confessors and martyrs for the faith, learned philosophers, full of Christian wisdom, ascetics whose entire life is a continuous prayer. Why then did you cast us away?" But whatever the poor wanderer could say, the work had been done: the schism had occurred. *By its very action (that is, by the arbitrary change of the Creed) the Roman world made an implicit assertion that in its eyes the entire East was not more than a world of helots in matters of faith and doctrine. Life in the church ended for an entire half of the church.*[12]

Rozanov has already remarked that the wanderer came to the West in the nineteenth rather than in the ninth century, and that his heart was full of sentiments other than love.[13]

"WE" AND "THEY" — PHILOSOPHICAL AND LOGICAL

The Slavophile psychology of contrast, antagonism, and battle formed an excellent combination with the romantic philosophy of the period, which was based on the principle of opposition, on the rhythm of thesis — antithesis — synthesis: everything might be posited against something else. The technique used by the Slavophiles cannot be classified with precision. Chizhevskii stated that Khomiakov's scheme resembled the Hegelian, but that his synthesis was not really a synthesis because one of the two contrasting elements was simply destroyed.[14] So also N. Rubinstein made the Marxist criticism that the Slavophiles used Hegel's technique, but

[12] Kh., vol. II, pp. 48–49.   [13] Rozanov, *op. cit.*, p. 15.
[14] Chizhevskii, *op. cit.*, p. 188.

failed to grasp the meaning of his dialectic.[15] The Slavophiles used romantic patterns of development through opposition and struggle in every aspect of their ideology: religion, philosophy, art, history — all grew according to the new organic laws of growth, all marched to romantic rhythms. "The Roman world," "Catholicism," "ancient Russia," "the contemporary West," as well as numerous other concepts, became rungs on the various dialectical ladders constructed by the Slavophiles.

Even literary appreciation and psychology came to be involved in similar systems. Ivan Kireevskii spoiled his talent as literary critic through extreme schematism, a great desire to have all the writers and all their works neatly arranged on the thesis-antithesis-synthesis pattern. As to psychology, the favorite scheme, the one which Ivan Kireevskii sought all his life, moved from unconscious affirmation and synthesis to struggle and duality and then to conscious synthesis resolving all former tensions.

The following diatribe by Ivan Aksakov is a typical example of the use of romantic philosophy and logic by the Slavophiles:

St. Petersburg as the embodiment of a negative moment of history cannot create anything *positive* in the Russian sense. According to a well-known dialectical law it is possible to return to *the positive* only through *a negation of the negation itself*, in other words through a negation of the St. Petersburg period, through a negation of St. Petersburg as a political *principle* which guided Russian life for almost two centuries. The result will be a Russian nation freed from exclusiveness, and called into the arena of world history. Is that clear? [16]

"WE" AND "THEY" — HISTORICAL

The psychological enemy, the metaphysical opponent was bound to have a historical embodiment. And indeed it had only too many embodiments: it had appeared in a variety of forms and had used every conceivable disguise since the very dawn of human life. The enemy had always been opposed by the forces of good. The struggle of the two made history. The Slavophiles were

---

[15] N. Rubinstein, "Istoricheskaia teoriia slavinofilov i ee klassovye korni," in *Russkaia istoricheskaia literatura v klassovom osveshchenii*, a collection of articles edited by M. Pokrovskii, volume one, p. 73.

[16] I. A., vol. V, p. 632.

convinced that in their age they were the leading champions of good against evil, and that it was their task to unmask the enemy, to make Russia realize its real nature and its destiny, and thus to ensure the victory of the true principles over the false ones. Slavophile efforts of historical analysis fall into two types: those dealing with the enemy on the world stage, and those concerned with its activity in Russia.

The one contribution of the Slavophiles to world history was Khomiakov's huge compilation of notes, arguments, hypotheses, and examples, which was published in three volumes after his death. Khomiakov began to write his *History* probably in 1838, and he continued to work on it intermittently until his death in 1860. The manuscript had no title, but merely four letters at the top of the first page — "I, i, i, i," and it was not divided into volumes, books, chapters, or sections. Khomiakov did not indicate his sources; in composing the work he evidently relied on his memory, not on notes. The Slavophiles sometimes referred to Khomiakov's *History* as "Semiramis," after Gogol had on one occasion been struck by this name in the text and used it to denote the entire work.

The *History* remained unfinished, and its nature and purpose are not entirely clear. Some specialists argued that it had been designed only as a collection of random notes, and that Khomiakov had written it to satisfy his friends, who had demanded that he put down on paper some of the provocative thoughts which he had expressed in conversation. It has also been claimed that Khomiakov used his *History* primarily as source material for his theological tracts and various other articles. These explanations both misjudge the nature of the work and fail to justify the significance which Khomiakov and the other Slavophiles attached to "Semiramis." Incomplete and fragmentary as Khomiakov's *History* was, it represented an attempt at a synthesis of the entire life of humanity, and purported to give a clear outline of the course and meaning of world history. Berdiaev, Gratieux, and other students of Khomiakov emphasized that Khomiakov's *History* should be judged not as a work of historical research, but as a brilliant contribution to philosophical speculation and to ethical and religious

thought. They sometimes failed to consider the fact that Khomiakov himself had wanted his masterpiece to be an exact historical
study, and that he had always defended his views in terms of
scholarship as much as in terms of religious truth or metaphysical
knowledge.[17]

Khomiakov's opinion on historical writing was stated repeatedly
throughout his history, especially in the form of criticism of other
historians. He began by complaining that of the three subdivisions
of humanity, into races, states, and religions, the historians concentrated exclusively on the second. His main attack, however,
was directed against their method: they were dry, pedantic, and
formalistic; they managed to compile facts, but not to understand
them. "Many truths, and perhaps the most important truths which
a man can attain are passed from one person to another without
any logical argument, but by a mere hint which wakens the latent
powers in the soul. Dead would be the science which would deny
truth only because it did not appear in the form of a syllogism."[18]
The historians concentrated their attention on minute details, and
forgot that through the microscope one could see only a drop of
water, and not the flow of the Volga. They were also prejudiced;
German scholars in particular were determined to rob the Slavs
at least of their ancient glory if not of their modern power. The
true understanding of history required greater qualifications than
mere erudition and hard work.

Poetry is required to understand history. . . .[19] There is a certain bearing, certain movements which reveal the fraternal kinship of man; but
often this kinship, obvious to an artist and generally to a man living
in the simplicity of human truth, escapes the painstaking scholar who
strained his eyes and his feelings over the minute labor of comparative
criticism.[20]

[17] See A. Hilferding's *Introduction* to Khomiakov's *History* discussing the
nature and the purpose of the work: A. Hilferding, *Predislovie k pervomu
izdaniiu*, in Kh., vol. V, pp. XI–XXI. For a very favorable estimate of the
History see: A. Gratieux, *A. S. Khomiakov et le mouvement slavophile*, volume II. *Les doctrines*, pp. 50–101.   [18] Kh., vol. V, p. 51.
   [19] Kh., vol. V, p. 71.   [20] Kh., vol. V, p. 33.

And in the most complete statement of his principles:

The calling of a historian demands a rare combination of different qualities: learning, impartiality, a broad point of view, Leibnitz' ability to draw together the most distant items and events, Grimm's patience in analyzing the minutest details, and so on, and so forth. Higher and more useful than all these merits is the feeling of a poet and of an artist. Learning may deceive, acuteness of intellect tends towards paradoxes: the feeling of an artist is the sense of the inner truth, which can not either deceive or be deceived.[21]

This infallible feeling revealed to Khomiakov the essence of the historical process: "Freedom and necessity compose the secret fundamental principles around which are concentrated, in various ways, all thoughts of man."[22] Khomiakov called the first principle the Iranian and the second the Kushite, for he believed that its original home had been in Ethiopia, and the Bible referred to Ethiopia as "the land of Kush."[23] The proponents of the two principles formed two hostile camps, based on spiritual affinity rather than on blood ties or political allegiance, and were engaged in a constant and manifold struggle for the world. The Iranian principle expressed itself in the belief in creation and in spiritual religion, in the alphabet, literature, and song. The Bible belonged to it, and Christianity was its logical culmination. Typically Iranian details included the legend of the great flood and enmity against the serpent. The link which united the Iranians was their faith, but they also belonged to the same white race which alone preserved the tradition of true spirituality.

The Kushites were mute men who believed in necessity, and directed their efforts towards enormous constructions, such as the pyramids of Egypt or the temples of Southern India. They were engaged in hewing out of stone rather than talking; they wrote little, and they wrote only in hieroglyphics. They worshipped the serpent. The Kushites were slaves of nature, whether in the form

[21] Kh., vol. V, p. 31.
[22] Kh., vol. V, p. 217.
[23] Koliupanov suggested that Khomiakov borrowed his view of Ethiopia as the cradle of ancient civilization from Diodorus of Sicily. Koliupanov, *op. cit.*, vol. II, pp. 185–186.

of stone or in the sensuous form of a serpent. They developed phallic religions; often they gave themselves up to complete sensuality, as, for instance, in Indian Shivaism. Sometimes, however, Kushitism evolved in what appeared to be the opposite direction. Thus Buddhism denied the world and all its attractions. In reality, Shivaism and Buddhism represented the two sides of the same medal: both were based on the same principle, on the recognition of necessity, be it in a sensuous abandon or in Nirvana. Kushite elements penetrated into the Iranian tradition itself. They always revealed themselves in formalism, legalism, and necessity, as opposed to free creativity and life. Through the Kushite Roman state they entered the Roman church, and from Catholicism they were taken up by Protestantism.

Khomiakov did not bring his *History* up to modern times, but he made it clear nevertheless that Kushitism had found its latest stronghold in German idealistic philosophy. The guiding idea of his *History* may be summed up in Samarin's words:

The struggle of *the religion of moral freedom* (the Iranian principle finally realized in the plenitude of divine revelation preserved by the Orthodox Church) with *the religion of necessity, material or logical* (the Kushite principle, the latest and the most complete expression of which is presented by the newest philosophical schools of Germany), this struggle, embodied in religious doctrines and in the historical fate of the leading peoples of humanity — such is the basic theme, which binds separate studies together into one organic whole.[24]

Khomiakov tried to make his *History* as inclusive as possible. He began by criticizing the historians for their exclusive preoccupation with Europe, and he was not going to repeat their mistake: the Iranian and the Kushite principles were revealed in action, not only in Europe, Africa, and Asia, but also in Central and South America, and there were references to Australia and to Polynesia. Khomiakov did not depict Kushites as monsters: they could be amiable children of nature, as in Ethiopia, or they could construct a highly organized and effective state, such as China. Still, their religion of subservience to material necessity was wrong and clashed with the principle of spiritual creativity.

[24] S., vol. I, p. 251.

On the historical plane this struggle occurred within nations and between nations. The two principles could not be found in a pure form, but were always intermingled, and that added to the complexity and the difficulty of the struggle. The most violent passions were brought to bear and the worst excesses were committed precisely where the conflict between Iranianism and Kushitism was at its sharpest. This was especially true of India, where the great Iranian bearers of Sanskrit and Brahmanism fought against extreme Kushitism in its twin form of Shivaism and Buddhism, but similar developments took place in other lands.

The Iranian could defeat the Kushite in battle, but in one important respect he was much more vulnerable than his opponent. Kushitism could not be corrupted any more than the material necessity, the facts themselves could be. But the free spirit of Iranianism demanded the greatest effort, and the highest purity; it was constantly in danger of contamination, and the slightest taint was noxious. History provided numerous examples of this degeneration of Iranian elements and their subsequent revival to meet once more the challenge of Kushitism, which remained always massive and solid, in spite, or rather because of the fact that it was essentially dead.

Khomiakov's *History* assigned an extremely important role to Slavdom. The Slavs had performed many very significant functions with which biased historians failed to credit them. They were a most ancient tribe, closely related to the Brahmans of India, whose Sanskrit presented the nearest parallel to the Slavonic. They were also the largest subdivision of humanity and the original settlers of the entire European continent. Waves of later migrants had pushed them out of most of western Europe into the mountains and the swamps, but much evidence remained to tell an impartial scholar about the former Slavic expansion.[25]

[25] Khomiakov's *History* was a peculiar combination of history, philology, and fantasy, but chiefly fantasy. The following account of the Slavic settlement in Europe is a typical example of Khomiakov's exposition of history: "At the furthest West, differing from the Celts in customs, language, and character, live Wendic tribes (the Wends, the Antes, the Unalians, the Menapians, the Morenes, the Nantuatians, the Veragrians, the Serbs). There lay a land of swamps, forests, and rivers, a land which was unpleasant and

The Slavs retained their racial character and their independence only in eastern Europe, but their historical role had by no means been limited to the lands east of the Vistula. The Angles had been Slavs. The Slavic element had been an important ingredient in the formation of the Saxons, and it had dominated Scandinavia for several centuries. The Slavs had played a leading role in the formation of Hellenic civilization as well as of the modern Greek people. Troy had been a Slavic city, and through Troy the Slavs had been largely responsible for the foundation of Rome and of the Roman state. The Etruscans, the Huns, the Bulgars, the Khazars had been Slavs. Slavic heroes had included Attila, Siegfried, and Parsifal. Thor, Apollo, Venus, and Diana were Slavic gods and goddesses; in fact, most goddesses were liable to be Slavic since leadership of women was a peculiarly Slavic trait. Anthropomorphism in religion had been another characteristically Slavic development.

The Slavs had contributed the most important elements of civi-

---

unattractive to the Celts; but the revolutionary wars and the struggle of Vendée against the entire might of raging France proved that the ancient Slavs had chosen a dependable retreat. In the South, too, the tribes (the Goritians, the Lusatians, the Rus, and others) in their Prigorie (Perigord), Pogorie (Bigorre), Kogorie (Cahors), Kalagorie (Calagorris), and Zagorie (Sigurris), and in their wild fastnesses of the Pyrennees found refuge from the Celtic onslaught. The retreating Iberians willingly ceded to them the bare rocks and joined the main mass of the Iberian people, which populated all the wide spaces of the Hispanic peninsula. Further East, the marshes of the Rhone estuary with the islands Piplas and Blascon or Lencate (Poplesie and Bleskun) and the snowy Alps of the Savoy and the Piedmont protected for a long time the freedom of the Ligurian Wends, the Lusians (Lysii), the Zalusians (Silysii), the Zalesians (Salassii), the Nantuatians, the Veragrians, and others from the violence of their bellicose neighbors. For a long time Antium (the city of the Antes, the present-day Genoa) flourished as a trading center and was famous for the originality of its people, while the larger part of the banks of the Rodan (Eridan) and the defenseless western area had already passed under the dominion of the Gauls, leaving to us the memory of the former inhabitants only in the name of the town Arles (Thelina, dolina), in Vindamum, and the Vienna of the Allobrogians, in the rivers Eridan, Skoras, or Prygun (Isere), etc. I shall say the same thing about the entire Alpine range where the Slavs, the Great Wends (Vindelici), the Kraintsy (Corni), and others, opposed the German onslaught and based themselves on their southern brothers, connecting themselves in an unbroken chain with the Wends of Liguria and the Adriatic." Kh., vol. V, pp. 92–93.

lization. In contrast to the German conquerors, whose aim had been the exploitation of the vanquished, the Slavs lived in peaceful communes and were engaged in agriculture. They also developed arts and crafts, fostered commerce and navigation, and built towns. Slavic influences could be seen in every phase of European history, from the trade of Hanseatic towns to the institution of the jury in England. Khomiakov was convinced that agriculture, trade, navigation, towns, all indicated the presence of the Slavs. The peasant commune, strong family ties, and worship of water also pointed to them. Their role in history was further attested by numerous place names of Slavic origin, especially those connected with such denotations of the Slavs themselves as *Antes*, *Wends*, *Rus*, e.g. — Vendée, Antibes, Russilon, Venetia, and so on.

To Khomiakov, correspondence or even superficial resemblance meant Slavic origin. Thus the Latin language was derived from the Slavonic. Such specifically Slavic traits as the high position of woman were also irrefutable proofs of the presence of the Slavic element, linking with Slavdom even the Phoenician goddess Astarte and the Babylonian princess Semiramis who, moreover, had been associated with the typically Slavic symbol of the dove. The Slavs were the best singers and the most musical people on the face of the earth, and therefore one could expect Orpheus to be a Slav. Mythology often helped, where history was powerless: thus Homeric mythology and the nature of the gods, who favored Troy, indicated beyond dispute the Slavic character of the city. Siegfried had to be a Slav for several reasons; one of them was that he possessed all the attributes of Slavic mythology, such as the maiden-ruler, the dragon, the cap of invisibility, the dwarfs, the magicians, and the priceless treasures.

In spite of their cultural superiority and great contributions to civilization, the Slavs in most European lands were gradually absorbed by other tribes. This happened because of the special pliability of the Slavs, their gift for associating with other peoples and reflecting their interests, and their great communicativeness, especially their facility in learning foreign languages, a trait in which they were the very opposite of the English. Furthermore, although conquest could rapidly create states, and compulsion could effectively organize societies, the higher principles of Slavdom made the Slavs shun this path and made them believe in a more noble and harmonious way of life.

Was the fate of the Slavonic tribe to bring to life, to awaken the dormant elements in other peoples, while remaining itself without glory and without historical records, but only with a certain kind of semi-yearnings which attain no goal, with a certain semi-life which resembles a dream? Perhaps this semi-life, these semi-yearnings represent the inner vice of the entire Slavonic family. Perhaps they are merely a result of the excessive demands of the inner spirit, which is incapable of a one-sided development and requires a full harmony of life for which humanity has not matured yet. Oh, if it were so! [26]

While Khomiakov wrote the Slavophile world history, Konstantin Aksakov contributed most to the Slavophile elaboration of Russian history. Khomiakov's study stood apart, however, whereas Konstantin Aksakov was assisted by the other Slavophiles, more often in articles dealing with religion, literature, philosophy, education, or politics than with history proper.

In Russian history, as in the history of the world, the basic principles were all-important:

[26] Kh., vol. V, p. 307.

Khomiakov's *History*, both in its method and in its content, was a typical product of the Romantic Age. It was written on the basis of artistic insight, and intuition, with a special reliance on mythology, and on the folk element, and it contained most outrageous generalizations and analogies in all fields of knowledge. Khomiakov regarded history as an organic process, as the dialectical struggle of two spiritual principles, and he treated separate races and nations as organisms with a special mission to accomplish. Abundant details also reflected the romantic spirit of the time, and had their origin in the West, especially in Germany. For instance, Khomiakov was influenced by the idea of the primitive Golden Age, very popular with the romanticists, and present in the writings of Schelling, among others. Strictly speaking, Khomiakov's *History* referred to two distinct Golden Ages: the Golden Age at the very dawn of human history, when humanity formed a single family and worshipped the free spirit; and the Slavonic Golden Age in Europe before other races came. Khomiakov's *History* was based on numerous Western romantic sources, but it may have borrowed most, its main idea included, from Friedrich Schlegel. See the Appendix for a comparison between Khomiakov's *History* and Schlegel's *Philosophy of History*.

A fearsome play of material forces strikes one at first glance, but it is a mirage; an attentive gaze will see only one force, which moves everything, which is present everywhere, but which makes its way slowly — the idea. . . .[27]

History was moral as well as metaphysical:

The moral task of life belongs not only to every man, but also to nations, and every man and every nation performs it in its own manner, selecting this or that path for its accomplishment.[28]

Russia had its principles and its moral path:

The history of the Russian people is the only history in the world of a Christian people, Christian not only in its profession of faith, but also in its life, or at least in the aspirations of its life.[29]

Russia could not be separated from Orthodox Christianity, and it was useless to study the history of the Russian people apart from Orthodoxy. This religious element was of an absolutely higher order than any national or racial traits, and it provided the content and the gauge of Russia, Russian culture, and the Russians.

The Slavs had always been distinguished by their peaceful occupation of agriculture, their strong family ties, and their organization into communes. The idea of force, compulsion, law was foreign to them. The commune meant a harmonious social relationship, the very opposite of Western individualism; the communes were organic, not mechanical, and they represented true growth and life. Small communes organically united into larger ones. The largest was Russia itself. But because of the imperfection of human nature, the commune had needed something to keep order, and above all to protect it from its bellicose neighbors. So it had invited the state to perform these functions. This had been the calling of the Varangians.

The calling was voluntary. The State and the Commune-Land did not mix, but as separate units formed an alliance with each other. The

---

[27] K. A., vol. I, p. 1. The volume contains not only Konstantin Aksakov's published historical articles, but also the unpublished ones, as well as some rough drafts, notes, and so on.
[28] *Ibid.*   [29] K.A., vol. I, p. 19.

relations of the Land and the State were already defined by the spontaneous calling: mutual confidence on both sides. Not war, not enmity because of conquest, as was the case with the other nations, but peace because of voluntary invitation.[30]

Russia was so different from the West that its history had been *sui generis* "from the very first instant."

All European states are formed through conquest. Enmity is their fundamental principle. Government came there as an armed enemy and established itself *by force* among the conquered peoples. . . . The Russian state, on the contrary, was founded not by conquest, but by a *voluntary invitation* of the government. . . . Thus in the foundation of the Western state: *violence, slavery, and hostility*. In the foundation of the Russian state: *free will, liberty, and peace*.[31]

The historical development of the Russians had been guided by their profound comprehension of the spiritual and the temporal elements in human life and of their interrelation:

Having understood after the conversion to Christianity that freedom is only of the spirit, Russia continually stood up for her soul, for her faith. On the other hand, she knew that perfection was impossible on earth, she did not seek earthly perfection, and therefore she chose the best (that is the least evil) form of government and held to it constantly, without considering it as perfect. Recognizing the government freely, Russia did not rebel against it, and did not abase herself in front of it.[32]

The Slavophiles wrote little about the first period of Russian history, the Kievan, but they praised it highly. In his study of *The Bogatyri of the Time of Great Prince Vladimir According to Russian Songs*, Konstantin Aksakov stressed the fact that these heroes of Russian folklore had been inspired by the true Orthodox faith and by their love for their families. They had been the valiant defenders of the happy society similar to a "merry-go-round, moving harmoniously and melodiously, full of joy. . . . This spirit permeates, this form marks everything that comes from Russia; such is our song itself, such is its tune, such is the organization of our Land." [33]

[30] K.A., vol. I, p. 4.
[32] K.A., vol. I, p. 10.
[31] K.A., vol. I, p. 8.
[33] K.A., vol. I, p. 337.

After the Tartar invasion and the Period of the Apanages, Moscow had united Russia around itself, and had thus performed its great historical task. The principles of Russian life remained exactly the same. The free opinion of the Land, which had formerly expressed istelf at numerous town meetings, was directed instead to the Zemskii Sobor and the Zemskaia Duma, which spoke to the tsar with the voice of the entire Land. The spheres of activity of the State and of the Land remained strictly separate. The State used the necessary force and compulsion; the Land, that is the people, enjoyed the free life of the spirit. This arrangement proved to be extremely satisfactory:

Throughout the whole course of Russian history, the Russian people never betrayed the government, never betrayed the monarchy. If there were disturbances, they concerned the question of the legitimacy of a particular ruler: of Boris, of the False Dimitrii, or of Shuiskii. But a voice never sounded among the people: we do not want monarchy, we do not want autocracy, we do not want the tsar. On the contrary, in 1612, having defeated the enemy and being left without a tsar, the people, unanimously and loudly, again called the tsar.[34]

The year 1612 was the favorite Slavophile year because they considered it to be the clearest affirmation of the true Russian principles: after the State had been betrayed and destroyed, when Russia was on the brink of annihilation from the hands of its foes, the Catholic Poles in particular, the Commune, the Land itself rose for its faith and its way of life, defeated all enemies, and reëstablished the old system. Then it again retired from political activity to its proper sphere of the spirit, and the first Romanovs continued in the footsteps of the former Moscow Tsars.

Thus had lived Russia, homogeneous, harmonious, and organic, without Western class divisions, without aristocracy and democracy, without enmity and compulsion. Russian society and Russian life had been distinguished by simplicity, by a complete absence of theatrical effects, so prevalent in the West. Russian education had been based on the true learning of the Orthodox Church.

[34] K.A., vol. I, p. 12.

All Holy Greek Fathers, not excluding the most profound writers, were translated, read, copied, and studied in the quiet of our monasteries, these sacred embryos of the universities which were not to be. . . . And these monasteries were in a living, continuous contact with the people. What enlightenment in our common people are we not entitled to deduce from this single fact! [35]

And yet this order of things did not last, the harmony was broken, the organic, Russian way of life destroyed. Peter the Great appeared on the scene.

The Slavophiles could never quite understand what enabled Peter the Great to sweep away old Russia, and to institute an oppressive, mechanistic, rationalistic, Western regime in its stead. Konstantin Aksakov in particular, made of Peter the Great a titan, who introduced, practically single-handed, everything evil, even serfdom, into Russia. He spent much time and effort trying to prove from ancient documents that freedom, harmony, and happiness existed in abundance in ancient Russia, but disappeared after Peter the Great. Other Slavophiles, led by Khomiakov and Ivan Kireevskii, were more willing to concede that pre-Petrine Russia had its defects. According to them, it showed a certain one-sided exclusiveness, and it lacked consciousness of itself and of its mission.

Ivan Kireevskii tried to trace the origin of these weaknesses:

One fact in our history explains to us the cause of this unfortunate cataclysm; this fact is the Stoglav Council. As soon as heresy appeared in the church, the discord of the spirit had to be reflected in life. Parties, which deviated less or more from the truth, appeared. The party of innovation overcame the party of tradition precisely because tradition was torn asunder by dissidence. Therefore, as the inner, spiritual link was destroyed, there arose the need of a material, formal link; therefore the system of precedence, the Oprichniks of Ivan the Terrible, serfdom, etc. Therefore, the perversion of books through error and ignorance, and their correction by private opinion and arbitrary criticism. Therefore the government before Peter dissented in opinion from the majority of the people, who were cast away under the label of Old Believers. Therefore Peter, as the leader of a party within the state, creates a society within society, and everything that follows from that.[36]

[35] I.K., vol. I, p. 119.   [36] I.K., vol. I, p. 120.

Kireevskii believed that Ivan the Terrible had been a heretic, and that the corruption of Russia could be dated from his reign. The very excellence of the old Russian system had invited corruption:

As to my personal opinion, I think that the originality of Russia consisted in the very fullness and purity of expression, which the Christian teaching received in it — in the entire compass of her public and her private life. The purity of expression became so blended with the spirit expressed, that one could easily mix the significance of the two, and respect the outer form as much as the inner meaning. . . . And indeed we see that in the sixteenth century the respect for the form already exceeds in many ways the respect for the spirit.[37]

The Slavophiles were opposed to Peter the Great and his reforms, to contemporary Russian government and society. Peter the Great was a despot, who interrupted the organic development of the country, and who wanted to mold Russia like clay in accordance with his rationalistic and utilitarian notions, and in direct imitation of the West. His reforms robbed Russia of its independent role in history, and made it an appendix to the West, split educated society from the people, and led to such evils as formalism and bureaucracy.

St. Petersburg was a perfect expression of and the natural successor to his work. This city was the very essence of rationalism, formalism, materialism, legalism, and compulsion: it had been built out of nothing, without spiritual sanctification or historical tradition, even the ground on which it stood was Finnish rather than Russian; yet this artificial, foreign city ruled the whole land, entire Holy Russia, by means of its compulsory decrees borrowed from the West and quite inapplicable to the Russian way of life. "We" and "They" formed a simple pattern as far as cities were concerned: "We" was represented by Moscow, "They" by St. Petersburg. The Slavophiles made numerous attacks on the enemy. Their approach ranged from exclamations of hate against "that city, that way of life, that activity, those people," and suggestions that St. Petersburg should drown itself, to the elucidation of the fact that St. Petersburg represented a merely negative

[37] I.K., vol. I, p. 219.

phase of Russian history and, therefore, could not contribute anything of positive value. Time and again the Slavophiles demanded that the capital be transferred back to Moscow.

Peter the Great was a common target of the Slavophiles. Petr Kireevskii was grieved because his own first name was Peter. When Soloviev and other historians demonstrated that Peter the Great was not as revolutionary as he was supposed to have been, and that Moscovite Russia had been developing her connections with the West, that too became an item in the indictment.

This is perfectly correct, and everything that is true in Peter's reforms was, of course, started before him. But Peter was not merely a continuer, and precisely this forms the characteristic of his epoch. Before him only the useful had been taken from the foreigners. Foreign life had not been borrowed, our own principles of life had been left intact, and Russia had remained independent. Peter, on the other hand, began to take everything from the foreigners, not only the useful and the universal, but also the particular and the national, foreign life itself with all its accidental details. . . . Therefore even the most useful, which had been accepted in Russia before Peter the Great, became of necessity not a free borrowing, but a slavish imitation. Still another circumstance was added to this: namely coercion, an inalienable attribute of Peter's actions. This coercion, in turn, changed the whole process; what had been done freely and naturally until then, began to be performed through compulsion and force. Therefore, the reforms of Peter are definitively *an overturning, a revolution*, in this lies the originality and the historical significance of his work. . . . National exclusiveness (which Russia had never known before) appeared on the part of Peter. It was Peter who stood for exclusive nationality, only not for that of his own people, but for those of the West; he attempted to destroy every manifestation of Russian life, everything Russian.[38]

The Slavophile denunciation of Peter the Great came to be regarded as the watchword of the movement, as its most characteristic trait and as its main contrast with the Westernizers. But at the same time the Slavophiles were forced by their romantic philosophy of history to accept Peter the Great and the St. Petersburg period of Russian life. Every period of history had its purpose and was bound to contribute to the development and the triumph of the true principles. Even Konstantin Aksakov had to

[38] K.A., vol. I, pp. 41–42.

admit that Peter the Great had been necessary.[39] The other Slavo-philes variously developed the same idea. Peter the Great rep-resented the inevitable reaction against the nationalistic ex-clusiveness, the ignorant respect for form, and various other vices of Moscovite Russia. This reaction was extreme, negative, and essentially wrong, but it was nevertheless bound to contribute to the higher synthesis. Even the new capital served a useful purpose:

Petersburg was and will remain exclusively the city of the government, and perhaps this split in the very center of the state will not be useless for the healthy and intelligent development of Russia. The life of the power of the state and the life of the spirit of the people became di-vided even as to the place of their concentration.[40]

Moscow, which was characterized by a luminous inner intelli-gence rather than by superficial gaiety, and by depth and honesty rather than by bustle and speed, was thus left free to develop the life of the Russian people, the life of the spirit. Furthermore, the fact that it was no longer the capital, but only an equal of other Russian lands, contributed to the indispensable virtue of humility. In Moscow "was now constantly developed the thought of the Russian society of tomorrow." [41]

In addition to curing certain ills of Moscovite Russia and en-abling Moscow to devote itself wholly to the life of the spirit, the St. Petersburg episode of Russian history may have conferred an even greater benefit on the country:

Look at Germany. More than any other people of Europe she denied her nationality, was even partly ashamed of herself, and what hap-pened? . . . Was this temporary renunciation really fruitless? No: Ger-many was rewarded by the fact that when she returned to self-con-sciousness and self-respect, she brought with her from the period of her humiliation the ability to understand other peoples much better than a Frenchman, an Englishman, or an Italian understands them. She practically discovered Shakespeare. We also renounced ourselves, and humiliated ourselves more, a hundred times more than Germany.

[39] This he did very sharply and in strikingly Hegelian terms, e.g., in his article "About a Contemporary Literary Argument." K.A., "O sovremennom 'literaturnom spore," in *Rus*, 1883, no. 7. The article was written in 1847.
[40] Kh., vol. III, p. 27.   [41] Kh., vol. III, p. 434.

I hope, I am certain that when we return home (and we shall return home — and soon), we shall bring with ourselves a clear understanding of the entire world, such as the Germans did not even dream of.[42]

Whatever defects may have brought about Peter the Great's reforms, and whatever ends the St. Petersburg period of Russian history may have served, the Slavophiles were convinced that that period had to end soon: Russia would then return to its organic development, to its true path in history, and it was bound to be stronger, fuller of wisdom, and more conscious of itself and its place in the world than ever before. Slavophilism was a thoroughly optimistic doctrine: the Slavophiles believed that the organic, Orthodox, Russian civilization would certainly triumph over its opponent, the materialistic and rationalistic civilization of the West, and that they were destined to lead Russia to its glorious future. To the Slavophiles Russian history was primarily a battle of civilizations: first, between Russia and outside opponents, then, still more significantly, within Russia herself, after the Western principle had entered Russia and had seized the government.

The same attitude pervaded the literary works of the Slavophiles whenever they dealt with Russian history. Khomiakov's only two completed tragedies, *Ermak* and *The False Dimitrii*, are especially interesting. Written in 1829 and in 1833 respectively, they preceded the formulation of the Slavophile ideology, and expressed in poetic language the views which came later to dominate Slavophile historical writing. The argument of *The False Dimitrii* may be summed up as follows: the False Dimitrii is seated after many trials and tribulations on the throne of Russia; he has to choose between the Russian and the Polish party, between Russian civilization and Polish; he chooses Poland; he dies a villain, and his cause is lost. The story of *Ermak* is a variation on the same theme: Ermak after many trials and tribulations

[42] Kh., vol. III, p. 210. This passage shows the measure of Khomiakov's willingness to make the best of the St. Petersburg period of Russian history. It is extremely interesting, in connection with the later development of the idea of Russian Messiahship by Dostoevskii, Soloviev, and others, but it is not typical of the Slavophiles who usually condemned unreservedly self-renunciation and imitation in any nation.

conquers Western Siberia; he has to choose between Russia, where he is wanted as a criminal, and Siberia, where he is promised power and glory, between Russian civilization and Siberian; he chooses Russia; he dies a hero, and his cause is won. "Siberian civilization," invented for the purpose, is competently represented by a shaman, who offers Ermak rule over the whole of Siberia, and untold riches, power, and glory, if only he would renounce Russia and link his fortunes with the Siberian principle.[43]

"WE" AND "THEY" — POLITICAL

The historic enemies were still very active, still plotting against Russia. The romantic foreign policy of the Slavophiles followed logically from their view of history, and their philosophy in general. Spurred by such events as the Crimean War, the Polish rebellion of 1863, the Balkan crisis of 1875–1878, and the Bulgarian crisis of 1885, Ivan Aksakov, who was especially determined to defend Russian and Slavic interests in the Balkans, kept repeating the following basic premises.

It is time to realize that we shall not purchase the favor of the West by any amount of willingness to please; it is time to understand that the hatred, not seldom instinctive, of the West towards the Orthodox Slavonic world stems from other, and deeply hidden causes; these causes are the antagonism of the two opposite spiritual principles of enlightenment, and the envy felt by the decrepit world of the new one to which the future belongs. . . ."[44] The hatred of the West towards the East and towards Orthodoxy is a traditional, instinctive, and peculiarly spontaneous feeling and motive force in the history of the world.[45]

There was no limit to the hostility and the contempt with which the West regarded the East:

---

[43] *Dimitrii Samozvanets* occupies pages 117–292 and *Ermak* pages 303–418 of the fourth volume of Khomiakov's *Works*. Both are characteristic examples of the romantic historical drama so popular at the time. Belinskii complained that Khomiakov's cossacks resembled German university students. Khomiakov's brother Fedor was also one of those who criticized the author for the absence of realism. See his letter to A. S. Khomiakov published in: "Pisma k A. S. Khomiakovu," *Russkii Arkhiv*, 1884, book three, pp. 221–225.
[44] I.A., vol. I, p. 5.   [45] I.A., vol. I, p. 322.

We are not even the plebeians, we are the pariahs of humanity, a cast-out tribe to which the laws of justice and the demands of humanitarianism do not extend, and in the case of which no moral principles developed by the Christian civilization of the European peoples are applicable.[46]

Russia could not escape Western hatred:

In the face of Europe Russia is guilty by the very fact that it exists.[47]

The West was conspiring against Russia all the time and under various guises, even that of an International Exhibition.[48] Russian enemies were numerous. There was, for instance, France, which represented in the Near East the interests of the Catholic world. But the greatest opponent was Austria:

Here is the state the very existence of which — artificial, based on violence and injustice — is an embodied contradiction of the idea of peace.[49]

Orthodox Christianity was the very essence of the Slavs, and therefore Austria was determined to destroy and assimilate Slavdom by making it Catholic. The other European nations were only too willing to support this policy of Catholic Pan-Slavism under the sceptre of the Austrian monarchy:

The Germanic and the Romance tribes often quarrel among themselves, but, as soon as the Slavs or Russia are in question, they immediately unite in the common feeling of hatred towards the Slavonic element. . . .[50] It is time for Russian diplomacy to become finally convinced that everything that is happening in Europe is nothing but a plot against us, against the natural moral and political influence of Russia on the Balkan peninsula, against its most legitimate claims and interests.[51]

The entire West was thus hostile to Russia.

[46] I.A., vol. II, p. 363.

[47] I.A., vol. III, pp. 176–181. This was the title of one of Aksakov's editorials.

[48] "Europe is forging different plans under the cover of a peaceful triumph of industry and art which is being prepared in Paris." I.A., vol. I, p. 147. [49] I.A., vol. I, p. 428.

[50] I.A., vol. VI, p. 6. [51] I.A., vol. I, p. 648.

We have no friends, sincere to any extent, among the powers of Western Europe; Russian frontiers with the West are almost completely open. Our natural and only allies, and besides partly adjoining our lands, are the Slavs.[52]

The outcome of this hostility was obvious: "We are convinced that the Eastern question will not be settled by anything, except the sword. . . ." [53] And the line was clearly drawn:

more than once in the future Europe will be divided into two camps: on one side Russia, with all Orthodox, Slavic tribes (not excluding Greece), on the other — the entire Protestant, Catholic, and even Mohammedan and Jewish Europe put together. Therefore Russia must care only about the strengthening of its own Orthodox-Slavic camp.[54]

While Ivan Aksakov was primarily interested in the Balkan Slavs, Samarin's main preoccupation was the Baltic provinces and Poland. The approach of the two was very similar, although Samarin preferred scholarly, documented studies to popular articles. In Poland the main enemy was Catholicism, which had seduced the Poles, and made this Slavic tribe betray the East, and throw itself into the service of the West. The Slavophiles were not certain whether Poland itself could be redeemed, but in any case they were determined to eliminate the Polish element from the Ukrainian and the White Russian areas. They demanded that the Poles be forbidden to own estates there, that a thorough Russian educational system be organized there under the aegis of the church, and so on.

In the Baltic provinces the Germanic element was the great opponent. Samarin fought against it from the late forties until his death in 1876. He wrote a learned monograph to demonstrate the outrageous nature of the organization of the city of Riga, where German privilege ran roughshod over the miserable natives of the area, the unfortunate Russians who had moved in, and even over all laws and orders of the government. He studied the land question, and the problems of religion and education. As a publicist, he did his best to further the conversion of the Letts to

[52] I.A., vol. I, p. 718.
[53] I.A., vol. VII, p. 99.
[54] I.A., vol. VII, p. 32.

Orthodoxy, and hinder their return to Lutheranism. He was engaged for many years in a vigorous polemic on the "Borderlands" against the Baltic Germans, against the policy of the Russian government, and against the prevailing opinion of Russian society. His brief imprisonment in the Peter and Paul fortress, the angry rebuke which he received from Nicholas I in person, constant censorship difficulties, and strain in personal relations only strengthened Samarin's conviction of the importance of his mission. Behind the Baltic barons, the Lutheran pastors, and the burghers of Riga, Samarin saw the mighty shadow of Germany. No risks could be taken. The Western borderlands of Russia had to be prepared for the coming battle of the German and the Slav.[55]

The Slavophiles emphasized that Russia had to fight two kinds of enemies: outside foes, and, from the time of Peter the Great, the destructive Western element within itself. The Germans provided the best illustration of the interdependence of the two problems: they formed two mighty, inimical states on the Russian border; they dominated and ruled to their liking the Baltic provinces of the Russian empire; moreover, they occupied the highest offices and exercised the determining influence in the Russian government itself. The Slavophiles never tired of denouncing them. Samarin, for instance, was willing to admit that many individuals of German origin had performed and were performing sterling services for Russia,

but as to the system inaugurated and represented by the Germans, as a political party, it is a razor's edge passed between the heart and the head of the nation, it is poison injected into the most sensitive fibers of the social body, it is a disintegrator, dangerous in quite a different manner from Herzen's propaganda, perhaps the only disintegrator which we have to fear.[56]

[55] Samarin's writings on Riga, and on the borderlands constitute volumes VII, VIII, IX, and X of his *Works*. His articles on Poland form a part of volume I. Samarin's study of Jesuitism and the Jesuits, published in volume VI, has a direct bearing on Poland.

[56] *Correspondence de G. Samarine avec la Baronne de Rahden, 1861–1876*, p. 29. Cf. the following entry in the diary of Vera Aksakov, a sister of the Slavophiles: "Today is Liuba's birthday. At dinner we congratulated one another and expressed the wish that the German party in Russia would be destroyed." *1854–1855: Dnevnik Very Sergeevny Aksakovoi*, p. 13.

The danger was by no means limited to German names: after Peter the Great, the orientation of the Russian government, and of the Russian educated class in general became overwhelmingly foreign, anti-Russian. A prince Gorchakov or a count Shuvalov at the Congress of Berlin, a prince Suvorov as governor-general of the Baltic provinces were worse than any German baron in Russian service.[57]

"WE" AND "THEY" — THE OPPONENTS

The Slavophiles are linked in Russian history with the Westernizers. The two movements rose together, out of the same background, and developed their respective ideologies in close contact and in sharp opposition to each other. Although they came to denote the two opposite poles of Russian thought, they had much in common, and it was this common element which made their intercourse fruitful. Both drew their knowledge and their philosophy from the West: the Westernizers were avowed disciples of Western thought, but the Slavophiles were more than their equals

[57] As far as their views on the borderlands were concerned, the Slavophiles were struggling against the current, and only Samarin and Ivan Aksakov lived to see the change of policy. When in the latter part of Alexander II's reign and especially in the reigns of Alexander III and Nicholas II, Russification became a standard government practice, the Slavophiles were given credit for formulating it first, and were described as the forerunners of the chauvinists and the Pan-Slavs of the end of the nineteenth and the beginning of the twentieth century. This statement has to be qualified: the Slavophiles stressed the religious element much more than the later nationalists, and they were very reluctant to use compulsion. Furthermore, the Slavophile inspiration, notably that of Samarin, was often not only nationalist, but also liberal. The Letts may have preferred Lutheranism to Orthodoxy, but the fact that they were exploited by the landlords could not be gainsaid. The institutions of Riga did represent special and archaic privilege. The peasants of White Russia really did have very little protection against the Polonized gentry. When, as in the case of Poland proper, the Slavophiles were forced to realize that most of the people were not with them, they found it difficult to decide what course to follow. Khomiakov, Ivan Aksakov, and Samarin all came to the conclusion that it might be best to set Poland perfectly free from Russia, although they had their misgivings about this course of action, and thought that it should apply to other powers as well, in the Balkans and elsewhere. Khomiakov, and Ivan Aksakov argued that the Poles should be allowed to decide their own fate by a plebiscite. See an outline of the Slavophile views on Poland in the fourth chapter of this work.

in Western learning. German idealistic philosophy, and especially
the romantic concept of nation and national mission, provided
an ideological framework for the doctrines of both groups. Only
the Westernizers believed that in order to accomplish her task
Russia had to follow the Western pattern of development, while
the Slavophiles maintained that Russia had a road of her own,
and that the imitation of the West led to disaster.

The Slavophiles were initially good personal friends of such
men as Chaadaev, Stankevich, Herzen, Granovskii, Belinskii, and
other Westernizers. They read the same books, attended the
same lectures, argued in the same salons, even wrote in the
same periodicals. They appeared to be a single, friendly, although
quarrelsome, society. Monday evenings were usually spent at
Chaadaev's, Friday at the Sverbeevs', Sunday at the Elagins',
Thursday at the Pavlovs'.

The whole large literary society of the capital assembled there on
Thursdays. There enthusiastic arguments continued late into the night:
Redkin with Shevyrev, Kavelin with Aksakov, Herzen and Kriukov
with Khomiakov. There the Kireevskiis used to appear, also Iurii Samarin, then still a young man. Chaadaev was a constant guest there, with
his head as bald as his hand, his unexceptionable society manners, his
civilized and original mind, and his eternal posing. This was the most
brilliant literary time of Moscow. All questions, philosophical, historical,
and political, everything that interested the most advanced contemporary minds, were discussed at these assemblies, to which the com-
petitors came fully armed, with opposed views, but with a store of
knowledge and the charm of eloquence. At that time Khomiakov led
a fierce struggle against Hegel's Logic. . . . Similarly vehement dis-
putations concerned the key problem of Russian history, the reforms
of Peter the Great. Circles of listeners formed around the debaters;
this was a constant tournament in the course of which knowledge, intelligence and resourcefulness were all displayed. . . .[58]

Gradually the two groups began to draw apart. The split was
made inevitable by the fact that the Slavophiles assigned the
highest place to religion, while the Westernizers moved more
and more toward atheism. Various incidents served as pretexts

[58] This autobiographical description belongs to Chicherin. Quoted from
Chizhevskii, *op. cit.*, pp. 61–62.

for quarrels: there was a violent argument connected with the participation of the Westernizers in *The Moscovite*; more bitterness was provoked by Granovskii's dissertation *Volin, Iomburg, and Vineta*, which proved that the famous Slavic town of Vineta was only a myth; the Westernizers accused Pogodin and Shevyrev of denunciation, which prevented Granovskii from obtaining permission for a new review; Khomiakov's brother-in-law, the poet Iazykov, wrote abusive verses "To those, who are not of us," and the ensuing argument almost resulted in a duel between Petr Kireevskii and Granovskii; Khomiakov opposed Granovskii on the subject of the Burgundian migrations and the nature of the Franks, and their dispute assumed a personal character. Reconciliations proved to be only temporary, and by 1846 the break was more or less complete. Even the personal relations of the Westernizers and the Slavophiles were coming to an end.[59]

The Westernizers were the most famous opponents of the Slavophiles, but there were very many others. As a matter of fact, most of the Slavophile writings were polemical in nature, and they were aimed against extremely varied groups: the Jesuits, and the proponents of the secular state, the radical Left and

[59] Konstantin Aksakov's formal partings from his Westernizer friends were particularly pathetic. See Herzen, *op. cit.*, pp. 306–307, and P. Annenkov, *Literaturnye vospominaniia*, pp. 244–245.

The Westernizers and the Slavophiles retained mutual high regard for life. Ivan Aksakov used to measure degeneration in the camp of his enemies by comparing the latest Russian radicals to Granovskii. After Granovskii's death Khomiakov had some kind words to say about "the good opponent." In his turn, Herzen in *The Bell* marked the deaths of Khomiakov and of Konstantin Aksakov as follows: "It is painful for those persons who loved them to know that these noble, tireless workers are no longer, that these *opponents*, who were closer to us than many of *ours*, no longer exist. The Kireevskiis, Khomiakov, and Aksakov *accomplished their task* . . . . they stopped the stampeded public opinion and made all serious men think. With them begins *the turning point of Russian thought*. . . . Yes, we were their opponents, but very strange opponents: we had *one love*, but *not an identical one*. Both they and we conceived from early years one powerful, unaccountable, physiological, passionate feeling, which they took to be a recollection, and we — a prophecy, the feeling of boundless, all-encompassing love for the Russian people, Russian life, the Russian turn of mind. Like Janus, or like a two-headed eagle, we were looking in different directions while *a single heart was beating in us*." Herzen, *Works*, the Lemke edition, vol. XI, p. 11.

the conservative Right, the Russian officials and the German philosophers. Although the Slavophile range of opponents was extremely wide, the Slavophiles were equally uncompromising to them all. The "We" and "They" pattern allowed of no third possibility in personal ideology any more than it did in history, politics, or religion: the world was divided into "We" and "They," and "We" were only those who faithfully believed in the Slavophile doctrine. Even when the Slavophiles agreed with somebody else on a particular point, they found it necessary to emphasize the fact that their opinion was based on their own peculiar views, and that they had really nothing in common with their chance associates. Ivan Aksakov could well complain at the end of his life that he was left alone in a hostile world.

In the teaching of the Slavophiles, the problem of Russia and the West had numerous and complex aspects, religious as well as political, and philosophical as well as personal. But all these varied aspects were united by the same basic approach: Russia was always "We," the West was always "They."

CHAPTER IV

THE SLAVOPHILE IDEOLOGY

THEY

THE FOUNDATIONS AND THE DEVELOPMENT OF THE WEST

"They" were guilty of a multitude of sins. Egoism, communism, rationalism, sensuality, pride, affectation, superficiality, cruelty, bellicosity, exploitation, luxury, deceptiveness, rapacity, treachery, lechery, corruption, and decay were among "Their" attributes. These sins were all related, and could be deduced from a single postulate: the history of the West was nothing but a logical development of the perverse spiritual principles which formed its foundation.

At the basis of the entire multiform civilization of the West lay the ancient spirit of Kushitism, the worship of necessity, matter, form, and the absence of freedom, spirit, life. To the Kushites faith was "a transcendental physics," a magical formula to manipulate matter and plan human life. Legalistic, oppressive, and militant Rome was an eminently Kushite state, and from Rome Kushitism passed into the Roman church.

Thus Western Europe developed not under the influence of Christianity, but under the influence of Latinism, that is, of Christianity interpreted one-sidedly as the law of external unity.[1]

The church therefore became something external to its members; religion, a completely Roman idea as well as the word itself, replaced faith; good works acquired the significance of deeds and were buttressed by a precise scale of rewards; sin became a transgression, not a sign of corruption; and in general, the supreme truths of Christianity were reduced to the crude postulates of Kushite knowledge.

[1] Kh., vol. I, p. 148.

Thus rationalism or the narrowly logical analysis became the nature of the Western church, in contrast to contemplative cognition, which was preserved in the East. . . . Prayer, ritual, sacrament, good works acquired, in the relationship of man to God, the nature of merit and of exorcising power, in perfect correspondence to the magic of Kushitism.[2]

Once this rationalistic principle was accepted by the West, it attained a dreadful ascendancy and determined all Western history:

for such is the nature of that logical mechanism, that "self-propelled knife" which is called rationalism — once it is admitted into the heart of human thinking and into the highest sphere of religious ideas, it must of necessity cut down and crush everything living and unconditioned, the entire, so to speak, organic vegetation of the soul, and leave nothing but a cheerless desert behind it.[3]

The cardinal principles of the West were the following:

one-sided rationalism and a dichotomy of the principle of enlightenment and, in a perfect correspondence with it, *a dichotomy of the social element composed of the conquerors and of the conquered.*[4]

Kushite rationalism and legalism came to the West from Rome. Conquest was the main characteristic of Germanic society. In contrast to the Slavs, the Germans did not want to till the land peacefully, but were always bent on conquering other peoples, even other Germans, and on exploiting them and their resources. Western society rose out of such Germanic conquests in the first centuries of the Christian era. It was based on compulsion as the fundamental principle of the state, on aristocracy as a highly developed and precisely formulated class apart from and opposed to the rest of the people, on the exploitation of the masses, on hatred and antagonism.

The Western world was very different from the Eastern, and could not continue to form one church with it. The circumstances of the schism were extremely important: the West arrogated to itself the right to change in an arbitrary manner the universal

[2] Kh., vol. VII, p. 212.   [3] Kh., vol. I, p. 203.
[4] Kh., vol. I, p. 211.

Christian creed, and thus broke the Christian bonds of love, cast away disdainfully its Eastern brothers, and rent Christendom asunder. This fatal Western act determined the subsequent historical path of the West.

A private opinion, personal or local (that is the same), which usurped for itself the right of an independent solution of a dogmatic question in the domain of the universal Church, contained in itself the formulation and the legalization of Protestantism, that is of the freedom of investigation divorced from the living tradition of unity based on mutual love. Thus Romanism, at the very moment of its origin, proclaimed itself as Protestantism. . . .[5] Romanism was the first to create a new type of heresy, a heresy against the dogma about the essence of the Church, against its belief in itself; the Reformation was merely a continuation of the same heresy under a different form.[6]

Khomiakov and the other Slavophiles emphasized strongly the continuity of Western development, the organic connection between Catholicism and Protestantism. According to them, Orthodoxy was in no way a middle ground between the two Western denominations: it was rather truth itself, the very opposite of the Western falsehood of rationalism, of which Catholicism and Protestantism were successive instances. In Western rationalistic dialectic, Protestantism came as the logical antithesis of Catholicism. As soon as the Western church broke the harmonious unity of Christendom based on love, it acquired a pressing need of some other authority. Catholicism found its authority in the person of the Roman bishop, and in the rigid, hierarchical organization of the church.

Such was the first period of Western history, the second was a period of reaction. The one-sidedness of Latinism provoked a counteraction, and little by little, after many unsuccessful attempts, after a long struggle, came the period of Protestantism, one-sided like Latinism, but one-sided in the opposite direction: for Protestantism retained the idea of freedom and sacrificed to it the idea of unity. It could not be otherwise, for reconciliation was impossible for the West brought up on the principle of Latinism, under the conditions of Germanic conquest and Roman legal formalism. The whole modern history of Europe belongs to Protestantism, even in the lands which pass for Catholic. Just as the

[5] Kh., vol. II, p. 50.   [6] Kh., vol. II, p. 66.

Latin idea of unity was that of external unity, so also the Protestant idea of freedom was that of external freedom, because freedom, separated from the idea of intelligent content, is a purely negative and therefore an external concept. In the course of several centuries, Protestantism was restrained from complete self-destruction only through arbitrary circumstances; but it carried within itself the seeds of its own ruin, and these seeds were bound to develop. They have developed.[7]

As is every antithesis of a dialectical ladder, Protestantism was determined by its thesis, that is by Catholicism:

Protestantism is a world which denies another world. Deprive it of this other world denied by it, and Protestantism will die: for its entire life is in negation.[8]

The Slavophiles described Catholicism as rationalism in materialism or rationalism in despotism, and Protestantism as rationalism in idealism or rationalism in anarchism, but rationalism always remained the common denominator. Anglicanism, in their opinion, was merely a transitional stage between Catholicism and Protestantism, which could not last much longer than Gallicanism had lasted. But although the Slavophiles regarded Catholicism and Protestantism as two successive dialectical instances of the same Western rationalism, they definitely preferred the latter to the former. They believed that the Catholic error was the deeper and the more dangerous one, and that it was especially characterized by hypocrisy and lying.

In times of trial the old, instinctive unity of all Western denominations, as opposed to the East, reasserted itself. Khomiakov emphasized that in a letter to Palmer, who was considering joining the Orthodox church:

A very weak conviction in points of doctrine can bring over a Romanist to Protestantism, or a Protestant to Romanism. A Frenchman, an Englishman will go over to Presbyterianism, to Lutheranism, to the Independents, to the Cameronians, and indeed to almost every form of belief or misbelief; he will not go over to Orthodoxy. As long as he does not step out of the circles of doctrines which have taken their origin in the Western world, he feels himself at home; notwithstanding his apparent change, he does not feel that dread of apostasy which renders

[7] Kh., vol. I, p. 149.   [8] Kh., vol. II, p. 44.

sometimes the passage from error to faith as difficult as from truth to error. He will be condemned by his former brethren, who will call his action a rash one, perhaps a bad one; but it will not be utter madness, depriving him, as it were, of his rights of citizenship in the civilized world of the West. And that is natural. All the Western doctrine is born out of Romanism; it feels (though unconsciously) its solidarity with the past; it feels its dependence from one science, from one creed, from one line of life; and that creed, that science, that life was the Latin one. . . . In short, if it was to be expressed in the concise language of algebra, all the West knew but one datum, a; whether it be preceded by the positive sign +, as with the Romanists, or with the negative −, as with the Protestants, the a remains the same. Now a passage to Orthodoxy seems indeed like an apostasy from the past, from its science, creed, and life. It is rushing into a new and unknown world, a bold step to take, or even to advise.[9]

The Western dialectic continued its inexorable course beyond Protestantism.

Rationalism has to end in the Protestant negation, because analysis moves by way of dissolution and negation. In its final result Protestantism must pass into a purely philosophic analysis with all its consequences. . . .[10]

The unfortunate people of the West could not be held responsible for their loss of faith "because sad disbelief becomes a virtue in the face of religious error." [11] German idealistic philosophy grew directly out of Protestantism:

Luther, or rather the Reformation, destroyed the inner calm of human spirit in Germany, it undermined not only the faith based on the one-sided foundation of authority, but the very feeling of faith, which was thrown to the mercy of private criticism. . . . Germany vaguely recognized in itself a complete lack of religion, and transferred little by little into the bosom of philosophy all requirements, which had hitherto been supplied by religion. Kant was a direct and a necessary continuer of Luther.[12]

Such was, according to Khomiakov, the course of Western development from Roman Kushitism to the nineteenth century.

The other Slavophiles, Ivan Kireevskii in particular, supported

---

[9] *Russia and the English Church*, p. 67.
[11] Kh., vol. II, p. 140.
[10] Kh., vol. VII, p. 213.
[12] Kh., vol. I, p. 298.

and developed Khomiakov's analysis of the West. Ivan Kireevskii, whose outline of the subject proved to be very important
in the history of Russian thought, emphasized as much as Khomiakov did the continuity of Western historical development based
on the fundamental rationalistic assumptions:

This classical world of ancient paganism, which Russia lacked in her
inheritance, represented in its essence a triumph of formal human reason over everything that is to be found inside and outside of it. This
pure, naked reason was based on itself, recognized nothing above itself
and outside itself, and appeared in two forms, characteristic of it: — in
the form of formal abstraction and in the form of abstract sensualism.
The effect of classicism on European enlightenment had to correspond
to the same character. But whether because the Christians in the West
fell lawlessly under the influence of the classical world, or because
heresy happened to correspond to paganism, the Roman church in its
deviation from the Eastern is characterized by precisely the same triumph of rationalism over tradition, of outer reason over inner spiritual
comprehension. Thus the dogma concerning the Trinity was changed
contrary to the spiritual meaning and tradition, changed as a result of
this external syllogism, deduced from the concept of divine equality of
the Father and of the Son. Thus, as a result of another syllogism, the
pope became the head of the church instead of Jesus Christ, then a
temporal sovereign, finally infallible; the existence of God was being
proved by a syllogism throughout entire Christendom; the whole totality
of faith was supported by syllogistic scholasticism; the Inquisition,
Jesuitry, in one word, all peculiarities of Catholicism developed through
the power of the same formal process of reasoning, so that Protestantism
itself, which the Catholics reproach with rationalism, developed directly
out of the rationalism of Catholicism. A perspicacious mind could see in
advance, in this final triumph of formal reason over faith and tradition,
the entire present fate of Europe, as a result of a fallacious principle:
Strauss and new philosophy in all of its aspects; industrialism as the
mainspring of social life; philanthropy based on calculated self-interest;
the system of education accelerated by the power of aroused jealousy;
Goethe, the crown of German poesy, the literary Talleyrand, who
changes his beauty, as the other one changes his governments; Napoleon; the hero of our time, the ideal of soulless calculation; the numeri-
cal majority, a fruit of rationalistic politics; and Louis Philippe, the
latest result of such hopes and such expensive experiments! [13]

[13] I.K., vol. I, pp. 111–112. The beginning of this passage indicates that
Ivan Kireevskii continued to believe, as he had believed in 1832, when he
wrote the article on "The Nineteenth Century" discussed in the first chapter

Konstantin Aksakov, in his championing of the true Russian principles, both in history and in contemporary society, invariably presented them in contrast with the perverse Western principles. Ivan Aksakov stressed repeatedly in his voluminous journalistic writings the peculiar nature of Catholicism and the crucial role which it played in Poland, in the Eastern Question, in the Austrian policy in the Balkans, and in the general attitude of the West towards Russia.[14] He believed that the Catholic church was

all entirely pervaded by *Western one-sidedness*. It is nothing else, but the *West* itself, but Rome, which elevates itself to *universal* significance, claims universal dominion, and demands the subjugation of the entire universe to itself.[15]

Samarin assimilated thoroughly Khomiakov's exposition of Catholicism and Protestantism, which he considered to be Khomiakov's most precious contribution to Orthodoxy, and used it to assail Lutheranism in the Baltic provinces and Catholicism in Poland.[16]

He made a study of Jesuitism which he regarded as

the last and the most legitimate offspring of Latinism. One can say that all the life juices, the entire soul of Latinism went into it, and that from the first minute of its appearance in the world Jesuitry embodied in itself the entire essence, the entire meaning of Latinism, and took over its place.[17]

Jesuitry represented the logical development of the rationalistic Catholic compromise: it was a most comprehensive attempt to efface the dividing line between good and evil, to replace truth by verisimilitude, and to reconcile all human sins and foibles with

---

of this study, that the main difference between Russia and the West was that Russia lacked the classical heritage, but he came to interpret it as an advantage rather than a disadvantage for Russia.

[14] Ivan Aksakov was also deeply interested in the Roman question and in the activities of the popes. See his editorials on "The Roman Question as the Papal Question," I. A., vol. VII, pp. 136–143, and on a papal encyclical, I. A., vol. IV, pp. 305–316.

[15] I. A., vol. I, p. 559.

[16] It was because of Khomiakov's definitions of Catholicism and of Protestantism that Samarin proclaimed Khomiakov to be "a doctor of the Church." See Samarin's *Introduction* to Khomiakov's theological works: Kh., vol. II, pp. I–XXXVI. Also published in: S., vol. VI, pp. 327–370.

[17] S., vol. VI, p. 194.

religion by means of ingenious sophisms and artful practices. Samarin was convinced that the Jesuits were the ideal emissaries and the most dangerous agents of Romanism in Poland and elsewhere.

Western civilization was based on false premises, on rationalism, on a split in the consciousness of man instead of the complete and integral comprehension characteristic of Orthodoxy, and this fatal defect had horrible consequences:

Because of it intelligence turns into clever cunning, the feeling of the heart into a blind passion, beauty into a dream, truth into mere opinion; learning into a syllogism; reality into a pretext for imagination; virtue into conceit, while theatricalism is the inseparable companion of life, the outer cover of falsehood, just as revery serves as its inner mask.[18]

The Slavophiles claimed to have detected this fundamental perversity in all manifestations of Western culture. Khomiakov saw it, for instance, as "the strange phenomenon of flesh simulating spirit," which permeated Western sculpture as much as Western painting, and the devotional life of Western saints and mystics as much as "the moral escapades of the George Sands." [19]

The West was extremely individualistic, and it was based on competition, strife, and conquest.

The entire private and public life of the West is founded on the concept of separate, individual independence which assumes individual isolation. Thence the sanctity of the external, formal relations, the sanctity of property and of conditional enactments are more important than human personality. Each individual — a private person, a knight, a prince, or a city — is, *within his rights*, a despotic unlimited individual, who is the law unto himself. The first step of every man in society is to surround himself with a fortress, from the depth of which he begins negotiations with other and independent powers.[20]

Conquest left an indelible mark on the Western man:

Conquering peoples, following their original character, always retain the feeling of personal pride and contempt, not only for everything vanquished, but also for everything alien.[21]

[18] I. K., vol. I, p. 216.

[19] See Khomiakov's article on the Russian painter Ivanov in Kh., vol. III, pp. 346–365.

[20] I.K., vol. I, p. 113.　　　　　　　　　　　　　[21] Kh., vol. V, p. 106.

The West was also very petty and unstable. In contrast to the Russian solidity of manner and clarity of purpose, the European "was always ready for extreme transports, always fussy, when not theatrical, always fidgety in his external and his inner movements to which he can render their proper measure only by a pre-meditated effort." [22] At the same time the Western man was too well satisfied with himself:

The Westerner, speaking generally, is almost always satisfied with his moral condition; almost every European is always ready to tell himself and others, beating himself proudly on the breast, that he is perfectly pure in the face of God and men, that he asks only one thing from God, namely that the other people be like him. If, however, it happens that his outward actions themselves are in a contradiction with the generally accepted concepts of morality, then he invents for himself a special, original system of morality, as a result of which his conscience again becomes pacified. [23]

The outward splendor of Western society did not stand in contradiction with its inner corruption; the two were in fact the opposite sides of the same medal. The principle of rationalism, utterly destructive in its ultimate results, served as a great temporary incentive for human society. In the words of Khomiakov:

The conditional, as the creation of reason (conscious or unconscious, a fruit of a profound calculation, or of an instinctive accommodation, that is all the same), easily assumes the appearance of a shapely form, easily unites material forces around itself and goes straight to its always one-sided goal. An invention of one locality or of one people, it is easily accepted and adopted by others because it does not bear the signs or the stamp of any locality or of any people. It is a fruit of reason, which is everywhere the same, not of the complete organism, which is every-where different. Its power and its seduction are in its weakness and its lifelessness. [24]

Ivan Kireevskii's appreciation of the situation was similar to Khomiakov's:

But this falling apart of the mind into particular forces, this domination of reason over the other activities of the spirit, which ultimately had to destroy the entire edifice of medieval European learning, at first had

[22] I.K., vol. I, p. 252.   [23] I.K., vol. I, p. 216.
[24] Kh., vol. VII, p. 325.

the opposite effect, and caused a development which was the more rapid, the more it was one-sided. Such is the law of the deviation of the human mind: the appearance of brilliance and the inner dimness.[25]

The glorious outward development of the West was most impressive, but it was also fatal. The temporary achievements of rationalism were bound to pass, the relentless dialectic of Western history was unfolding towards its ultimate stage of utter negation and destruction. The Slavophiles saw doom hanging over the West.

Western history and Western society formed an organic whole. The same principle of growth and the same logic of development ruled Europe from Norway to Spain, from the Vistula to the Atlantic. The Western man carried them with himself to North America and everywhere else he went. In the Slavophile ideology the West was one complete whole posited against Russia, Slavdom, or the Orthodox East. This organic whole was in turn composed of organic entities, nations. The nations were all infected by the cancer of rationalism, and in times of stress they demonstrated their spiritual solidarity against the Orthodox world, but they presented nevertheless great variations within the common framework of Western civilization, variations all the more significant because they were logical and organic, not arbitrary and artificial.

ENGLAND

Of the Western countries, the Slavophiles liked England best.[26] Khomiakov had a number of English friends, visited England in 1847, and wrote a long "Letter about England." [27] English people, English manners, English customs, even English buildings and lawns struck a responsive chord in his soul.

[25] I.K., vol. I, p. 193.

[26] Anglophilism in Russia was already widespread among the landlords at the time of Catherine the Great. England was unique in appealing to both liberals and conservatives. The empress herself was a leading Anglophile. See: E. Simmons, *English Literature and Culture in Russia (1553–1840).*

[27] This "Letter about England," which occupies pp. 103–129 of the first volume of Khomiakov's *Works*, represents the most thorough Slavophile discussion of England.

Soon I came to know London reasonably well, and I became comfortable, as if at home. I saw the Tower of London with its centuries-old fortifications, saw Westminster Abbey with its hundreds of tombs, a small part of which would be sufficient for the glory of an entire people, and I saw how the English revere the greatness of their past; I saw Christ's Hospital, where the students wear even now the strange costume of Tudor times; and I understood London: the summits are there, but then the roots are there too.[28]

The observation of Sunday in England indicated the same organic character of English life:

Strange is the sight of this emptiness, strange is the silence of this enormous, noisy, always bustling city, but on the other hand it is hardly possible to imagine anything more majestic than this silence. . . . Two million men, the most enterprising and the most active in the whole world, stopped their occupations, interrupted their amusements, and all that because of obedience to one high idea. I was glad to see that; I was happy for the high morality of the popular will, for the nobility of the human soul.[29]

Khomiakov discovered that the English were badly misunderstood by the rest of the world: they had no aversion to foreigners, but simply were careful in selecting their friends because they placed a high value on friendship. He continued:

Of course, it can not be said that the English show a great liking for foreigners, but it is not too clear to me why any people at all must like foreigners especially well. A certain land likes them as its educated teachers; the German likes them as his students; the Frenchman likes them as spectators to whom he can show himself. The Englishman does not need them, and therefore he remains rather indifferent towards them; this is very natural.[30]

The accusation of starchiness and ceremoniousness was again misdirected, and the white tie and the dinner jacket deserved every respect as the popular dress of England. It was ridiculous to charge "merry old England" with dullness and boredom, unless one preferred the superficial jokes of a French vaudeville to a true tradition of merriment.

[28] Kh., vol. I, p. 108.   [29] Kh., vol. I, p. 109.
[30] Kh., vol. I, p. 112.

The English were practical and businesslike, they were ruthless imperialists and hard-headed traders, and they amassed tremendous riches and power. The other countries were quick to notice this materialism because they admired it and wanted to emulate it, forgetting that England was also the land of Wilberforce, and of numerous missionaries, of political figures such as Cobden, and determined inventors such as Arkwright, of spiritual life, of love for nature, revealed in the unsurpassed English gardens, and of Shakespeare and the glorious old literature which was still flourishing. The English were a religious rather than a rationalistic people:

In the English character there is a deep and a highly justified disbelief in human reason. In this respect an Englishman reminds one of a Russian. Rationalism does not enter into his character.[31]

Oxford could indicate best the real nature and the true worth of England:

In a quiet summer evening, when the setting sun illuminates with its ruddy light all the twenty-two colleges of ancient Oxford, with their Gothic spires, gabled windows, and transparent arcades, when long shadows of ancient oaks and chestnuts fall on the green meadows of a park, and herds of deer play on the lighted meadow and on the shadows, and themselves flicker like shadows and trustfully run up to the university buildings and the cells of the students — at that time, believe me, Oxford is more magical than Venice itself. In Venice there is luxury and voluptuousness: over Oxford there hovers a certain disciplined and luminous thought. The top of the tree rustles and bends: in calm and silence grow and gather strength its centuries-old roots. The university discipline is similar to the monastic, the games of the students still retain the entire character of children's play; but for this reason this long childhood prepares a strong and intelligent manhood; therefore, from the severe monastic quiet come out those powerful and daring minds, who develop on such an enormous scope the spiritual and the material might of England, and who govern it through the tumult and the tempest of commercial and political life. . . . Very few Englishmen would ask you whether you have seen Liverpool or Birmingham; everyone would ask whether you have seen Oxford and Cambridge.[32]

[31] Kh., vol. I. p. 135.   [32] Kh., vol. I, pp. 133–134.

But, in spite of its many excellent traits, England was a part of the West, and its fate was linked with the fate of the West. Khomiakov thought that the Angles themselves had originally been a Slavonic tribe, and that their name was a variant of the tribal name of the Uglichi. They joined with the Saxons, who were a Germanic tribe with Scandinavian and Slavic admixtures, and with the Jutes, another Germanic tribe with a possible Cimmerian tinge. Together they established in England an organic, agricultural society, not a military camp of conquerors, so typical of the Germanic tribes on the continent. Celtic Christianity was spontaneous and organic, not mechanical and imposed, like the Roman; rulers such as the great King Alfred were worthy leaders of this promising young society; and national institutions, for instance, the Slavonic custom of jury based on unanimity, provided excellent material for future development. But England was not allowed to follow its proper path; it was conquered by the Benedictines, and it was conquered by the Normans.

The Normans, homeless, without family, and without soul, before the judgment of those who appraise impartially animal courage and animal valor, the Normans destroyed old England, and brought into it the entire odious corruption, and the entire inhuman way of life, which they learned in France, and which the Franks were teaching to all Europe.[33]

The Benedictine conquest had been even more ominous: England became a part of the Roman world with its rationalism, legalism, formalism, and artificiality. The Protestant reaction was a logical consequence of Romanism.

In modern English history the two principles struggling for the possession of England, the old organic one, and the new rationalistic, were represented by the Tories and the Whigs respectively.

One, organic, living, historical, already weakened by the decline of the rural communal life, and by the unconsciously admitted Protestant skepticism, formed Toryism. The other, personal and analytic, distrusting the past, prepared long ago by the decline of communal life, and strengthened by the entire decomposing power of Protestantism, formed Whiggery.[34]

[33] Kh., vol. III, p. 134.   [34] Kh., vol. I, p. 128.

Whiggery appeared to mean liberty and progress only on the surface:

> To a more educated and impartial observer, to a Russian, the deadening dryness of Whiggery, when it is destroying the past, and its barrenness and, so to speak, soullessness, when it thinks of creating, are too obvious. At its bottom lies skepticism, which does not believe in history, and does not like it, rationalism, which does not recognize the lawfulness of natural and simple feelings, when they do not have a strictly logical foundation. . . .[35]

The growth of Whiggery was fortunately slowed down by the fact that: "In most cases a Whig is still a Tory a little, because he is an Englishman." [36] Whiggery meant daily bread, Toryism meant human joy and human happiness, all popular customs and games,

> the calm and the smiling sanctity of the family circle, the entire poetry, the entire fragrance of life. In England every old oak with its long branches, every bell tower silhouetted from afar against the sky, is a Tory. Many past generations made merry under this oak, prayed in that ancient church.[37]

The very fact of the struggle of the two principles was to the great credit of the English: in other Western lands there was no struggle, rationalism was there in complete control. "The other countries of Europe submitted to the chemical and the mechanical laws, England alone lives according to the physiological law." [38] Still, the battle was not an even one, Whiggery was definitely winning it:

> Of course, England is still strong, many living and fresh saps flow in her veins; but the work of the Whigs moves relentlessly forward. The blows of the Protestant axe ring loud and regularly, thousand year old roots are severed, the majestic tree groans.[39]

Khomiakov was not certain whether or not England, which formed a part of the materialistic and rationalistic West, but which also contained other and high principles, could be saved

[35] Kh., vol. I, pp. 128–129.
[37] Kh., vol. I, p. 130.
[39] Kh., vol. I, p. 139.
[36] Kh., vol. I, p. 129.
[38] Kh., vol. III, p. 470.

from Western doom. Her salvation depended on her ability to become conscious of herself, to realize that she was proceeding along a fatal path, and turn to "the inner sanctum of her spirit," which she still fortunately possessed.

Next to Khomiakov, Koshelev was the greatest Slavophile admirer of England. Koshelev's father had been educated at Oxford, and Koshelev himself visited England several times, and was especially interested in industrial and scientific exhibitions, in meeting prominent Englishmen, and in the Parliament, where he happened to be in the House of Commons when the Reform Bill of 1832 was passed. Koshelev's references to England were briefer and more businesslike than Khomiakov's, but they were equally full of praise.[40]

The other Slavophiles reëchoed the same high evaluation of England. Konstantin Aksakov, for instance, explained on one occasion the nature of the glorious English freedom:

Thus, on the one hand, the moral principle in family, society, and religion; on the other hand, respect for the past, and for tradition: there is the source of the calm freedom of England.[41]

Ivan Aksakov's advice was to learn from England especially:

the combination of a true enlightenment, and of a respect for the customs of the entire people, for ancient traditions, for the originality and the peculiarity of the organic development of the people. . . .[42]

FRANCE

France stood at the opposite pole from England in the Slavophile estimate. In 1826, at the age of twenty-one, Khomiakov described France as follows in a letter from Paris:

Centuries of glory, blood, brilliant enlightenment, and pleasures, not moral, but lively, passed over France, and she weakened, as a man after shocks disproportionate to his strength. I shall continue the comparison. All his impressions, all his concepts mixed into some colorless chaos, from which he tries to extricate himself, but cannot because he does not have a clear purpose. Similarly in France there is a certain

---

[40] See especially Koshelev, *op. cit.*, appendix, pp. 25–26.

[41] K. A., Brodskii, *op. cit.*, p. 121.   [42] I. A., vol. II, p. 499.

fermentation, not, however, the powerful, ardent sort, which marks the youth of the people, but rather the impotent, cold sort, incapable of creating anything high and original. That is why their works of art are so colorless, their ideas about their political existence so disjointed, their desires so vague. I think though that the provinces do not resemble Paris.[43]

Soon Khomiakov decided that the origin, the basic principles, not the provinces, were important.

The giddy assuredness of the Celt, the proud aristocratism of the German, and the everyday aridity of the Roman character fused into one in the composition of a Frenchman.[44]

Especially dreadful was the Frankish legacy of cruelty and depravity. France developed into a Western nation par excellence. In a rationalistic society institutions, customs, laws, everything in fact, could be borrowed, the more readily, the more abstract and artificial it was, the fewer traces it had of the organic originality of a people. "Such were the disadvantages and the advantages of the French language and the French way of life. They had to become a possession of the entire Western world." [45] The French, in turn, could borrow anything from anybody. They took, for instance, the organic English institution of trial by jury, and heedlessly mutilated it by substituting the majority rule for unanimity. Even French national heroes were borrowed:

It is impossible not to notice this peculiar relation of France to the greatest accomplishers of her destiny. She was an effective instrument of greatness which she could not create, probably because of the shallowness and the incoherence of her inner principles.[46]

Charles the Great and Napoleon were not Frenchmen. Later Ivan Aksakov maintained that even Gambetta was really an Italian.

The French had no originality and no spontaneity at all; they were always imitating, always posing, always artificial. They could not even understand German philosophy, and they were in general incapable of comprehending anything abstract. Their creative impotence was strikingly manifest in the field of arts and

[43] Kh., vol. VIII, pp. 9–10.
[44] Kh., vol. V, p. 120.
[45] Kh., vol. VII, p. 326.
[46] Kh., vol. VII, p. 250.

letters. The French people never composed "a single living melody." It had no real poetry.

As a matter of fact, as popular art becomes less and less possible, art in general gradually dries up. France had been of necessity, always, and to the highest degree, an anti-artistic land, unable not only to create, but also to understand the beautiful in any field of art.[47]

Khomiakov was convinced that:

France, gay, witty, and foppish, always self-satisfied in her scholastic mediocrity and her artistic nothingness, ready to accept or deny everything new indiscriminately, France, which knows from Cousin about the immortal works of the German philosophers, and from newspapers about all discoveries in the world of learning, requires long and great lessons of humility, before human feeling, capable of understanding human truth and of sympathizing with it, can be resuscitated in her.[48]

It was natural that a nation such as France would have the French Revolution.[49] Ivan Aksakov paid special attention to it:

The First French Revolution provided the most tremendous example of violent application of theory to practice, this immolation of life on the altar of abstract theory: it was an orgy of theory feasting on the ruins of the existing and the living, a Bacchanalia of the despotism of abstract, self-confident thought of separate individuals, who sacrificed to the theoretically understood ideal of a people the real, apolitical, inner freedom of life, to the idea of a people, the people of France itself, which, as was demonstrated by the revolution of 1848, still cannot understand the whole extent of evil of such a despotism.[50]

The extent was frightful indeed. The French Revolution

deprived life of the freedom of organic regeneration, scorned the rights of life, installed a tyranny of an abstract doctrine over life. It destroyed all historically developed social differentiations and forms of social life, instead of eliminating merely the falsehood in their mutual relations, it

[47] Kh., vol. I, p. 19. This judgment was all the more severe because Khomiakov himself had studied art in Paris. He did, however, elsewhere make an exception for French medieval architecture.

[48] Kh., vol. V, pp. 532–533.

[49] Samarin made the sharpest Slavophile definition of revolution: "Revolution is nothing but *rationalism in action*, in other words: a formally correct syllogism turned into a battering ram against the freedom of a living way of life." Iu. Samarin and F. Dmitriev, *Revolutsionnyi konservatism*, p. 10.

[50] I.A., vol. II, p. 267.

leveled everything to an external uniformity; it scattered the people into *individuals*, and replaced the concept of a people as an organism with a variety and freedom of functions by the concept of an agglomerate, an arithmetical sum of impersonal individuals, the sum, the thoughts, wishes, and will of which must be determined also, arithmetically, *by a count* of votes. History, tradition, popular custom — down with them; all moral factors of the life of a people many centuries old — down with them; instead of quality — quantity; instead of moral truth — external, legal truth; instead of a historical, living system — a formally legalistic system; in one word, instead of living, personal rule, living, popular, organic union — a state mechanism.[51]

France proceeded rapidly to change her forms of government, but all to no avail. The basic principle was false, and France could not escape the logic of its growth:

wearing a crown, a bourgeois hat, or a Phrygian cap, it is still the same bureaucratic and parliamentary despotism.[52]

One could only pity France,

The miserable land called to warn by her fate the rest of mankind, a country flinging herself about between popery and atheism, between superstition and disbelief, between slavery and revolt![53]

SPAIN

Spain was very different from France, but essentially it was as wicked a nation as France. It too represented the Kushite spirit of Rome, but from another angle. In fact — "In no other area of the ancient Roman world did the Roman mental character predominate to such an extent."[54] France was characterized by a great flair for imitation, superficiality, frivolity, and skepticism; the distinctive traits of Spain were fanaticism, superstition, aristocratic individualism, and pride. The Spanish view of the Catholic church was the most Kushite of all:

[51] I.A., vol. V, p. 557. Ivan Aksakov's criticism of the French Revolution was typical of the Romantic Age, and reminds one of Burke, among others. The most important single influence on Aksakov's appraisal of the French Revolution may have been that of De Maistre. For De Maistre's influence on Ivan Aksakov see: P. M-ev, "Zhozef de Mestr i ego politicheskaia doktrina," in *Russkii Vestnik*, volume Two Hundred Two, 1889, May, pp. 220–238; June, pp. 74–95, pp. 237–238.   [52] I.A., vol. II, p. 481.
[53] I.A., vol. VII, p. 348.   [54] Kh., vol. VII, p. 468.

For the more spiritual Germany and England, and perhaps for the best minds of France, Popery represented the high idea of the spiritual unity of the entire Christian world; for France in general it represented the dry and barren concept of the administrative unity of the church; for Italy it represented a symbol of her own greatness and world dominion; for Spain it represented the culmination of the entire world of exorcism.[55]

France developed the rationalistic, secular state. Spain was completely priest-ridden. It provided the best example of the horrible, and typically Kushite corruption of the church by the world and worldly affairs. Spain rose as the Western bastion of Christendom in a bitter struggle against Islam, and the Spanish character, already permeated by Romanism and by the horrible depravity of the Goths, the Franks of Spain, assumed its final shape in the course of this struggle. Its main elements became cruelty and pride, typical of an aristocratic band of warriors convinced of their high mission. The long contact with Arabic civilization added another vice, rationalism of form. The sombre, proud Spaniard would not tolerate any competition, and he had no sense of humor. He eliminated his rivals by fire and sword. He was even jealous of their national heroes, and had to compose the miserable fiction of Bernardo di Carpio's victory over Roland. It was only natural that the Spaniards created the Holy Inquisition, that the Spaniards bathed the New World in blood, that the Spaniards produced the dogma of *Filioque*, which marked the rift between the East and the West.

GERMANY

The Slavophile treatment of Germany indicated the extent to which the Slavophiles were influenced and impressed by German romantic thought: to the Slavophiles Germany meant German philosophy. This philosophy was the highest achievement of the human mind. It gave Germany the intellectual leadership of mankind, and made it a great country, comparable to England. Next to German philosophy stood the extremely extensive, honest, and

[55] Kh., vol. VII, p. 470. The best Slavophile discussion of Spain is in Khomiakov's *History*. Khomiakov mentioned that as a child he had been a bitter enemy of Spain and an enthusiastic admirer of the English freebooters.

thorough, although plodding and dull German scholarship. At times the Slavophiles agreed with Hegel, and other German thinkers, in considering Germany as the fullest historical revelation of the Spirit. But they were certain that the future did not belong to Germany: German philosophy was very great, but it had its limitations, and so did German scholarship. The two were, after all, products of the fundamental rationalism and formalism of the West. In Germany books had acquired excessive authority, thinkers were worshipped as prophets, and spiritual creativity was stifled by pedantic learning and one-sided rationalism. German scholars were divided into those who were engaged in constructing fantastic a priori philosophic systems, and those who were devoted to the minutest research in all fields of knowledge: neither group could escape from the vicious circle of rationalism.[56] The next stage of universal history belonged to the land which could transcend rationalism, and replace it by the development of all human faculties and the resulting fullness of life.

The Slavophiles both loved and hated romantic Germany. In either case they had a very high appreciation of it.[57] Late in life Samarin was deeply grieved to see the disappearance of the Germany of philosophy, and the arrival of the harsh, practical, and cynical German empire.

THE OTHER EUROPEAN NATIONS

The Slavophiles refused to take Italy seriously.

As to modern Italy, no matter how one strains one's mind, there is so far nothing to say, except perhaps that there *die Citronen bluehen*, that it is a land of wonderful nature, a treasury of art (not contemporary, however), a storehouse of majestic historical reminiscences, the eternal *dahin* for the inhabitants of the North. . . .[58]

The development of Italy was plagued by the dreadful ulcer of popery. The Italians, because of their position in the center of the Catholic world, cared little about their own land.

---

[56] See Chapter V for the Slavophile criticism of German idealistic philosophy.

[57] See the Kireevkiis' letters from Germany discussed in " 'We' and 'They' — Psychological," Chapter III, for the expression of this Slavophile attitude.

[58] I.A., vol. VII, p. 339.

Small countries were summarily dismissed by the Slavophiles. Such were, for instance, "the sterile flower called Switzerland," and "the half-French Belgium, which imagines that she has created a life for herself because five powers invented boundaries for her in order to avoid a European war." [59] Scandinavia was discussed only in Khomiakov's *History*, which gave an account of the tribal migrations, and of the Scandinavian heroic age, and advanced a theory of the Slavonic origin of Scandinavian religion and culture. Austria was not really a nation, not really an organism, although it found a certain binding element in Catholicism and in the Jews. The Hungarians remained essentially a proud, militant, wild, and cruel Asiatic horde. The Slavic peoples of the Habsburg Empire belonged to "We" rather than to "They." Even when Catholic, they had been forced into Catholicism, and they manifested their resistance by such means as John Huss and the Hussite movement.

Poland occupied a peculiar position. It was a Slavic land, but it had betrayed the Slavs, and had sold itself willingly to Catholicism and the West. This act of foul treachery, and the acceptance of the poisonous doctrines of Catholicism led gradually to the decline of Polish culture and of the Polish state, and eventually to the complete collapse and partition of Poland.[60] In his article on Glinka's opera *A Life for the Tsar*, Khomiakov described Poland as

a part of the West, full of aristocratic knighthood, dashing and gay, soft as silk and hard as iron, which worships individuality and might, which scorns the family, which broke away from the communal life, and which threatens with its entire force (and even more with its seductiveness) every land still retaining the family and the communal brotherhood.[61]

[59] Kh., vol. V, p. 533.

[60] "But the stigma laid upon Poland by her recognition of the rights of the emperor and of the pope, by her petition for a royal title and crown, by her request for permission to fight and conquer the pagan Northern Slavs, and by her assumption of the state of a vassal, was not and could not be erased. Moral subjugation and bondage, moral so-to-speak incompetence of the people and of the state were admitted and recognized forever." Kh., vol. VII, p. 309.

[61] Kh., vol. III, p. 100.

Ivan Aksakov often saw no hope for "the Poles, this miserable, haughty, arrogant, and thoughtless tribe, which in addition has been burnt through and through with the Catholic-Jesuit morality." [62] Samarin, the leading Slavophile expert on Poland, was more optimistic. It was too early to despair: "As two souls imprisoned in the same body, Slavicism and Latinism have waged and are waging inside Poland herself an implacable life or death struggle." [63] Samarin believed that the Slavic principle would prevail.

THE UNITED STATES OF AMERICA

The Slavophiles showed a considerable interest in the United States of America. As early as 1830, in his "Review of Russian Letters for the Year 1829," Ivan Kireevskii observed that:

Out of the entire enlightened humanity two nations do not participate in the general slumber; two nations, young and fresh, flourish with hope; these are the United States of America and our fatherland. But the distance, geographic and political, and above all the one-sided character of English culture of the United States, transfer all European hopes to Russia.[64]

Gradually the Slavophiles came to occupy an emphatically hostile position toward the United States. The United States represented rationalism, legalism, and materialism in their most outrageous form. The country had no background, no real nationality, nothing traditional or organic. Ivan Kireevskii gave an incisive evaluation of this experiment of bare reason:

The experiment has already been made. What a brilliant future appeared to belong to the United States of America, built on such a reasonable foundation, after such a great beginning! — And what happened? Only the external forms of society, deprived of the inner source of life, developed, and they crushed the man under the external mechanism. The literature of the United States, according to the reports of the most impartial judges, is a clear expression of this condition. An enormous factory of talentless poems, without a shadow of poesy; trite epithets signifying nothing and yet constantly repeated; a total absence of feeling for everything artistic; an obvious contempt for all thinking,

[62] I.A., vol. III, p. 581.   [63] S., vol. I, p. 335.
[64] I.K., vol. II, p. 39.

which does not lead to material gains; petty personalities without general foundations; puffed up sentences with a most trifling content, a profanation of the sacred words, *humanity, fatherland, common good, nationality,* to such an extent that their use has become not even hypocrisy, but simply a recognized stamp for selfish interests; a superficial respect for the external side of the laws combined with most insolent violations of them; a spirit of coöperation for private gains combined with an unblushing unfaithfulness of the coöperating individuals, and an obvious disrespect for all moral principles, so that it is evident that at the basis of all this mental activity lies the most petty life, cut off from everything that lifts the heart above personal profit, sunk in the work of egoism, and recognizing material comfort together with its subsidiary elements as the highest goal. No! If indeed a Russian is fated, for some impenitent sins, to exchange his great future for the one-sided life of the West, then I would rather fall into revery with the abstract German in his involved theories; I would rather fall into indolence until death under the warm sky, in the artistic atmosphere of Italy; I would rather start whirling with the Frenchman in his impulsive, momentary desires; I would rather turn into stone with an Englishman and his stubborn and unaccountable habits than I would suffocate in this prose of factory relations, in this mechanism of selfish worry.[65]

Konstantin Aksakov shared Kireevskii's view on the American nation:

This external order may appear very brilliant, but it is a superficial glitter; it may appear free, but it is the individual freedom, a mutually limited licence. No, freedom is not there: where the spirit of God is, there is freedom.[66]

Ivan Aksakov continued the work of the earlier Slavophiles in analyzing the United States of America. His main contribution was an article "Concerning the Absence of Spiritual Content in the American People," published in *The Day,* on January 30th, 1865. America was engaged in a civil war, and Ivan Aksakov observed it with much interest:

But evidently not the external freedom alone is necessary for man or, to put it more correctly, the freedom itself is not created on a merely contractual foundation! The free citizens themselves, of their own free will, after arming themselves with all the weapons of the despotic states,

[65] I.K., vol. I, pp. 153–154.   [66] K.A., vol. I, p. 58.

have already harassed, tormented, and killed one another three years in succession. The principle of personal freedom, deprived of its moral content, turned out to consist of purely material urges, and became simply a means for the attainment of personal, material well-being. . . .[67]

The dreadful war was

quite worthy of America. This is some kind of madness, an orgy of fratricide, for which the entire luxury of civilization has been adapted. As if the final purpose of the latter were to invent the greatest comfort and convenience for the self-destruction of mankind![68]

America had added nothing of real value to the treasury of humanity:

It brought nothing, except machines and goods, except mechanical inventions, except material improvements. Art, science, philosophy, are not the lot of North America, they are not in its province.[69]

America was still living on the traditions, on the scraps of organic life brought over from the Old World.

When these traditions disappear, a truly American people will be formed, and an American state will be organized, without faith, without moral principles and ideals; it will either fall apart, from the unruliness of personal egoism and the lack of faith of the individuals, or it will coalesce into a horrible despotism of the New World. . . .[70]

THE JEWS

The Jewish problem attracted the attention of the Slavophiles, and its treatment in their ideology underwent an interesting development.

[67] I.A., vol. VII, p. 55. The article occupies pp. 52–65.
[68] I.A., vol. VII, p. 64.   [69] I.A., vol. VII, p. 56.
[70] I.A., vol. VII, p. 65. Comparisons between Russia and America were frequent at the time and were often influenced by Tocqueville. The view of the United States as a perfectly materialistic and utilitarian land had been expressed, e.g., by V. Odoevskii, who had stressed that money was the basic principle of America.

Khomiakov, who wrote more about foreign nations than any other Slavophile, had very little to say about America. One of his remarks began with the typical "I do not like the Americans. . . ." There was also a reference to some American acquaintances: "In Moscow I became acquainted with some American men and women. Quite a special people; there is something savage in them, in spite of education: ladies and gentlemen who went wild. They liked me very much." Kh., vol. VIII, p. 329.

Khomiakov was not at all anti-Semitic. He believed that the Jews were an Iranian tribe, as attested above all by their great religion, and that they had made at the time of the Old Testament a most important contribution to humanity, but he thought that by denying Christ they had denied their own tradition, and had thus terminated the creative period of their history.[71] Ivan Kireevskii did not like the Jews, but he left only chance remarks on the subject. Anti-Semitism acquired a definite place in the Slavophile ideology only after the death of the early Slavophiles.

In one of his last letters, in March, 1876, Samarin wrote from Berlin:

You must certainly know that today there is practically no Berlin left, there is a new Jerusalem which speaks German. When it is the question of Judaism, which is enthroned in the Reichstag, which Bismarck *suffers*, while pretending to utilize it, which directs higher education, which occupies the place close to woman as the family doctor, the family teacher, or in all simplicity as a confidant, the place which had been occupied by the directors of conscience of the seventeenth and the eighteenth centuries, which pays and inspires the majority of the periodicals, it is not, you understand, a question of either the Old Testament, or of nationality raised to the height of an elected race. It is something intangible and elusive as a whole, it is the most complete extract which has ever existed of the elements fundamentally hostile to a moral and social system built on a Christian foundation. Certainly these elements are to be found everywhere, to a greater or lesser extent, but in order to divine their presence, to extract them from the farthest corners of society, and the deepest recesses of human consciousness, to bring them to the light of day, and above all to teach them not to blush, finally to form them into a body of doctrine and into a political party, an element was lacking which only the Jews could bring into play: an infallible flair and an absolute disregard of consequences in the negation of everything existing. Only the Jews possess this quality, or at least they possess it to an incomparably higher degree than anybody else because it is a part of their immemorial, growing historical tradition, unbroken since the creation of the world, and of the thoroughly *extra-Christian* (I say *extra-* and not only *anti-*Christian) constitution of the entire race. It is impossible not to admire the variety of forms and colors which this movement has at its disposal, without ever breaking its unity. In politics it is the adoration of success, and the cult of the golden calf;

[71] See Khomiakov's *History* and his article "Concerning Bunsen's Biblical Studies," Kh., vol. II, pp. 249–289.

in philosophy it is matter, which develops from itself to the fullest self-consciousness; on the social plane it is the remaking of all historical institutions on the basis of the pure Manchester doctrines, or of the rise in productivity, understood quite abstractly as the highest purpose in and for itself; in the domain of the family it is individual desire as the sole foundation of all relations; in the field of education it is the development and the direction of instincts: stimulus and response, nothing more, and as the aim, a battle of parasites exploiting useful people. That is how it is.[72]

Ivan Aksakov developed the same ideas in his journalistic struggle against the Jews and their defenders.

Judaism, in our days, is not only a material force, but also a spiritual one, entering all spiritual and moral folds of the Christian existence. It rules not only the stock exchange, but also the press, for instance, in Austria, it penetrates, especially in Germany, into the fields of art, literature, science, and internal social development of European societies, carrying always and everywhere its spirit of negation with it.[73] . . . Jewish noxiousness is a *national* quality, a quality of Jews as a nation.[74]

The Jews were bent on destroying Christendom not only because of malice and hate, but also because they were preparing their own universal dominion which they had never renounced. All radical and revolutionary elements were their natural allies.

Christian societies by their rebellion against Christianity bring down Jewish power on their own heads, and themselves forge the Jewish chains: this is already becoming a reality. It is remarkable that the enemies of Christianity, and even of religion in general, in short, the most desperate radicals, are at the same time the most enthusiastic friends of the Jews.[75]

[72] *Correspondence de G. Samarine avec la Baronne de Rhaden. 1861–1876*, pp. 241–243. In S., vol. VI, pp. 487–488 this letter was published in an abbreviated form.

[73] I.A., vol. III, p. 731. Ivan Aksakov's writings on the Jewish problem were collected in I.A., vol. III, pp. 685–844, but there are important references to the Jews in the other volumes as well. Ivan Aksakov was anti-Semitic throughout his journalistic career, and his anti-Semitism gradually increased. As a young man Aksakov had already hated the Jews. See the second volume of his *Letters* covering the years 1848–1851. E.g., "But it is a strange feeling that they (the Jews) arouse in me; I cannot get rid of the thought that every Jew continues to crucify Christ!" I.A., *Pisma*, vol. II, p. 36.

[74] I.A., vol. III, p. 790.   [75] I.A., vol. III, p. 825.

Ivan Aksakov felt certain that the Talmud was the most important part of Jewish faith, Jewish professions to the contrary notwithstanding, and that the Talmud taught the Jews to regard the
rest of mankind as material for their exploitation and subsequent
conquest. He also believed that the Jews of the whole world
were guided by the World Israelite Alliance, which always had
dark designs against Russia.

Ivan Aksakov was extremely hostile to the Russian Jews, who
formed a large minority in the western provinces of Russia, but
his hostility was mitigated a little by the more humane considerations inherent in the Slavophile view of the world. The Jews were
to have civil rights, receive an opportunity to earn their livelihood, and to be allowed to hold those offices, which did not put
them in a position to affect "the Christian way of life." A Jew
could become a real, not merely a nominal, citizen of Russia by
joining the Orthodox Church. Ivan Aksakov stressed that con-
verted Jews were much more Russian than the scions of ancient
Russian families, who had turned Catholic. He had to disapprove
of Jewish pogroms on religious and on legal grounds, but maintained, nevertheless, that the rapacity of the Jews was solely
responsible for the pogroms, that the Christians suffered much
more from the Jews than the Jews did from the Christians, and
that very little damage was inflicted in the course of the pogroms,
while the Jews declared fictitious heavy losses.

THE DECLINE OF THE WEST

The Slavophiles were intensely interested in the West; they
had a profound appreciation of Western culture, and of German
philosophy in particular. Khomiakov's description of the West as
"the land of holy miracles" is especially famous. The West was
based on one-sided rationalism, and therefore it had to cede its
place to the bearers of a higher principle, but the Slavophiles
could not determine how much of Western culture was perma-
nently valid and desirable. At times they were prepared to renounce all of it. On other occasions they spoke of the peerless
intellectual training provided by German philosophy, of many

glorious achievements of Western scholarship, and expressed the belief that the spark of true faith could bring back to life the entire dying body of the West, and animate its rich and varied civilization.

If the Slavophiles were to observe the Hegelian pattern strictly, if the West were the thesis, Russia the antithesis, and the happy society of the future the synthesis, then the West had a very important place, for the synthesis had to combine organically and on a higher plane the main antagonistic characteristics of both the thesis and the antithesis. But the Slavophile dialectic was not strictly Hegelian. Khomiakov and the other Slavophiles often showed a desire to annihilate one of the opposing forces rather than incorporate it into a higher synthesis. The historical role of the West was thus never precisely determined. The Slavophiles wavered between the obliteration and the incorporation of the West, between the total denial of the West and the recognition of its great value. In addition to "the land of holy miracles," the West was called numerous other things, good and bad; once or twice it was described as an imbecile.

Of one thing the Slavophiles were certain: whether the West had contributed much or little, whether it was "the land of holy miracles" or an imbecile, its role belonged to the past, and not to the future. "The land of holy miracles" was only a line in Khomiakov's poem which expressed this basic Slavophile conviction:

Sadness, sadness comes over me! Thick darkness is falling on the distant West, the land of holy miracles: former suns become pale as they burn out, and the greatest stars fall from the sky. . . . Woe! The age has ended, and the entire West is covered with the shroud of death. There darkness will be deep. . . . Hear then the call of fate, spring up in a new radiance, awake, oh somnolent East![76]

The West was torn between revolution and despotism, between compulsion and anarchy, between aristocracy and democracy, between abject submission and war. All these phenomena were opposites only in a sense; on a deeper level they revealed themselves

[76] Kh., vol. IV, p. 27.

as different aspects of the same basic corruption of rationalism.[77] The dialectical development of the West had passed the stages of Kushite Roman culture and German conquest, of Catholicism, and of Protestantism, and the period of idealistic philosophy was in its turn drawing to a close. This philosophy, as represented by Hegel, expressed the ultimate development of rationalism, the farthest reaches which it could attain, and therefore it marked the end of the dialectical process, and the end of the West. One-sided reason had finally revealed itself in its complete, pure form, and had once for all demonstrated its own false nature. Schelling already realized that and appealed to other principles, but the West had no principles except rationalism.[78] Once reason became bankrupt, the only possible course for the West was dissolution and death.

The Western man did not comprehend his own tragedy, but he was smitten by it, and he was at the end of his wits.

It is painful to see what a subtle, but inevitable and justly sent madness now drives the Western man. He feels his darkness, and, like a moth, he flies into the fire, which he takes to be the sun. He cries like a frog and barks like a dog, when he hears the Word of God. And this gibbering idiot they want to upbraid in accordance with Hegel! [79]

"They" had no hope left. The future belonged to "We."

WE

When the tired, old West, eaten by the cancer of rationalism, could no longer maintain its dominant position in the world, Russia was quite prepared to take its place. Russia was young, fresh, vigorous, and organic.

Russia is a different story; she experienced no struggle, no conquest, no eternal war, no endless treaties; she is not a creation of circumstance, but the product of a living, organic development; she has not been constructed, she grew. . . .[80] Not a single nation in the world is such an integral living organism, as the Russian, not a single one perhaps has

[77] For a concise summary of the characteristics of the West as contrasted with those of Russia see: I.K., vol. I, pp. 217–218.

[78] See Chapter V for the Slavophile evaluation of German idealistic philosophy.

[79] I. K., vol. II, p. 250.　　　　　　　　[80] Kh., vol. III, p. 110.

been granted such a treasure of capacities, and such a power of organic, natural concretion and attraction.[81]

Russia was the country which possessed that happy, organic life of which the West could only dream. The West

is agitated, tormented by political and social problems for which it can find practically no solution, except through bloody violence; we have, so to speak in the *natural* state, everything which is for them only a dream, something sought for, a subject of abstract thought.[82]

THE RUSSIAN PEOPLE

The Russian people was the only truly Christian people on earth; according to Konstantin Aksakov, Russian history could be read as one of the lives of the saints. Russia could not stop short of the Christian ideal:

Nothing can be done about it, Russia must either be the most moral, that is the most Christian, of all human societies, or nothing; but it is easier for her not to be than to be nothing.[83]

Humility was the basic Russian characteristic.

It is from this standpoint, from the standpoint of Christian humility that one must look at the Russian people and at its history. Man and his work are not praised by such a people, only God is praised.[84]

One could not deny the high mission of the people,

whose communal way of life is so near to the ideal of brotherly love, which forms the essence of Christianity, the people, which could produce the proverb "in Holy Russia one does not starve to death," which immediately begins to regard *condemned* criminals as unfortunates, which does not even preserve in its memory a record of its glorious deeds, which sees in its history only the action of Divine Providence, pardoning and punishing the sins of the people. . . .[85]

Of course the Russians were only human, they committed many unworthy deeds, and were guilty of numerous moral transgressions, but these were particular sins rather than vices. They were

[81] I.A., vol. II, p. 249.
[83] Kh., vol. III, p. 337.
[85] I.A., vol. IV, p. 251.

[82] I.A., vol. II, p. 687.
[84] K.A., vol. I, p. 18.

merely deviations from the true path, which always remained dear to the Russian heart. The Russians never bragged about their evil doings, they were never content with their moral state, but always aspired to a more Christian existence, and in that they were the very opposite of the corrupt and self-satisfied Westerners.

Because the Russians were true Christians, they were free. To the Slavophiles Christianity meant freedom: the real, inner freedom as distinct from all political and legal enactments.

The Russian people is not a people; it is humanity; it is a people only because it is surrounded by peoples with exclusively national essences, and its humanity is therefore represented as nationality. The Russian people is free, it has no state element in itself, it contains nothing relative. . . .[86] *Freedom* is the general essence of the Russian, true freedom and the absence of conditionality everywhere.[87]

The idea that the Russian people was in fact Humanity and that it was able to understand and represent all mankind, the idea which later in the century became a favorite theme of the proponents of Russian Messiahship, was repeatedly stated, but not developed by the Slavophiles. Khomiakov alluded to it in his emphasis on the absence of racial discrimination in Russia, and in his evaluation of Peter the Great's reforms, Konstantin Aksakov postulated it as the essence and the promise of Russian greatness, and Ivan Aksakov used it to prove that Russian foreign policy could never be one of exclusive and egoistic national interest.

This Christian understanding of the other nations by the Russians was the very reverse of hostility, and the Slavophiles were deeply offended whenever somebody suggested that the Russians hated foreigners, the Germans for instance:

Now really, what could be the origin of this absurd fable about hatred toward the Germans, *Deutschenhetze*, which, it is alleged, has seized our Russia? The Russian people, probably more so than any other people in the world, is a stranger to any hatred of human beings in general, and of foreigners in particular.[88]

[86] K.A., vol. I, p. 630.   [87] *Ibid.*
[88] I.A., vol. II, p. 595.

The specific characteristic of the spirit of the Russian people consists precisely in its many-sidedness, breadth, and its expression of the principles of mankind at large. It feels no tribal enmity either to a particular German or to *the German in general.*[89]

The same was true in the domain of religion: to a Russian, Orthodoxy was everything, but this boundless devotion to the true faith was combined with the greatest religious tolerance.

True Christianity meant humility and simplicity.

In the Russian world there is nothing proud, nothing brilliant, not a single striking effect. All is simple. Words are sparing; you will find as many words as are necessary for action, even less than necessary. Great deeds are accomplished without vaunting and bragging.[90]

The Russian spirit was opposed to luxury:

The Russian respected more the rags of a beggarly and weak-minded man of God than the golden brocade of a courtier. Luxury used to penetrate into Russia as an infection from the neighbors. People apologized for it; they succumbed to it as to a vice, and always felt its unlawfulness, not only religious, but also moral and social.[91]

Ivan Aksakov asserted that the conscience of Russia was merciless and incorruptible, and that the Russians were especially sensitive "to every lie, falsehood, insincerity of speech, to everything stilted and learned by rote." [92] He suggested that Russian diplomatic failures were sometimes due to this basic integrity of the Russian spirit, which was easily lost on the devious diplomatic paths, where corrupt Westerners felt quite at home.

The Russians preserved their youth, freshness, and vigor. The West, on the contrary, was very old and decrepit. It exhibited: "Boredom and indifference, a lack of energy in all its bloodshed and upheavals." [93] The Kireevskii brothers, Petr in particular, stressed that the divine spark of exaltation and enthusiasm was practically extinct in the apathetic West and was retained only by the Russians. Petr Kireevskii's only article was written in defense of Russian energy and enthusiasm against Pogodin's de-

[89] I.A., vol. II, p. 596.
[91] I.K., vol. I, p. 214.
[93] K.A., vol. I, p. 22.

[90] K.A., vol. I, p. 19.
[92] I.A., vol. III, p. 135.

piction of the Russian historical character as passive and resigned to its fate. So also in 1830 Petr Kireevskii wrote from Munich:

Only after one has visited Germany, can one understand the great significance of the Russian people, the freshness and the flexibility of its faculties, its spiritedness . . . . — and do you know that at Moscow University you will hardly find a dozen of such plain, and soulless faces, which compose the entire University of Munich? Do you know that in the whole University you will barely find five students with whom it is not a shame to become acquainted? That the majority of the students sleep at Oken's lectures and read novels at the lectures of Goerres? . . . .[94]

In addition to being full of enthusiasm, the Russian was stately, calm, and relaxed. This was again a result of the true religious and intellectual principles of life.

The Westerner cannot understand this living synthesis of the higher intellectual capacities, when none of them move without a sympathetic response of all others; this balance of inner life which marks even the most superficial movements of a man, brought up in the customary tradition of the Orthodox world: for all motions of the latter reflect, even at the most critical turns of life, something profoundly calm, a certain artless measure and dignity combined with humility, which testify to the balance of the spirit, to the depth and integrity of self-consciousness.[95]

The Russian people felt clearly its moral, Christian mission and was not interested in the inferior, material aims. Khomiakov wrote on the subject of the Crimean War:

The Russian people does not think of conquest at all, conquest has never seduced it. The Russian people gives no thought to glory, this feeling never moved its heart. It thinks of its duty, it thinks of a sacred war. I shall not call it a crusade, I shall not dishonor it by that name.[96]

The state itself was only a means to the high moral end:

In general the Slavic tribes, by their nature, are tribes of *the social life* so to speak, rather than of *the political*. They regard the state not as in itself the highest *goal* of existence, but only as a means to a free, peaceful, and happy life based primarily on the internal truth, and not on legalism.[97]

[94] Quoted from Liaskovskii, *Bratia Kireevskie*, p. 23.
[95] I.K., vol. I, pp. 201–202.
[96] *Russia and the English Church*, p. 169.   [97] I.A., vol. I, p. 562.

The favorite nationalist arguments of Russian size and power were incorporated into the Slavophile doctrine, although in a subordinate role.

We are assisted by the extraordinary receptivity and giftedness of the Russian character, the complete security of our external, political position, the instinctive feeling of our national might, the consciousness of being a great people with a world mission, finally by our physical size itself which exercises an undeniable influence on our moral nature, free from petty narrowness.[98]

Ivan Kireevskii delighted in the fact that, "In general, everything Russian has in common with everything enormous the quality that it can be surveyed only at a distance."[99] Khomiakov believed that there was "a secret (but perhaps understandable) sympathy between the spirit of man and the size of society — greatness of intellect and of thought belong only to great peoples."[100]

The intellectual and the artistic gifts of the Russians were as outstanding as their moral character. The Russian peasant had a much higher native intelligence than the peasant of any other nation. The Russians were particularly distinguished by their vivid imagination, and their great talent in literature, the arts, music, and song. The ancient Russian way of life had expressed the aesthetic nature as much as the moral ideal of Russia, and the gay and happy mood as well as the serious purpose of the Russian people.[101]

The Slavophiles did not concentrate their attention on the defects of the Russian character, with one exception. The only negative trait which they discussed at length was a certain incapacity

---

[98] I.A., vol. II, p. 740.   [99] I.K., vol. I, p. 48.   [100] Kh., vol. I, p. 227.

[101] See also Ivan Aksakov's "Speech about A. S. Pushkin" delivered to the Society of the Friends of Russian Letters on June 7, 1880. I.A., vol. VII, pp. 813–833. Aksakov described Pushkin as "the most Russian of all our poets," and emphasized the simplicity, sobriety, balance, objectivity, and optimism of Pushkin's writings as a deep revelation of the national Russian character.

Khomiakov commented on one occasion that the position which Pushkin came to occupy in Russian culture and life was in itself a proof of the universal, inclusive nature of Russia and the Russians: because he had some Negro blood, Pushkin could not have married in the United States of America, even "a white-faced daughter of a German washerwoman or of an English butcher." Kh., vol. V, p. 107.

for sustained effort, a peculiar inability to work much and consistently. Ivan Kireevskii described its metaphysical background:

But it is necessary to confess that this constant longing for integral wholeness of all moral forces could also have its dangerous side. For only in the society where all classes are equally permeated by the same spirit, where universally respected and numerous monasteries, these popular schools and the highest universities of a religious state, wholly control the minds; where, in consequence, men mature in spiritual wisdom can guide others not yet mature, only there such an attitude of man must lead him to the highest perfection. But when he is deprived of the guiding care of a higher mind, before his inner life had attained originality and maturity, his life may represent an unfortunate combination of excessive efforts with excessive prostrations. Therefore, we see sometimes that a Russian by concentrating all his strength on work can accomplish more in three days than a cautious German would accomplish in thirty; but, on the other hand, he cannot for a long time afterwards resume his work voluntarily. That is why in many cases a Russian, in such an immature state and deprived of a proper guide, may regulate his own work worse than the most mediocre German mind, which would measure for him the amount and the intensity of his efforts according to hours and tables.[102]

Russian laziness was most exasperating. Khomiakov once angrily commented that:

The faculties of the mind, given by God, are left in a peculiar state of criminal neglect, because of the eternal expectation of miracles. This is our disease.[103]

Khomiakov's own work indicated much interest and enthusiasm, but it usually lacked finish, consistency, and continuity, and Khomiakov had to be locked in by his friends for an hour a day in order to begin the writing of his *History*. A disastrous inability to produce was exhibited by Ivan and especially by Petr Kireevskii, and in general this trait in the characters of several Slavophiles proved to be as damaging to the Slavophile publications as the censorship. Ivan Aksakov joined Khomiakov and the Kireevskiis in the complaint: "We do not know how to work, we do not respect industry, and that is why with all our talents we produce so

[102] I.K., vol. I, pp. 211–212. [103] Kh., vol. VIII, p. 142.

little." [104] For a Slav, especially for a Russian, "the modest and tedious work of a mason" proved more difficult than the storming of the Kars fortress, or the forced crossing of the Balkans in winter. An appeal for hard prosaic work formed a dominant theme of Ivan Aksakov's poetry as well as of his journalistic writings:

And I understood that the time of living deeds, brilliant sacrifices, and magnanimous struggle has passed, and that instead of it our lot consisted in the deed of a muffled and tedious struggle! Daring forces are not needed in our days! And the deceptive impulses of youth are dangerous for us because they are all so good, so brilliant, so beautiful.[105]

The Slavs, especially the Orthodox Slavs, were usually treated on the same plane with the Russians, although in the capacity of younger and weaker brothers. The Russians were the greatest family of the Slavic race; Russian traits were really Slavic, and Slavic traits Russian. Occasionally the Slavophiles even stated that the Balkan Slavs had better retained some of the original Slavic principles, such as brotherhood, than had the Russians. Individual Slavic peoples, the Bulgarians, the Serbs, the Montenegrins, also usually received high praise. For instance, Ivan Aksakov was convinced that:

The Bulgarian people contains in itself all qualities necessary for healthy civic growth. It is a serious people, sensible, peaceful, industrious, persistent in its efforts to attain a goal; it does not tolerate rhetoric, or anything showy, any external theatrical demonstrations or manifestations. It *is not ashamed* of gratitude.[106]

Gratitude happened to be particularly important in the case of the Bulgarians because it determined their attitude toward Russia. All other "typically Bulgarian qualities" were equally prominent in the Slavophile description of the Russians.

THE RUSSIAN LANGUAGE

Like most romanticists, the Slavophiles were fascinated by language.

[104] I.A., vol. VII, p. 788.   [105] I.A., *Sbornik stikhotvorenii*, p. 24.
[106] I.A., vol. I, p. 329.

Man did not invent, did not construct the word. The word is inseparably connected with his being, with the spirit which God had put into him; it is the voice of conscious reason bestowed from on high. The word appeared together with man. It is a living expression of consciousness; it is inseparable from consciousness as consciousness is inseparable from man. The word and man are one.[107]

Just as the Russian nation was the most organic of all the nations, the Russian language was the most organic of all the languages:

Indeed the Russian word is not some chance growing together of the national essences with different principles and characters, as, for instance, are the French, the Italian, and the English languages, but a living expression of original and independent thought; it is no more possible to tell a Russian "speak thus" than it is to tell him "think thus." [108]

The Russian language was closer to the original language of mankind than any other tongue, and it revealed the Russian soul, the Russian spirit, and the Russian way of life. According to Konstantin Aksakov, its outstanding characteristics were the spirit of freedom, profound meaning and perfect logic, and the ability to combine a very great variety of particular forms into an organic unity.[109]

THE ORTHODOX CHURCH

The Russian people was above all a people of life, growth, development, activity, in contrast to the mechanical, formalistic, and petrified West. The Russians lived in the church, in the family, and in the commune, ranging from the local agricultural commune to the great commune of the entire land. The Orthodox Church was the most important of these institutions, and it was very much more than an institution.

[107] K.A., vol. III, p. 1.
[108] Kh., vol. III, p. 452. The Slavophiles liked England, but they did not like the difficult English language, "that ugly English writing, in which letters, it seems, are placed not to indicate which sounds should be pronounced, but rather to tell the reader which sounds should not be pronounced." Kh., vol. III, p. 197.
[109] Konstantin Aksakov's linguistic studies compose the second and the third volume of his *Works*. A high estimate of them is given in V. Vinogradov, *op. cit.*, pp. 61–68.

The Church is a revelation of the Holy Spirit, given to the mutual love of Christians, that love, which leads them up to the Father through His incarnated Word, Our Lord Jesus Christ.[110]

The Church was truth, truth intrinsically connected with love and freedom.

Khomiakov's attention was centered on the position of man in the Church:

A man, however, does not find in the Church something foreign to himself. He finds himself in it, himself not in the impotence of spiritual solitude, but in the might of his spiritual, sincere union with his brothers, with his Savior. He finds himself in it in his perfection, or rather he finds in it that which is perfect in himself, the Divine inspiration, which constantly evaporates in the crude impurity of every separate, individual existence. This purification happens through the invincible power of the mutual love in Jesus Christ of the Christians, for this love is the Holy Spirit.[111]

No external, legal expression of these bonds of love which formed the essence of the Church was necessary or possible:

We confess the one and free Church. It remains one, although it has no official representative of its unity, and it remains free, although its freedom is not expressed by a division of its members.[112]

This inner freedom could be seen in every manifestation of the life of the Orthodox Church, whereas it was totally absent in the rationalistic and formalistic religions of the West. The Western man could not even understand the meaning of the true Church, the realm of freedom:

Poor Romanist! Poor Protestant! No! Church is not authority, just as God is not authority, just as Christ is not authority; because authority is something external to us. Not authority, I say, but truth, and at the same time the life of a Christian, his inner life; for God, Christ, Church live in him a life which is more real than the heart which beats in his breast, or blood which flows in his veins; but they live in him only inasmuch as he himself lives an ecumenical life of love and unity, that is the life of the Church.[113]

[110] Kh., vol. II, p. 220.
[112] Ibid.

[111] Kh., vol. II, p. 112.
[113] Kh., vol. II, p. 53.

Khomiakov emphasized that every single member of the Church formed an organic part of it. No man or group of men stood at its head; the Orthodox Church knew no pope in any form, but only Jesus Christ. There was no excessive differentiation between the clergy and the laity, no assertion that the hierarchy had the exclusive right of teaching, while the masses were entitled only to the passive reactions of listening and following. Khomiakov was overjoyed by the Encyclical of the Eastern Patriarchs in 1848, which was directed against the growing papal claims in the domain of the Christian dogma, and which proclaimed that both the immutability of the dogma and the purity of the rite were entrusted not to the hierarchy alone, but also to the entire people of the Church, who were the Body of Christ.[114]

Truth as revealed in Orthodoxy was incomparably superior to everything else: Russian nationality, Slavdom, forms of government and social institutions, as well as all individual matters, were valuable precisely to the extent to which they were Christian, that is Orthodox. In theory at least, the Slavophiles always insisted on this single standard, and in contrast to many later nationalists, they never allowed any change or qualification of their basic formula.

Slavdom also had its whole significance in Orthodoxy. The Slavophiles especially emphasized this consideration because many Slavs were Catholics:

That is precisely the point: the single physiological fact of Slavonic origin, even together with the Slavonic language, means nothing by itself; it does not create strength, does not give content to nationality, does not raise it to universal significance. Everything depends on the inner content of the national spirit. A Latinizing Slav is merely a spiritual appendix to the Romano-Germanic West, and will not reach higher than the West; he has no lot except crawling in the wake of a *foreign* world mission. He has nothing *of his own* to tell to the world.[115]

The Russians, the Slavs in general, had a natural character particularly propitious for the acceptance of true Christianity, and

[114] Recently a brief article in English was published by Edward Every on "Khomiakoff and the Encyclical of the Eastern Patriarchs in 1848," in *Sobornost*, series 3, no. 3, summer, 1948, pp. 102–104.

[115] I.A., vol. I, p. 566.

the development of a Christian society, but the content of this society, its message and meaning, were Orthodox rather than Slavic. The dynamic spiritual principle which led Russia and Slavdom had been brought into the world by Jesus of Nazareth, and not by any original Slavic ancestors.

The state was entirely secondary to the church. Konstantin Aksakov gloried in the fact that to a Russian even fatherland was of little significance compared with faith. As to government proper, the Slavophiles had a low opinion of it. The Slavophile ethos included religious, racial, national, philosophical, and even linguistic elements, but government and power were not admitted. Theocracy, however, was no solution. It was typical of the rationalistic West, and it signified the final surrender of the church to the world. The Slavophiles, who were opposed to force and compulsion on every plane, could never admit them into the sacred precincts of the church. The only way, then, was to create a lay state, which would base itself to the greatest possible extent on the Christian principles, and would always follow them as its guiding light. The state had to put itself in accord with the church not by persecuting heretics, but

by positing the following as the chief aim of its existence: to be perpetually permeated more and more by the spirit of the Church, and not only not consider the Church as a means for making its own existence more comfortable, but, on the contrary, regard its own existence as only a means for the most complete and convenient establishment of the Church of God on earth.[116]

The Slavophiles were deeply concerned with the actual position of the Orthodox Church in Russia, and they strongly resented the government policy of treating religion as one of its bureaucratic departments. They complained that, although the government never pretended to play any part in the fundamental issues of faith and dogma, thus invalidating any charge of caesaropapism, state interference in church affairs, as far as it went, was quite obnoxious. The church showed a most unbecoming servility toward the tsar and the government. The state was formalistic and legalistic, it stifled liberty and creative life within the church, as

[116] I. K., vol. II, p. 271.

everywhere else, and it was at its worst when it tried to protect and guide the church. Khomiakov, in his correspondence with Palmer and elsewhere, as well as the other Slavophiles, repeatedly expressed both their basic conviction as to the righteousness and the excellence of the Orthodox Church in Russia, and their irritation with the state interference in religious matters.[117]

Within the Russian church itself, the Slavophiles favored all democratic, popular elements, and were invariably opposed to centralization, regimentation, and bureaucracy. They were especially hostile to the Holy Synod, which they regarded as a typical creation of Peter the Great, and which came to embody in their eyes everything undesirable in the church. The Slavophiles were horrified by the project of establishing a standard salary for all priests, and charging a set fee from the people for church sacraments and ceremonies. In a series of unusually bitter articles Ivan Aksakov suggested that the priests should also have decorations, uniforms, and swords, and inquired about the price of the human soul according to the new tariff.[118]

It was especially important that the people participate as much as possible in their church. The Slavophiles emphasized that the early Christian world had been centered around the parish commune, and that the parish commune had played a very important role in ancient Russia. In such a commune, the parishioners elected their priest and lived their lives together, bound by Christian love. The Slavophiles hoped for the revival of this life of religious communes, and Ivan Aksakov expressed an expectation that, in the future, parish communes would become the basic units of the life and organization of Russia.

The church had a particularly important mission in the field of education, especially in the borderlands, where Orthodoxy had to face Catholicism and Lutheranism, and in those parts of Russia which were infested by heresy, and the Slavophiles insisted that the state should let church schools develop freely. Because Russia had no meaning for them apart from Orthodoxy, the Slavophiles

[117] See, e.g., *Russia and the English Church*, pp. 95–96.
[118] Ivan Aksakov's articles dealing with the Church were published in the fourth volume of his *Works*.

were particularly perturbed by the Old Believers and by Russian sectarians of all kinds, of whom some of them, notably Ivan Aksakov, had a firsthand knowledge. The Slavophiles emphasized positive measures to disseminate Orthodoxy rather than negative ones to suppress heresy. Although they attached a very high significance to the conversion of all the Russians to Orthodoxy, and although they sometimes advocated various methods of pressure toward that end, they were not willing to condone direct compulsion.

THE FAMILY

Life in the church meant to the Slavophiles life in truth and fullness, the only life worthy of man. In the church man willingly renounced his individualism, egoism, and exclusiveness, and became through this act of self-sacrifice an organic part of an immeasurably greater whole. His individuality was not lost. On the contrary, it was strengthened, transfigured, and transposed to an incomparably higher level. Through his abnegation and humility, man came into real contact with other human beings, man learned how to love, man became man. Nothing could replace or rival the church in this task of transfiguration, but other institutions could offer their more modest contributions to the same end, and their value depended on their offering.

The family was especially important: it represented the bonds of love in their most direct and obvious form, it formed the foundation of every healthy society, and its decay was a very significant feature of the decline of the West. The Slavs had a special predilection for the family, which formed the basis of their social life:

They did not know the chance nature of the organization of military bands, founded on brute force and unchecked by any moral laws. Family sanctity and human feelings were developed in a simple manner between the graves of the fathers and the cradles of the children.[119]

The family forged bonds of love in time as well as in space, it united successive generations and made tradition and society possible.

[119] Kh., vol. III, p. 135.

THE PEASANT COMMUNE

In addition to living in the church, and in the family, a man, or at least a Slav, lived in the commune. In nineteenth-century Russia the commune meant the peasant commune, which owned land and parceled it out to its members, and which settled its own affairs at communal meetings. The problem of the commune became of paramount importance in connection with the emancipation of the serfs and the reorganization of Russia in the reign of Alexander II. A strong current of opinion, especially liberal opinion, considered it to be an archaic institution, which stifled individual initiative, hindered the development of agriculture in Russia, and retarded the entire progress of the country. The Slavophiles were among the earliest and the strongest opponents of this view. Samarin in particular defended the commune with great energy and determination both as a publicist and as a leading executor of the emancipation reform, and exercised a considerable influence on the extremely important role assigned to the commune in the Emancipation edict and its translation into practice. Samarin's arguments were primarily economic: the commune, through its periodic redistribution of land, ensured a permanent proper adjustment between land and labor; it represented the only security for the peasant, who was not strong enough to stand on his own in the competitive world; it guaranteed to the government the collection of taxes, and so on.[120]

Behind Samarin's practical considerations stood the Slavophile doctrine of the commune, which had been developed mainly by Khomiakov and by Konstantin Aksakov, and which upheld the commune on the religious, the metaphysical, and the historical, as well as on the economic and administrative planes. Khomiakov, who did not live to see the emancipation reform and the decision of the government about the commune, described the two contending views as follows:

[120] Samarin's writings dealing with the peasant problem and the emancipation reform compose the third, fourth, and fifth volumes of his *Works*. Important material on the commune is also contained in volume one, which consists of Samarin's articles on miscellaneous subjects.

Thus the following things are posited against each other: the retention of an age-old custom, based on the fundamental principles of life and feeling, the right of all to own land and of each one to use it, the moral link among people, and the moral, ennobling education of the people in the social sense by means of constant practice in communal justice and administration, with full publicity and rights of conscience, and against what is this posited? Against the violation of all popular customs and feelings, the concentration of property in relatively few hands, and the proletarization or at least the hireling status of all the rest, the dissolution of mutual ties among the people, and the absence of any social and moral education.[121]

The Slavophiles were convinced that the interference of the state could only injure the commune.

Undoubtedly a creation of the moral freedom of the people should not be enclosed within a Chinese wall of administrative institutions, just as iron hoops should not be made to gird a young tree, or an iron stake should not be driven into its heart in order to prevent it bending from the wind: this would be senseless. Freedom, which we respect in the past, must be respected in the future. It must be given the right to change, contract, or expand the forms of its expression. . . .[122]

Konstantin Aksakov was especially provoked by attempts to define the commune and its functions legally:

You take it upon yourself to decide: *when a commune is a commune*. This is the first example of nonsense and of insolence to the people. A *commune is a commune when it recognizes itself as such*. There can be no other definition. . . .[123] Rest in peace. The commune has existed for a long time; we had self-styled tsars, but no self-styled commune.[124]

Alleged improvements, such as the projected introduction of the majority rule, were bound to cause incalculable damage:

You dare to define for the commune what is its own decision, you dare to violate the principle which constitutes its basic strength, the secret of its life, namely: unanimity. You introduce *majority*, that crude, material force, which we do not recognize as such mainly because of our base servility to Europe — majority, which is so opposed to the spirit of the Russian land.[125]

---

[121] Kh., vol. III, p. 290.   [122] Kh., vol. I, pp. 287–288.
[123] Konstantin Aksakov, *Zamechaniia na novoe administrativnoe ustroistvo krestian v Rossii*, p. 9.
[124] K. A., *Zamechaniia*, p. 14.   [125] K. A., *Zamechaniia*, p. 11.

The commune was a priceless treasure. "Western thinkers turn in a vicious circle solely because it is impossible for them to attain the idea of the commune."[126] The Slavs possessed the commune because of the social nature of their native character, and above all because they were guided by the Orthodox Church and its ideal of Christian brotherhood. Konstantin Aksakov insisted that: "The commune is that highest true principle, which is not destined to find anything higher than itself, but which is destined only to flourish, purify, and elevate itself."[127] His summary description of the commune was probably the most significant one in Slavophile literature:

A commune is a union of the people, who have renounced their egoism, their individuality, and who express their common accord; this is an act of love, a noble Christian act, which expresses itself more or less clearly in its various other manifestations. A commune thus represents a moral choir, and just as in a choir a voice is not lost, but follows the general pattern and is heard in the harmony of all voices: so in the commune the individual is not lost, but renounces his exclusiveness in favor of the general accord — and there arises the noble phenomenon of harmonious, joint existence of rational beings (consciousnesses); there arises a brotherhood, a commune — a triumph of human spirit.[128]

Berdiaev remarked most appropriately:

The Slavophiles were under the influence of their *narodnik* illusions. To them the commune was not a fact of history, but something imposing which stands outside the realm of history; it is the "other world" so to speak within this world.[129]

LANDED PROPERTY

The Slavophile concept of the commune determined their attitude toward landed property. The land belonged really to the commune: Russian land belonged to the great commune of all Russia, local communes were the masters of local holdings. The Roman concept of property, which had been inherited by the materialistic and legalistic West, did not apply to Russia, where man came first and property rights second. The peasant commune was

---

[126] Kh., vol. I, p. 50.
[128] K. A., vol. I, pp. 291–292.
[127] K. A., vol. I, p. 291.
[129] Berdiaev, *The Russian Idea*, p. 50.

the best example of the Christian attitude to life, which considered property as a means to satisfy human wants, and not as an independent principle; the land was held jointly by the commune and was periodically redistributed among its members according to their needs and their ability to cultivate it.

The Slavophiles argued that the Russian landlords, as well as the Russian peasants, did not own their land, but merely used it: historically, landlords' service to the state came first, their rights to the land followed from it, and these rights were never absolute, but always conditioned by the state on which they depended and by the rights of the peasant commune; the power of the landlords over the peasants was also a function of their service to the state, and not a property right. The relativity and conditionality of land ownership pervaded the whole structure of Russian society:

> The tsar does not possess land as an owner, he merely uses it, and this concept of use, this relation is also transferred to the peasants, for in accordance with the Russian view land in general is not property, but only an object of use.[130]

The Slavophiles asserted that the Russian attitude towards landed property was a guarantee against pauperism and against the growth of the proletariat in Russia. Ivan Aksakov maintained that because Russian land belonged to the Orthodox Russian people, foreigners and non-Orthodox Russian landlords in Orthodox areas had land only on sufferance, and were required to give it up on demand for a proper compensation.[131]

THE EMANCIPATION OF THE SERFS

The Slavophiles were unconditionally opposed to serfdom. It was incompatible with their religion, their philosophy, and their view of Russia and the Russian people. Besides, it had outlived its economic usefulness and was especially detrimental to such pro-

---

[130] K. A., vol. I, p. 433.

[131] Throughout their discussion of property, the Slavophiles used the term *vladet* as the concept contrasted with absolute ownership. Vladet means *own* or *possess*, but because to the Slavophiles *vladet* signified a relative, functional possession of land, while the real ownership resided elsewhere, I translated it by *use*.

gressive landowners as Khomiakov and Koshelev. The Slavophiles showed an early interest in its abolition, and discussed measures to that end.

Even Petr Kireevskii, who wrote very little, and whose opinions have usually to be conjectured, expressed himself in unmistakable terms as to the immorality of serfdom and the necessity of reform. Suspicious of the landlords, and hostile to bureaucracy, he put his trust in drastic action by the government, as distinct from all voluntary arrangements and partial measures.

To rectify the general direction of Russian life is beyond the strength of a private individual; this can be done only from the center, that is, only by the government. . . .[132] Only a basic, centralized, and therefore governmental, reform can help, because only the government can stop at the same time all sources of abuse, which feed one another. It alone can simultaneously abolish both bureaucracy and serfdom. . . .[133] As to the nature of the change, which I would like the government to promulgate all over Russia, it should not be the intermediate stage of bondsmen, because mediation between the landlord and the peasants is impossible, but *a complete division between the landlord and the peasants*: I think it would be just to give them half of the land.[134]

Petr Kireevskii did not mention any compensation to the landlords for the lost half of the land, and he urged haste:

I not only do not share the opinion of those who think that our people is not sufficiently mature for legality, but I think on the contrary that it is in a stage in which it has not yet lost this maturity, which it is losing more and more with every year.[135]

Most of the other Slavophiles also championed emancipation as a thorough government reform, specific, standard, and obligatory for all Russia. Their uncompromising hostility to serfdom can be measured by the fact that, in their struggle against it, they appealed to the government, to legality, and to compulsion, the prin-

---

[132] Petr Kireevskii expounded his project of emancipating the serfs in a letter to Koshelev written as early as 1847. See: "Ob otmene krepostnogo prava. Pismo Petra Vasilievicha Kireevskogo k A. I. Koshelevu," in *Russkii Arkhiv*, 1873, columns 1345–1360, esp. column 1358.

[133] P.K., "Ob otmene krepostnogo prava," column 1359.

[134] P.K., "Ob otmene krepostnogo prava," column 1356.

[135] P.K., "Ob otmene krepostnogo prava," column 1359.

ciples toward which they usually felt hatred. In his important memorandum "Concerning the Abolition of Serfdom in Russia," presented to Ia. Rostovtsev, a leading official dealing with emancipation, Khomiakov declared:

In the presence of mutually burdensome obligations, a voluntary agreement will be entirely to the advantage of the more powerful, who always profit in any case, whereas a standard norm will mean the salvation of the weak, who are precisely those in need of protection. . . .[136] A redemption, standard, compulsory, and in one act, is the only intelligent solution of the entire problem.[137]

With his usual love for detail, Khomiakov proceeded to specify the size of peasant allotments as two *desiatinas* each, described how the money for the reimbursement of the landlords could be obtained, and explained how the entire reform could be completed within four years.[138]

Samarin, who played a leading part in the actual abolition of serfdom, was also the chief Slavophile theoretician on the subject. The Slavophiles found it very difficult to explain the presence of serfdom in old Russia, and Konstantin Aksakov even outlined the fantastic theory that real serfdom had been introduced only by Peter the Great. Samarin emphasized that serfdom did not represent a logical development of true Russian principles, but was

[136] Kh., vol. III, p. 302.

[137] Kh., vol. III, p. 304.

[138] Ivan Kireevskii was a striking exception among the Slavophiles in that he was opposed to the emancipation of the serfs. He had to admit that Slavophilism and serfdom were incompatible, and he conceded that serfdom neither should nor could have been prolonged indefinitely, but during the last years of his life, obsessed by an unaccountable fear of all change, he pleaded constantly for the retention of serfdom for the time being, that is until the dominant Western spirit in the country would be replaced by a truly Russian orientation, which he promised would happen soon. I.K., vol. II, pp. 241–245, pp. 252–255. Ivan Kireevskii's views influenced his brother Petr. Koshelev, "Moi vospominaniia ob A. S. Khomiakove," column 267.

Koshelev was one of the most active Slavophile proponents of emancipation, but he favored voluntary agreement between the landlords and their serfs rather than government action. See Koshelev, *Zapiski*, appendix five, pp. 58–166. The appendix contains Koshelev's plan for the abolition of serfdom composed at the beginning of 1858.

merely a horrible accident, a by-product of administrative enactments:

Serfdom in Russia was an indirect, and one can say an unexpected result of two general legislative measures, which originated with the government. Each one of them was applied simultaneously in the entire country; we mean: the prohibition to leave the land, and the leveling of peasants with serfs during the first census.[139]

Samarin used the Slavophile theory of the commune and landed property to prove that the landlords did not have an absolute proprietory right to the land and the peasants, and he stressed the historical perspective. "The population of Russia was agricultural, and therefore settled, since the dawn of history."[140] Princely, church and private possessions were a later development, which tended to obscure, but could not replace the more ancient relationship of the peasant communes to the land which they tilled. Gradually the service gentry usurped great power over the land and the people:

In the conflict of interests of the common people with the interests of the service class, the powerful and the only organ of the state, the latter were bound to win.[141]

Serfdom itself, however, only underlined the right of the peasants to their land:

The peasants lost for a long time their personal freedom, the right to be their own masters: *but this sacrifice saved their right to the land for better times.*[142]

Serfdom had two fundamental aspects:

At its base, in my opinion, lies *the concept of inseparability of the peasant and the land*, a concept entirely foreign to Western Europe. This *inseparability* is manifested in a twofold manner: *as the dependence of the peasant on the land*, that is serfdom, and *as the dependence of the land on the peasant*, that is the inverse relationship, the realization of which belongs to the future.[143]

[139] S., vol. II, p. 196.
[141] S., vol. II, p. 151.
[143] S., vol. II, p. 15.

[140] S., vol. II, p. 147.
[142] *Ibid.*

This second aspect was extremely important. It expressed that part of the concept of serfdom, which was "*positive* and destined for further development, because a village can exist without a landlord, but it cannot hang in the air, have no soil under it."[144]

The economic argument was as powerful as the legal: peasants without land were unthinkable, and material security was more important than any personal rights, or any changes in form.

A whole estate, which is reliably secured in its means of livelihood, and the material well-being of which is constantly increasing, cannot remain long in a dependent status and cannot fail to attain a position proper to it in society; inversely, personal freedom and a model social organization fall far short of guaranteeing even daily bread.[145]

Samarin had made a detailed study of the Prussian land reform, and he supported his views with analogies and examples from Western, especially German, history. He was considered a liberal among the leading figures in the work of emancipation, and he often defended peasant interests against a majority of his colleagues.[146]

Samarin and the other Slavophiles had a good reason to be pleased with the reform of 1861: serfdom was abolished, the peasants were given land, redeemed by the state, in consideration of future payments from the peasants to the state, and the rural commune was recognized as the basic peasant unit in Russia. Ivan Aksakov contentedly affirmed that "the reform of the nineteenth of February is a product of fundamental Slavic principles."[147] The Russian solution was

broader, more liberal than the Western, original, Russian, answering to the problems of Russian history.[148] . . . . by our land reform we left behind us entire Western Europe with its higher culture and civilization.[149]

---

[144] S., vol. III, p. 19.   [145] S., vol. III, p. 439.

[146] The time element is extremely important in judging the "liberalism" of the various Slavophile projects dealing with the abolition of serfdom. For a period of time the development of thought on that subject was so rapid that "liberal" schemes became "conservative" in a few months.

[147] I. A., vol. III, p. 330.   [148] I.A., vol. V, p. 423.

[149] I.A., vol. VI, p. 134.

FREEDOM OF "THE LIFE OF THE SPIRIT"

The Slavophile religion and philosophy of freedom was reflected on the political and the social planes by a demand for freedom of conscience, speech, and the press, and in general by insistence on the complete liberty of "the life of the spirit," as distinct from the political sphere. The vagueness of this "domain of the spirit," and the fact that spiritual freedom was hardly compatible with political despotism, did not affect the conviction or the persistency of the Slavophile demand.

An absolute freedom of conscience followed directly from the religious views of the Slavophiles:

The Church says concerning conscience: it is free because it is *mine*, *God's*; the state says: it is free because it is *not mine, not Caesar's*.[150]

The necessity of freedom of speech appeared to them to be equally obvious. As Konstantin Aksakov tried to explain to the government: "Man was created by God as an intelligent and a talking being."[151] Freedom of speech, freedom of the press had nothing to do with any political or constitutional rights; it was just as natural and inseparable from man as walking or breathing.

This conviction permeated the Slavophile writings on the social and the political problems, as well as much of their poetry, notably Konstantin Aksakov's most famous piece — "The Free Word." The Slavophiles had good reason to protest against censorship, which interfered with their work and closed down most of their publications. But they opposed above all censorship as such rather than its specific tendency. In particular, they constantly remonstrated against restrictions imposed on their opponents, whether the opponents were Russian radicals or spokesmen of the Baltic barons. The Slavophiles were confident that truth was bound to win an open argument, and that every restriction encouraged falsehood.

In his capacity as the leading Slavophile publicist, Ivan Aksakov always argued for "freedom of the spirit," and against limitations on faith, belief, opinion, or their public expression. Following his brother, Konstantin, and the other Slavophiles, he tried to con-

[150] I.A., vol. IV, p. 112.   [151] K. A., Brodskii, *op. cit.*, p. 95.

vince the government that autocracy and freedom of the press
were perfectly compatible, even complementary:

Certain conditions are necessary for social life and creativity, and the
absence of these conditions constitutes the main source of our illness.
These conditions of life are freedom of the development of social intellect, and freedom of opinion and its expression, both orally and in print.
On the other hand, only an unlimited freedom of opinion can render
meaning to the unlimited freedom of government action.[152]

The government would not understand. Ivan Aksakov received
repeated warnings, his periodicals were temporarily suspended or
closed down one after another. A month before his death, Ivan
Aksakov, then the editor of *Rus*, was presented with another warning. He acknowledged it in a blistering editorial, in which he
restated once again the Slavophile principles of freedom, and assailed the oppressive measures of the government. Slavophilism
ended on the same sharp note of protest with which it had begun
against conditions in contemporary Russia.

The unqualified Slavophile opposition to capital punishment
represented a particular instance of their religious approach to
life, and their belief in freedom of the human spirit. As Konstantin
Aksakov proclaimed in one of his editorials in the *Common Talk*:

Death penalty is legalized murder, but murder never the less. . . . And
when you say that a criminal cannot repent, you are judging the soul
of man, a judgment which belongs only to God.[153]

Ivan Aksakov developed the ideas of his brother:

killing a man, even when it is done by the sword of the state, is contrary
to the spirit and the meaning of the teaching of Christ — Christ who
wanted mercy and not sacrifice, who did not desire the death of a
sinner.[154]

Freedom of the life of the spirit was not only an inalienable
human right, but also an indispensable prerequisite for the healthy
growth of society. The Slavophile doctrine laid a special emphasis
on the activity of society, and considered spontaneous social ini-

[152] I.A., vol. IV, p. 402.   [153] K. A., Brodskii, *op. cit.*, p. 117.
[154] I. A., vol. II, p. 407. See also Ivan Aksakov's editorial on "The Abolition of Capital Punishment" in I.A., vol. VII, pp. 467–473.

tiative preferable to government directives, in administration as much as in education, and in journalism as much as in styles of dress. In Russian history the Slavophiles emphasized the role of the commune, the town governments, and the zemskii sobor; in contemporary Russia they defended the commune, and worked hard in the zemstvo instituted by Alexander II, although they often objected to both the Right and the Left wings in the zemstvo, as well as to its general "Western orientation."

The Slavophiles wanted more, not less self-government for Russia. They believed that the problems confronting the nation could be solved only by a free and responsible participation of the entire society, the whole people, not by bureaucracy and government planning. This participation was to be, however, on the social, never on the political, constitutional plane.

LAW AND JUSTICE

The Slavophile views on law and justice formed an integral part of their ideology. Few ideas were as repellent to the Slavophiles as that of the abstract legal mind shaping life and society according to its own dictates. The Slavophiles denied that law had any value in and of itself. In the scale of values they stressed the Christian standard, complete inner truth, to which the external, legal truth could only be an unworthy servant. Historically they emphasized custom, tradition, the gradual growth of the life of the people, as opposed to the artificial and arid projects of legislators.

Law and custom rule the social life of the peoples. Law, written and armed with compulsion, brings the differing private wills into a conditional unity. Custom, unwritten and unarmed, is the expression of the most basic unity of society. It is as closely connected with the personality of a people as the habits of life are connected with the personality of a man. The broader the sphere of custom, the stronger and healthier the society, and the richer and more original the development of its jurisprudence.[155]

The Russian people was the most organic of all the peoples, and therefore its life was based much more on custom than on law.

[155] Kh., vol. III, p. 75.

In his article "On Legal Problems," and in other works Khomia-kov emphasized the Christian nature of Russia and the validity of law as measured by its contribution to the great end of establishing a truly Christian society on earth. He advocated public, oral pro-cedure, juries based on unanimity, arbitration whenever possible, and other measures designed to increase the moral and the social element in the court at the expense of legal formalism. Unanimity in the jury was in itself a great moral phenomenon:

Yes, the very faith in hunger, by which unanimity is extorted, is an ex-ample of a deep moral sense. Where no individual personalities are involved (they are eliminated by the very principle of the jury), one who wants to save an innocent person will willingly suffer three times more than one who wishes to punish a guilty person.[156]

Arbitration was also a highly moral practice: the arbiter repre-sented the contending parties themselves, deprived of their per-sonal prejudice in the case; most important was "the freedom of the arbitration court from the limitations imposed by the letter of the law." [157]

The Slavophiles welcomed the fundamental judicial reform promulgated by Alexander II. Khomiakov did not live to see the abolition of the system, which he had condemned as making Rus-sian courts "black with black injustice," and the introduction of some of the changes which he had championed most ardently, but Ivan Aksakov, who himself had had legal education and ex-perience, continued to represent the Slavophile point of view on legal matters. Aksakov criticized certain borrowings from the West, and some specific defects of the new judicial system, but he

[156] Kh., vol. III, p. 334.
[157] Kh., vol. III, p. 333.

The Slavophile treatment of law and justice found favor with religious thinkers rather than with legal scholars. Many of the latter condemned it as utterly Utopian in its failure to realize the great significance of the state and of legal institutions. However, the Slavophiles had some followers even among legal scholars, notably professors V. Leshkov and L. Vladimirov. See Vladi-mirov's monograph: *Aleksei Stepanovich Khomiakov i ego etiko-sotsialnoe uchenie.* Vladimirov admired both Khomiakov's general approach to law and many of his particular statements on the subject, among which he regarded particularly highly Khomiakov's insistence that the guilt of the parents should not affect the children.

rallied to the support of the new courts whenever their principle was challenged in favor of the old organization.[158]

EDUCATION

Education was even more important than law in the construction of a Christian commonwealth. The Slavophiles emphasized that education began very early and that its basis was always to be found in the family: "A child, whose first words were *God, daddy, mama,* will have a different frame of mind from the one whose first words were *money, apparel,* or *profit.*"[159] Russian education had to serve Russian needs:

Therefore education, in order to be Russian, must be in accord not with the principles of piety in general, not with the principles of Christianity in general, but with the principles of Orthodoxy, which is the only true Christianity, with the principles of family life, and with the requirements of the rural commune. . . .[160]

The Slavophiles favored both church schools and a strong emphasis on religion in all other types of schools. As usual, they distrusted government initiative: the basic principles of life and education could not be manufactured by the state, which could merely assist the growth of the Russian principles by eliminating obstacles in their way:

We see as yet no other solution except *complete freedom* of education: then schools will be formed which will be private, not state, which will belong to and reflect the needs of society; then each milieu will itself create the schools which it needs most.[161]

[158] Ivan Aksakov's articles on legal topics were collected in the fourth volume of his *Works.* See in particular the article "Concerning the Old Courts (in Connection with Increased Attacks on the New Courts in Society and in the Press)." Aksakov emphasized that he was not arguing from the standpoint of Western liberalism, but few liberals or radicals could have made as effective a condemnation. The keynote line came early in the article: "The old court! At the mere recollection of it one's hair stands on end and one's flesh begins to creep!" I.A., vol. IV, p. 655.

[159] Kh., vol. I, p. 347. The article "Concerning Public Education in Russia" occupies pp. 345–370.

[160] Kh., vol. I, p. 350.

[161] I. A., vol. II, p. 198.

The belief in the special national character of the Russians also played a part in the Slavophile consideration of education, e.g., in Ivan Aksakov's comparison of the Russian child and the German:

But the qualities of mind of the Russian child are quite different from those of, for instance, the German child, to whose spiritual image and likeness we are so forcibly fitting our Russian children. The German mind is formalistic by its very nature, and therefore the same formalism which at present deadens and destroys the talents of the Russian high school students, presents no obstacle to the German; the German student flourishes and exudes health, whereas our high school students look completely worn out. The mind of the Russian child is incomparably more lively, with a greater inclination towards concrete forms and images, with a greater demand for a synthesis, with an inalienable admixture of the element of artistic cognition.[162]

Christian upbringing could be successfully fostered only by the family and society as a whole, not by the school alone. The Slavophiles stressed the importance of the Christian pattern of daily life, with its fasts and its festivals, its customs and its rites, and Khomiakov himself, even as a young student of painting in Paris, invariably observed the fasts and the holidays of the Orthodox calendar. Teaching and research were entitled to complete freedom, but the Russian students were to be guarded from "the German superstition," which consisted in regarding the results produced by every scientific discipline at every given stage of its development as the final and incontrovertible truth.

ECONOMIC LIFE

The Slavophile attitude towards the economic development of Russia was ambiguous. As usual, the Slavophiles preached activity, development, growth in agriculture, industry, and commerce as much as in education, literature, and art. Personal inclination and interests supported this general tendency: Khomiakov, Koshelev, and some other Slavophiles were progressive landowners attracted by improved methods of agriculture, new machinery, and so on; Ivan Aksakov even became a bank executive, and as a publicist he often championed the merchant class, advocated the

[162] I. A., vol. VII, p. 739.

extension of railroads, a greater exploitation of the natural resources of Russia, and the like.

On the other hand, the Slavophiles could not approve the direction of the economic change: their doctrine was based on agriculture and the village commune, and it was unsuited to an industrial society. The Slavophiles disliked the town, and they were afraid of the proletariat. They attempted to prove that the proletariat could not develop in Russia because of the peasant commune, which provided land for all, and because of the artel, a communal organization of Russian craftsmen, but they were nevertheless worried by the trends in Russian economic and social life. Besides, they themselves belonged to the old landed gentry, and had a certain aversion to the capitalists, and to the *nouveaux riches* of all kinds. Although many of the Slavophiles managed their affairs well and took an active part in the economic development of Russia, they often felt an urge to escape from contemporary life to their studies of the Moscow of Ivan III, or the Kiev of Saint Vladimir.[163]

LITERATURE, ART, SCIENCE

The Slavophiles argued in romantic terms for the great significance of literature and art, and for the principle of art for art's sake, but they also remembered the great social purpose to be accomplished. Khomiakov resolved the difficulty by explaining that whereas art as such was not to serve any extraneous purpose, the artist was of necessity a man of his time and his society and reflected its problems and aspirations:

An artist is not a theory, not a sphere of thought or intellectual activity; he is a man, always a man of his time, usually its best representative, entirely permeated by its spirit and its clearly defined or potential aspirations.[164]

Literature directed towards the exposure and the eradication of social wrongs was therefore as legitimate as the so-called pure literature. Khomiakov made that point clear in 1859, at a meeting

---

[163] See Chapter VI for the treatment of the Slavophiles by Marxist historians from the class point of view.   [164] Kh., vol. III, p. 419.

of The Society of the Friends of Russian Letters, when as Chairman of the Society he welcomed two new members — I. Selivanov, who advocated literature with a social content, and Count L. Tolstoi, who presented himself as a proponent of art for art's sake.[165]

Literature and art had to be original in order to express the spirit of the nation, and the Slavophiles were bitterly opposed to imitation.

> Every age, every nation contains in itself the possibility of original art, provided it believes in something, provided it loves something, provided it has some religion, some ideal.[166]

The spirit was important and not the form: to be a truly Russian writer or artist one did not have to concentrate on folklore or try to reproduce the ways of the common people, one had simply to be a Russian, to believe and live as a Russian, and one's work was bound to reflect the principles which one cherished.

Khomiakov thought that the true, Christian spirit of Russia was revealed in Ivanov's painting "An Appearance of Christ to the People," which he regarded as the greatest creation in the history of art, and he considered that the best expression of the Russian spirit in literature was achieved by Gogol, and in music by Glinka. Some of the other Slavophiles judged Pushkin to be as important or even more important a writer than Gogol. The most pronounced literary bias of the Slavophiles was directed against the new naturalistic school, which, they felt, did a grievous injustice to the Russian people, even when its proponents were as competent as Grigorovich, Uspenskii, or Saltykov-Shchedrin.

In science and scholarship the Slavophiles also insisted on national originality. They admitted that scientific laws and discoveries were universally valid, but they argued that the scientific genius of a nation formed an integral part of its national spirit, which determined the lines and the success of research.[167]

---

[165] Kh., vol. III, pp. 414–419.   [166] Kh., vol. III, p. 96.

[167] See several articles by Samarin in the first volume of his *Works*. Samarin was challenged by a number of his contemporaries. See: M. Katkov, "Vopros o narodnosti v nauke," in *Russkii Vestnik*, 1856, book two, pp. 312–319.

THE GOVERNMENT

The Russian lived in the church, in the family, and in the commune. He was active in the social and in the economic spheres, in literature, art, and science. But the field of politics, the realm of the state, remained foreign to him. The Slavophiles were anarchists of a peculiar kind: they considered all formalism and compulsion and therefore every form of state as evil, but they were convinced that the state could not be avoided. The best one could do was to limit the scope of the evil, and Russian history represented a successful attempt to achieve just that.

The Russian people is not a political people, that is, it does not aspire to political power, does not want political rights, does not contain in itself even the germ of the love of power.[168]

The Russian people realized more clearly than any other the corrupting, stifling, deadening nature of government, and therefore it consciously established a separate government machine and retained for itself, in exclusiveness and purity, the social, creative sphere of life. Russian history began with the calling of the Varangians, Russian towns used to invite princes to rule them, and finally the entire Russian commune, through its representatives in Moscow, invited the Romanov dynasty to rule Russia.

History offers no other example of that kind; no other people desired the state so consciously, but on the other hand, no other people kept itself so consistently apart from the state.[169]

Supreme right and value rested definitely with the people, whereas the state, the government, had been merely invited to assist the people.

It was clearly understood that the people did not exist for the state, but the state for the people. The principle of life, of moral achievement, of the spirit is undoubtedly to be found in the commune, in the people. The state is of secondary importance, and according to its very idea it cannot put a soul into the people, at best it can communicate to the people mechanical motion.[170]

[168] K. A., Brodskii, *op. cit.*, p. 69. [169] K. A., vol. I, p. 594.
[170] K. A., vol. I, note to p. 251.

Khomiakov was at times as outspoken as Konstantin Aksakov. For instance, in a letter to Koshelev, after praising an article of Tiutchev, he added the following lines of criticism:

Reproach him for one thing, for his attack on the *souveraineté du peuple*. It indeed does contain the *souveraineté suprème*. Otherwise what is the meaning of the year 1612? [171]

Although the Slavophiles loved to discuss the year 1612, however, they were absolutely opposed to any formal guarantee of the supremacy of the people, any established machinery for the election or control of the tsars. This meant to them the worst kind of legalism of the Western type, the involvement of the people itself in politics, the corruption of the Russian soul.

If Slavophilism is characterized by a certain democratic element, its democracy is not formal, political, not state, legal, but mystical.[172]

The Slavophiles believed in autocracy.[173] This conclusion followed logically from their premises: if power was an evil burden, the fewer men who had to carry it the better. The Slavophiles

---

[171] Kh., vol. VIII, pp. 200–201.

[172] N. Ustrialov, "Politicheskaia doktrina slavianofilstva. (Ideia samoderzhaviia v slavianofilskoi postanovke)," in *Izvestiia iuridicheskogo fakulteta*, volume I, Harbin, 1925, pp. 47–74, esp. p. 66.

The Slavophiles were very hostile to political democracy. E.g.: "It is clear that the principle of majority is a principle which does not need harmony; it is a compulsory principle, which wins only through physical superiority; those who are *in the majority* overwhelm those who are *in the minority*." K.A., vol. I, p. 292. Or: "The essence of democracy is the most crude worship blinded by ambition of the principle of the state, of the external, material, compulsory, and relative truth, and the desire to introduce this principle into the inner life of the people." I. A., vol. II, p. 87.

[173] There may be one exception to this statement. Gershenzon suggested that Petr Kireevskii, about whose views little is known, was not in favor of autocracy. He quoted an aphorism found in Petr Kireevskii's unedited papers: "It is said that a people cannot exist without a single, autocratic ruler, as a herd cannot exist without a shepherd. But the shepherd in charge of a herd is *a man*; he is superior to the herd by his very nature, and he is therefore its legitimate ruler. It would have been insane to trust in the security of the herd, if an ox ruled a herd of oxen, or a ram of rams. (Therefore) Is it not clear that the analogy is false? and who, except God, is as superior by his very nature to man, as man is superior to a herd of beasts? For a man to occupy this position, either he must be raised to the level of God, or the people must be degraded to the state of beasts." Gershenzon, *op. cit.*, p. 97.

stressed the difficulty and the responsibility, not the power and the glory, of the supreme rule, and they "regarded the crown of the tsar as a certain kind of a martyr's crown, a sacrificial symbol of self-renouncement."[174] Ivan Aksakov emphasized the advantage of having a living man, a soul and a conscience, instead of formal institutions and legal bodies, at the head of the nation. Autocracy was also dear to the Slavophiles as a great Russian tradition, as an organic element of Russian history and life.

But all these Slavophile justifications of autocracy were historical and functional, therefore relative, never religious and absolute: the idea of a divine monarchy or of a mystical connection between the church and the tsar was entirely foreign to the Slavophile thought. Samarin underlined the fact that the church had nothing to do with any form of government:

The Church is indifferent to this form, to the question how power should be organized, to whom it should be entrusted; the Church restricts as little the freedom of political development as of the development of commerce or of language.[175]

The government had an important function to perform: it provided the necessary element of formalism and compulsion, it organized the defense of the people against its enemies. The Slavophiles were particularly insistent that the government should not overstep its bounds and encroach on the free life of the spirit of the people.

Thus the first relationship between the government and the people is the relationship of *mutual non-interference.*[176] . . . *Defense* in general, that is the meaning and the duty of the state. Its guardianship consists in providing greater comforts of life, and not at all in managing it. The State is in no way a preceptor. . . .[177] Its entire virtue must consist of its *negative* character, so that the less it exists as a state, the better it accomplishes its aim, as is the case in England.[178]

And to eliminate all possible doubt:

The fewer points of contact the government has with the people, and the people with the government, the better.[179]

---

[174] Ustrialov, *op. cit.*, p. 57.
[176] K. A., Brodskii, *op. cit.*, p. 80.
[178] I. K., vol. II, p. 272.

[175] S., vol. VI, pp. 557–558.
[177] K. A., vol. I, p. 552.
[179] K. A., *Zemechaniia*, p. 26.

Konstantin Aksakov's memorandum to Emperor Alexander II was meant to expound this truly Russian delineation of the spheres of activity, and the nature and the role of the Russian people and the Russian government. It concluded with the following words:

May the ancient union of the government and the people, of the state and the land be reëstablished on the firm foundation of true, fundamental Russian principles. To the government the unlimited freedom of *rule*, which is its exclusive possession, to the people the full freedom of both external and internal *life*, which the government safeguards. *To the government the right of action, and consequently of law; to the people the right of opinion, and consequently of speech.*[180]

THE SLAVOPHILE MISSION

The people of Russia meant to the Slavophiles the peasants, the members of the rural commune. The peasants were not a class, or an estate, but rather the whole body of the nation, the real incarnation of Russia, its history, and its tradition. In contradiction to this mystical, homogeneous mass of the people stood all particular classes, groups, parties, and interests. Classes were a natural phenomenon in the rationalistic and legalistic West, but they were alien to the Russian spirit, which was based on the higher principles of wholeness and organic unity. The presence of these particularist elements in Russian life was a symptom of the disease caused by the fact that Peter the Great had abandoned the true Russian principles, and that from his time on, the Russian government, the Russian intellectuals, the Russian landlords, all in fact, except the people, had been aping the West. The disease would pass, and then the upper classes of Russia would be organically absorbed by the great Russian commune. The Slavophiles gave no details of this process, but they were certain of its inevitability. In the meantime they opposed class privilege and class distinction. Ivan Aksakov gave a faithful expression to Slavophile principles when in 1862 he urged the Russian gentry to petition to the throne:

That the gentry be permitted to do the following: to perform solemnly, in the face of the whole of Russia, the great act of annihilating itself as

---

[180] K. A., Brodskii, *op. cit.*, p. 96. The complete text and the additions to the text of Konstantin Aksakov's *Memorandum* are reproduced on pp. 69–102.

an estate. That the gentry privileges be modified and extended to all estates in Russia.[181]

The Slavophiles were convinced that only they themselves and the common people were free of Western infection. The Westernizers, the liberals, and the radicals were outspoken lackeys of the West, but the conservatives were not really better. They too had no understanding of Russia, no connection with the Russian past, no place in the Russian future.

There they are, our real nihilists for whom Russian nationality, Orthodoxy, tradition do not exist . . . .[182] nihilism which is not religious, or social, but political, which flourishes not in student circles, but in those of Adjutant-Generals. It is composed of two elements: the adoration of comfort in the service, and complete disbelief in the historical future of Russia.[183]

The conservative ideal was "not the Russia of tomorrow, but the Austria of yesterday."[184]

The Slavophiles never tired of emphasizing the basic cleavage in Russia, the division between the people on the one hand and the educated society with all its parties and groupings on the other:

The public speaks French, the people speaks Russian. The public follows Paris fashions. The people has its Russian customs. The public (at least in its great part) eats meat; the people observes fasts. The public sleeps, the people has already arisen long since and works. The public works (mostly with its feet on the dance floor): the people sleeps or already rises again to work. The public despises the people: the people forgives the public. . . . The public and the people have their epithets: we call the public honorable, and the people Orthodox.[185]

The numerous and varied writings of the Slavophiles were all permeated by this spirit of righteous indignation and sweeping condemnation, and were dedicated to the exposure of evil and to the affirmation of the true Russian principles.[186]

---

[181] I. A., vol. V, p. 218.   [182] I. A., vol. I, p. 306.
[183] S., vol. IX, p. 204.   [184] S., vol. IX, p. 485.
[185] K. A., Brodskii, *op. cit.*, p. 122.

[186] Occasionally the Slavophiles were even capable of a graceful approach to the matter, e.g., in the story of Prince Lupovitskii, a comedy of Konstantin Aksakov, which described the debacle of its hero, a very well-meaning and ineffectual Russian aristocrat, who decided to bring the material and espe-

The Slavophiles suffered all the time from government restrictions and suppression.[187] They were independent and outspoken, and that in itself could not be tolerated; their criticism was much too extensive and bitter; but the real conflict was that of principle: the Slavophiles condemned the entire organization, policy, and class foundation of the state. They remained loyal to the monarch himself, but they had a peculiar view of autocracy. And there was an inherent contradiction in their doctrine between the idea of the Russian tsar, and the thoroughly anti-Russian nature of the government.

Khomiakov and the Slavophiles did not say openly and could not say openly that our historical government is an alien, foreign government, but they thought that, their entire teaching led to that conclusion.[188]

In spite of the difficulties of their struggle, the opposition of the bulk of Russian society, and the hostility of the government, the Slavophiles were optimistically inclined. They felt that their teaching was bound to spread all over Russia, and spread soon. If the converts were not as yet numerous, quality compensated for quantity. The march of history, the logic of events, the development of the dialectic made an early triumph of truth inevitable. Sometimes the Slavophiles were so excited by the developments in Europe that they believed the new age to be just around the corner, and

---

cially the moral advances of the West to his Russian peasants. Prince Lupovitskii had a strong sentiment for Russia and did not want to discuss its defects in public in Paris: "Somebody may overhear us here, we speak frankly about Russia; it is unpleasant, awkward, in front of, after all, foreigners. You see, the Frenchmen are still, however, after all, foreigners." Konstantin Aksakov, *Kniaz Lupovitskii ili priezd v derevniu*, p. 8.

[187] One can almost say that the Slavophile publications were suppressed as a rule and allowed as an exception. Many bizarre incidents resulted. Khomiakov's reference to England as "the favorite daughter of freedom" had to be published as "the favorite daughter of nature," — the reference was in a poem, and "freedom" and "nature" rhymed. Once a censor objected to the publishing by Konstantin Aksakov of an old popular song which contained some words of abuse directed at a ruler of a nomadic horde: "Although it is a hostile tsar, it is still unbecoming that the author should quote the following lines from the song. . . ." Smirnov, *op. cit.*, p. 65.

[188] Berdiaev, *Khomiakov*, p. 227. It is dangerous to guess what the Slavophiles "thought, but could not say openly," but their teaching did "lead to that conclusion."

in their moments of failure and dejection they were supported by
their conviction in the surpassing significance of their mission.[189]

The Slavophiles felt that their criticism itself was very important:

> its purpose is to expose falsehood, which settled on us, to free the spirit
> from its captivity, to clear a place for the action of truth, for the awak-
> ening of the popular instincts, which were smothered in us, for the com-
> prehension of the inner meaning of the historical and the social phe-
> nomena of the life of the people.[190]

Furthermore, the Slavophiles were convinced not only that they
were the first to understand and define the Russian disease, but
also that they could cure it. They were able to reveal the true
principles, the real essence of Russia. They could answer the
question of Russian destiny, and thus save Russia from the fate of
those peoples which

> disappeared from the face of the earth solely because they had unwit-
> tingly and instinctively asked themselves the question whether they
> were necessary to God or man, and had not been able to find a satisfac-
> tory answer.[191]

Ancient Russia had possessed the true principles, but it had lacked
this clear comprehension of itself and its destiny, — "in ancient
Russia intelligence lacked consciousness."[192] It was the mission of
the Slavophiles to supply this indispensable consciousness of the
self, which was the true strength of the people. This did not mean
a return to the dead past, but the attainment of a new and glorious
life:

> Then ancient Russia will be resurrected in the enlightened and har-
> monious form, in the original beauty of a society which unites a patri-
> archal local life with the deep meaning of the state representing the
> moral and the Christian person; but then it will be conscious of itself
> and not based on chance, full of living, organic forces, not wavering
> between existence and death.[193]

[189] For an example of extreme Slavophile optimism see Khomiakov's reaction to the revolutions of 1848. Kh., vol. VIII, p. 177.

[190] I. A., vol. V, p. 552.   [191] Kh., vol. III, p. 428.
[192] Kh., vol. I, p. 24.   [193] Kh., vol. III, p. 29.

The Slavophiles claimed to represent the bringing into consciousness, the all-important revelation of the ancient, deep, mighty, and mysterious essence of Russia, its true spirit. No romantic theory could ask or offer more.

CHAPTER V

THE SLAVOPHILE ARGUMENT

GOD AND MAN

Slavophilism was based on a specific religious view of man and the world. To the Slavophiles a man meant primarily his faith. This faith was determined not by the man's professed allegiance to a creed, not by his outward participation in the life of the church, but by the basic spiritual principles which resided in his heart of hearts, and which activated his whole being. The great fallacy of the West consisted in the fact that it failed to understand the fundamentally religious nature of man and that it regarded its superficial rationalist formulas, whether those of the Catholic theologians or those of the atheistic radicals, as the complete answer to the needs and problems of humanity. In the West, reason had suppressed all other human faculties, and because reason alone could never be sufficient, it had degenerated into an ingenious intellectual defense of the strangest assumptions and the weirdest prejudices. When one refused to recognize the claims of religion, when one would not believe in God, one ended up by believing in Utopias, or in the stock exchange. True Orthodox knowledge was the very opposite of the one-sided rationalism of the West:

The main characteristic of religious thinking consists in the effort to combine into a single force all separate parts of the soul, to discover that internal center of being, where intelligence, and will, and feeling, and conscience, and the beautiful, and the true, and the remarkable, and the desirable, and the just, and the merciful, and the entire range of intelligence merge into one living whole, and thus, reëstablish the substantial personality of man in its primeval indivisibility.[1]

Man was an organic whole. All his activities stemmed from the same basic principles which determined his being, and therefore

[1] I.K., vol. I, p. 275.

it was deceptive and misleading to segregate those activities into separate compartments. Khomiakov expressed a deep Slavophile conviction when, in his statement of the policy of the Slavophile periodical *The Russian Conversation*, he emphasized the fact that: "Moral problems must be always present at the solution of practically all intellectual problems."[2] Real knowledge was a complex phenomenon: intuition, love, participation through life and feeling, were all essential for the true comprehension of the world, of human society, of history, or of culture. The Slavophiles were certain that they understood Russia and the West in this profound, basic sense, and they could therefore discard the facts which did not seem to fit their pattern and remain deaf to the objections of the critics, who could not see beyond the external appearances.

The Slavophiles insisted that every human being had his faith, whether it was based on the Orthodox community of love, the Catholic submission to the authority of the Pope, the Protestant belief in the free inquiry into the Bible, the eighteenth-century cult of human reason, or the nineteenth-century conviction about the veracity of the allegedly "scientific" assertions of the positivists and the materialists. Samarin was especially skillful in detecting concealed assumptions in the reasoning of his opponents, and in reducing the argument to its basic premises. Of particular interest is Samarin's polemic with K. Kavelin, provoked by Kavelin's book

[2] Kh., vol. III, p. 200.

This doctrine of the organic interdependence of the different faculties of man made the Slavophiles pay special attention to the personality of various thinkers. In advising his sick friend, the poet Iazykov, against homeopathy, Ivan Kireevskii went to the extent of claiming that the lack of moral integrity in a man's character was bound to invalidate his ideas: "Has there ever been since the creation of the world a system which did not reflect the character of its inventor? It seems to me this is impossible. What then is the character of Hahnemann himself? The mind of a genius combined with the character of a charlatan. Therefore, one can tell in advance that all his inventions will contain partial truth and will be fake as a whole." I.K., vol. I, p. 65.

The Slavophiles have been ridiculed for this naïve assumption of a direct connection between a man's character and his doctrines. Modern psychology, however, demonstrates both the presence and the great extent and significance of this connection, although certainly not in the simple form suggested by the Slavophiles.

on *The Problems of Psychology*, which lasted three years (1872–1875) and dealt with the nature of man.[3]

Kavelin shared the enthusiasm of his age for science and for progress based on the application of the "scientific" method to all human needs. Psychology in particular was destined to determine and prescribe the proper norms of human behavior and to establish human personality and life on a solid, scientific foundation. Samarin demonstrated with a devastating logic that no amount of scientific observation could produce an ethical postulate, that even if it were possible to obtain ethical norms in such a manner these norms would carry no persuasive power with them for any individual who felt differently inclined, and that Kavelin had to look elsewhere for the moral principles on which he insisted. Kavelin's efforts to find a basis for human freedom and responsibility only further exposed the fundamental contradictions of his reasoning. Kavelin believed that human behavior was physiologically determined, but he made an exception for certain instances, when a man was in a state of calm, not driven by any impulses, and could therefore make a free choice. Samarin argued convincingly that such instances did not exist in fact, and that they could not be reconciled with the rest of Kavelin's own system.

Kavelin's main weakness was his inconsistency. Convinced materialists went further, and were willing to part with ethics and moral principles as such. The Slavophiles were quick to take up their challenge, and Samarin again proved to be the ablest exponent of the Slavophile point of view, in particular in his famous polemic with Herzen.[4] Samarin was willing to admit that Herzen's view of the world had internal consistency, but he was certain that there was a tragic contradiction between this view and Herzen's own life and activity. If moral values were merely a matter of

---

[3] For Samarin's polemic with Kavelin see: S., vol. VI, pp. 371–477; and K. Kavelin, *Sochineniia*, volume three, columns 375–874.

[4] Samarin's polemic with Herzen was not included in Samarin's *Works*. It was published in 1883 in *Rus*. Samarin's and Herzen's letters were arranged in their chronological sequence, and a historical account of the polemic was added to them. "Perepiska Iu. F. Samarina s A.I. Gertsenom," *Rus*, 1883, no. 1, pp. 30–42; no. 2, pp. 23–30.

subjective taste, Herzen had no right to hurl invectives at anybody. As a matter of fact, despotism represented a rule par excellence of personal taste. If determinism ruled the world, if freedom was merely a delusion, Herzen's life spent in a struggle for political freedom had indeed been wasted. The same fatal contradiction between philosophy and action which had ruined Herzen's life, could be detected, according to Samarin, in each particular aspect of Herzen's activity. For instance, Samarin objected:

Explain to me then: according to what right do you rise so passionately against *corporal* punishment? Could it be that you have in reserve some other punishments, which are *not corporal*?[5]

The truth of the matter was that Herzen did not believe the things which he professed to believe. He preached materialism and determinism, whereas his own basic convictions, his own faith had been formed from better elements, and he had always retained "a handful of earth from the other shore." This stolen handful, however, was not enough: its influence on Herzen was bound to weaken gradually, and it could have no effect on Herzen's disciples. Herzen could not believe in the ideals for which he struggled. Yet man could not live without faith: "The dumb animal is the only consistent and logical materialist in the entire world."[6] Deprived of its natural object, Herzen's faith took a pathological turn:

Positive goals disappeared from sight one after another, formulas faded, convictions shrank and were reduced to zero. Only the usual means remained: revolution as an end in itself, revolution for revolution's sake.[7]

[5] "Perepiska Samarina s Gertsenom, *op. cit.*, no. 1, p. 37.
[6] S., vol. VI, p. 546.
[7] "Perepiska Samarina s Gertsenom," no. 1, p. 41.
For the Slavophile criticism of materialism see also Khomiakov, *On Contemporary Developments in the Domain of Philosophy. A Letter to Iu. F. Samarin* (Kh., vol. I, pp. 283–314) and Samarin, *Letters about Materialism* (S., vol. VI, pp. 540–554). The Slavophiles often mentioned and briefly discussed materialism in connection with their discussion of the West and of philosophy. Ivan Aksakov often referred to it in his editorials dealing with Russian radicals and revolutionaries.

Thus, Herzen was on the road to exchanging all his former ideals and beliefs for a blind faith in the revolution itself, regardless of its character or aims. Samarin emphasized that the difference between him and Herzen was not merely or even primarily political, social, or economic: the fundamental cleavage was that between the religion of freedom and the religion of necessity, between the Iranian and the Kushite principles.

Man's faith, the basic spiritual principles which formed the very essence of man occupied a central position in the Slavophile ideology. In postulating these principles, and the character in which they should be revealed, the Slavophiles largely restated the Christian ideal. Christian love was the highest value, and because human personality was an organic whole this love was intrinsically connected with the entire nature of man, with his intellectual activity as well as with his emotional life. Humility, charity, compassion, and self-sacrifice all followed naturally from love, and all went into the formation of a true Christian. At the same time the Slavophiles were extremely sensitive to neurotic traits, and were determined to avoid them in their ideal of man. In particular they were opposed to every kind of rigidity and formalism as well as to everything theatrical, affected, or artificial. They attributed the highest importance to the quality of naturalness and spontaneity, which could be expressed in the burning enthusiasm eulogized by Petr Kireevskii, or in the stately manner especially admired by Petr's brother Ivan, but which was in either case an unaffected, immediate reaction of the entire personality, as contrasted with the strained, artificial behavior of a man in the throes of internal division and conflict.

Freedom, love, spontaneity, fullness, ease, and peace in one's inner life as well as in one's relations with one's fellow-beings constituted the most valuable assets of human character. Formalism, rigidity, artificiality, inhibition, and compulsion were the greatest evils to be avoided by man. The Slavophiles projected this conception of man, their experience, knowledge, and intuition in human psychology to the religious, the social, the political, the historical, and other planes.

Man outside society was a contradiction in terms, for only in society could he develop the basic human qualities of love, charity, and self-sacrifice. Even knowledge was a social phenomenon, not only in the technical, empirical, but also in the deeper, gnosiological sense. The Slavophiles laid a very heavy emphasis on the concept of *sobornost*, a term denoting the organic synthesis of multiplicity and unity in the Orthodox Church, and the fact that the church is based on the principle of councils. It was only through this *sobornost* founded on common Christian love and faith that man could attain the higher levels of truth and knowledge which were entirely outside the reach of an isolated individual. The commune in its turn supplied the deep experience and understanding of the real principles of Russian life and history which no man could achieve alone.

The same fundamental spiritual assumptions which determined the nature and life of man exercised the decisive influence on the development of human society, institutions, nations, races, and cultures. The Slavophiles particularly emphasized the fact that the improvement of man's life on earth, the progress of humanity, depended entirely on the recognition and development of Christian ideals. Christianity offered no political, social, or economic system, but it supplied the indispensable principle of freedom, morality, true and permanent values, which alone could make the advancement of mankind possible. A society which denied God could last and even develop for some time because of the previously accumulated moral capital, but eventually it was bound to revert to barbarism. "*A progress* which denies God and Christ ultimately becomes a *regress; civilization* culminates in *savagery;* freedom in despotism and slavery." [8]

For after the renunciation of God there follows inevitably a whole logical chain of renunciations: the renunciation of every absolute truth, and of every compelling law, and of moral responsibility, and of the concepts of good and evil with their substitution by the concepts of harm and utility. When man denies God, he inevitably ends up by denying

[8] I. A., vol. IV, p. 195.

the freedom of his own spirit; when he wipes out "the image of God" in himself, he unescapably tends to liken himself to an animal. . . . Exactly all that is taking place in front of our eyes.[9]

The fundamental religious and psychological preferences of the Slavophiles revealed themselves in a striking manner in the Slavophile doctrine of society and its institutions. The family was cherished because it meant a triumph of love, a natural association of people united by their spontaneous mutual affection. The peasant commune represented to the Slavophiles a further development of the same principle, a fellowship similar to the family, but on a larger scale. On the other hand, bureaucracy, for instance, was denounced as a product of legalism, formalism, and compulsion. Any form of government was bound to be based on the imposition of the external law as distinct from the internal moral truth, and therefore government was an evil, although an unavoidable one.

A distinction of the inner truth from the outer truth, of the moral law from the formal, juridical law is the favorite motif in the writings of the Slavophiles and is basic to their entire social philosophy. The Slavophiles develop it in countless variations on most varied occasions. It is characteristic of all of them — of Kireevskii, and of Khomiakov, and of Aksakov, and of Koshelev, and of Samarin. It contains the essence of the social message of the Slavophiles, it is used to deny the West, and to glorify ancient Russia, it forms the foundation for the hatred of the St. Petersburg period of Russian history.[10]

The Slavophiles did not limit themselves to the analysis of society in terms of their particular concept of man: they found in the contemporary world, as well as in history, superhuman personal entities, which were living organisms with their specific characters, processes of growth, tasks, and aims. Nations, races, civilizations belonged to this class of superior organisms, and the Slavophiles were especially concerned with the nation, the people. A nation, like a man, formed a synthetic organic whole; it was

[9] I. A., vol. IV, pp. 192–193.
[10] Ustrialov, *op. cit.*, p. 53.
This basic contrast between "morality" and "legalism" which pervades the Slavophile ideology has been discussed by most students of Slavophilism. One of the best analyses of it is contained in Gratieux, *op. cit.*, volume II, chapter VII, pp. 207–237, especially pp. 233–234.

activated by its basic religious assumptions, revealed its specific, inherent character, grew and functioned according to special physiological laws, and could be comprehended as a whole, but never through an analysis of its parts.

A nation is a separate, whole, independent organism, which is composed of the totality of individuals, past, present, and future, which is ruled by its own inner historical laws, which has its own growth, its own memory, its own development, desires, problems, and aims, its own intellectual and spiritual functions, which are performed in the course of ages. . . .[11]

Khomiakov complained that his contemporaries failed to realize "that every people is, as much as every man, a living person, and that its inner life is nothing but the development of some moral or intellectual principle. . . ."[12] History could be understood only in terms of nations: "Such is the mystery of historical destiny. . . . The universal task of humanity is divided not according to persons, but according to nations. . . ."[13] A nation had to retain its individuality, if it was going to play a part in world history: the value of a nation, as well as the value of a man, depended on its specific personality.

Nations are individuals within mankind, individuals not only in the physiological, but also and especially in the spiritual sense: nations, which have preserved and developed the specific qualities of their particular spirit, participate in an independent and fruitful manner in the general growth of humanity; nations which lack personality count for nothing — blotting paper in the book of history.[14]

The Slavophile ideology was based on the recognition of two types of organisms: human beings, and superpersonal entities — nations, races, civilizations. Because the two types were regarded as perfectly analogous in their nature and function, the Slavophiles could project their view of man, and their specific understanding of human character, to the superpersonal entities. The main antagonistic organism, the West, received all neurotic qualities which were in turn parceled out among its component parts. The West was especially characterized by its horrible inner conflicts,

[11] I.A., vol. I, p. 272.
[13] Kh., vol. III, p. 223.
[12] Kh., vol. I, p. 38.
[14] I.A., vol. I, p. 247.

its inability to have a natural feeling or a normal reaction, and its hatred of the East. Romantic doctrines, which provided the necessary framework for the direct transfer of the Slavophile views of man to nations, also offered ready schemes for the evolution of the superpersonal organisms, for their development in the past, the present, and the future.

The concepts of "We" and "They," which form the core of every aspect of Slavophile thought, and which bind all these aspects together, can be reduced to a fundamental psychological urge: an attraction to spontaneity, ease, freedom, and a revulsion from compulsive behavior, inner conflict, neurotic rigidity. Factors of personal psychology, the nature of which we can only conjecture, made the Slavophiles particularly aware of the contrast between the neurotic and the normal in human personality. Romantic ideology gave them an excellent opportunity to project directly and on a wide scale their personal conflicts and preferences onto social and historical planes. In discussing society and history the Slavophiles used two approaches: they measured institutions, nations, races, and civilizations by the contributions of the latter to the Slavophile ideal of human personality; they also considered these institutions, nations, races, and civilizations as themselves personalities with requirements analogous to the human. It is remarkable in what a direct and thorough manner the Slavophiles managed to project their characters into their view of the world. The conflict between the Iranian and the Kushite, between the religion of freedom and the religion of necessity, is indeed the key to the Slavophile ideology, provided it is considered in its proper context: as a conflict within Khomiakov himself, not as a struggle of two subdivisions of humanity throughout world history.

The Slavophile views can be further clarified by a reference to their sources, of which Western romantic literature composed both the bulk and the most significant part.

THE SLAVOPHILES AND THE WESTERN ROMANTICISTS

The fact that the Slavophiles were strongly influenced by the romantic ideology of the West is no longer open to doubt. There is much dispute, however, concerning the extent of this influence, the relation between it and other influences, notably that of the Eastern doctors of the church, and the degree to which the Slavophiles were original within the general romantic framework, or were able to "surpass" romanticism.

The writings of the Slavophiles testify to their thorough acquaintance with Western romanticism. An analysis of the biographical data leads to the same conclusion. In particular, the Slavophiles profited from their excellent training in foreign languages, their travels and, in the case of some, their studies in the West. The fact that only a small percentage of the works of the Western romanticists was translated into Russian, and that these translations were usually late in appearance, is, therefore, of little significance for the consideration of the sources of the Slavophile ideology. Some of the Slavophiles knew Schelling and other leading German romanticists personally; all of them were deeply interested in the intellectual life of Western Europe.

The mass of material left by the Slavophiles indicates, in the first place, the great range of the Slavophile knowledge of the romantic West. The Slavophiles were especially interested in the philosophers and the theologians, but they were also acquainted with the literary figures, the writers on politics, the historians, the economists, and the administrators. Like their German contemporaries, many of the Slavophiles went through a period of admiration of Schiller and Goethe, as well as of some other writers especially popular at the time. For instance, the letters of young Samarin tell of his particular love for Hoffman.

More important than all specific references to Western romanticists is the general romantic atmosphere which permeates the articles, the essays, and the correspondence of the Slavophiles. Romantic enthusiasm and the sense of mission, idealism, and inclination toward literature and esthetics, which had been very prominent in the Lovers of Wisdom, became component elements of Slavophilism. To speak of the influence of the romantic spirit on the Slavophiles is not quite adequate: it would be more correct to say that spiritually the Slavophiles were a part of the romantic movement.

Western romantic influences on Slavophilism have been gradually receiving more and more attention from historians, but this attention is still insufficient, particularly in the case of such major romantic writers as Friedrich Schlegel and Novalis, about whom, as distinct from Schelling and Hegel, the Slavophiles left only passing remarks. Although it is dangerous to go beyond direct evidence, it may be more dangerous to argue that the Slavophiles were not acquainted with a particular romantic thinker or school of thought. Their random comments about Western romanticists and their works often indicate a knowledge of the author or assume such knowledge in the reader.

The Slavophile ideology had so broad a romantic basis that it is extremely difficult to disentangle its sources beyond the general term of "romanticism." This broad background enabled the Slavophiles to escape the domination of any one Western thinker. Although Hegel and Schelling occupied a more important place in the Slavophile writings than any other philosophers, and exercised a profound influence on Slavophilism, none of the Slavophiles can be simply classified as Hegelians or as the followers of Schelling, except for Samarin and Konstantin Aksakov, who were devotees of Hegel in their youth, but even then only for a few years. In addition to Hegel and Schelling, the Slavophiles were constantly influenced by other romanticists, as well as by some nonromantic sources. The failure to recognize the extent of the romantic foundations of Slavophilism resulted not only from the caution of historians, but also from the efforts of the admirers of the Slavophiles to present them as original and unique, as the true spokesmen of Russia, a revelation of the Russian soul. It was difficult for men, who themselves argued in terms of organic nation, national spirit, national mission, and the like to recognize the romantic origin of their favorite concepts, which they preferred to regard as fundamental truths of life and history.

The Slavophile criticism of Hegel and Schelling formed an interesting aspect of their relations with Western romanticists.[15] The

[15] Slavophile writings contain numerous references to Hegel and Schelling. The most significant critical discussions of the two thinkers are to be found on the following pages: I.K., vol. I, pp. 91–93, pp. 127–131, pp. 257–264; vol. II, pp. 92–103. Kh., vol. 1, pp. 36–37, pp. 143–145, pp. 261–271, pp. 289–302.

Slavophiles attached particular importance to this criticism because they regarded Hegel and Schelling as the logical culmination of Western philosophy: in condemning these two "titans of thought" they were passing judgment on the entire intellectual development of the West, on the West itself. Ivan Kireevskii and Khomiakov, who evaluated Hegel and Schelling and assigned their roles in the Slavophile view of the world, had a deep appreciation of German idealistic philosophy, which they considered to be the greatest intellectual achievement in the history of humanity. This philosophy had run its full course, had revealed completely its nature and its value.

To it belongs inalienable and eternal glory in the history of learning. It covered and outlined clearly the circle of abstract, purely rationalistic thought; it determined definitely and precisely the laws of this thought, it determined them for the entire humanity and for all ages. No thinker can speak of it without reverent gratitude. . . .[16]

Ivan Kireevskii came to the following natural conclusion:

Therefore I think that German philosophy, in conjunction with the development which it received in Schelling's last system, may serve as the most convenient intellectual step from borrowed systems to an original philosophy based on the fundamental principles of the ancient Russian enlightenment and capable of subordinating the bifurcated civilization of the West to the complete cognition of believing reason.[17]

The Slavophiles always retained their high regard for German idealistic philosophy. Samarin was deeply upset to see the Germans turn from Kant, Schelling, and Hegel to Feuerbach and the materialists. Even Ivan Aksakov, the least philosophical of the Slavophiles, persistently advocated the study of the idealists and commented that the abandonment of such study was a significant characteristic of the new generation of Russian radicals and revolutionaries.

But the genius of the great German thinkers only helped to re-

[16] Kh., vol. I, pp. 270–271.

[17] I.K., vol. I, p. 264. This passage has often been quoted as an example of the determination on the part of the Slavophiles to create an original Russian philosophy. Some critics believe that the Slavophiles failed in their purpose only because of the sudden deaths of Ivan Kireevskii and of Khomiakov.

veal the fatal defect of their school, its rationalistic one-sidedness. The Slavophiles regarded Hegelianism as the final, complete and perfect expression of Western rationalism. Hegel was "the last of the great German philosophers, the man who demolished the entire edifice of Western philosophy by adding the last stone to it."[18] Schelling went one step further: like Hegel he had plodded his way to the very summit of rationalistic reasoning, but then, at that summit, he saw the limitations of rationalism and condemned the entire German idealistic philosophy, which had been largely his own creation. The Slavophiles were in accord with Schelling's indictment of all his predecessors, and they sympathized with Schelling's efforts to attain "complete knowledge," but they were certain that these efforts were bound to be futile because true principles of knowledge could be found only in Orthodoxy — the essence of the West was Hegelian, and therefore the West could not go beyond Hegelianism.[19]

In Hegelianism the substitution of formulas for life and of syllogisms for events reached fantastic dimensions: the entire system was nothing but an astounding tour de force of abstract reason, which developed from itself, without any reference to anything else. Hegel's system was clear, coherent, and most imposing, but it had no connection with any kind of reality. Hegel was the most complete, the only true rationalist in the world; he was daring enough to conclude that abstract thought meant life, that nothing existed except the logical formula. Khomiakov stressed the fact that Hegel's disciples were not able even to understand this absolute claim of reason which would not recognize any other reality, and that some of them in their search for a foundation for the Hegelian structure, for a substratum, came upon matter, and established the school of nineteenth-century materialism. Hegelianism remained as the most magnificent absurdity in human history: the most grandiose structure of human reason, and at the same time the most striking revelation of the limitations of this reason, of its inadequacy and falsehood, when it was separated from the

[18] Kh., vol. I, p. 16.
[19] Khomiakov in particular liked to identify Hegel and the West. See, especially, Kh., vol. I, p. 268.

higher human faculties. Khomiakov also analyzed some particular defects of Hegel's system: he noted that because in Hegel life depended on logic, Hegel understood history "inside out," that is, instead of tracing the activity of a nation, and compiling the results of this activity, Hegel reversed the cause-effect relationship, postulated his arbitrary logical formula first, and then regarded this formula as the cause of the activity of the nation. Khomiakov, however, never considered this criticism of Hegel applicable to his own writing of history.

The Slavophile criticism of the German philosophers has been often cited as a proof of their independence from Western thinkers and their ability to "surpass" romanticism.[20] In point of fact, this criticism is itself one of the most striking illustrations of the romantic origins of the Slavophile ideology. The main Slavophile accusation against Hegel, the charge that his system was based exclusively on one-sided rationalism, whereas it promised to provide "complete comprehension," had already been leveled by Fichte against Kant, by Hegel against Fichte, and by Schelling against Hegel. Furthermore, the same accusation had been made by all romantic philosophers against the Enlightenment of the eighteenth century. The Slavophiles were very well acquainted with this line of reasoning, and they admired in particular Schelling's criticism of Hegel. Special studies substantiate in detail the romantic nature of the Slavophile criticism of the German idealistic philosophers. Zenkovskii concluded that although Khomiakov had rebelled against German transcendental philosophy, he himself could never cast off the shackles of this philosophy.[21] Chizhevskii, whose monograph stresses the importance and the extent of Hegel's influence in Russia, exults in the fact that Samarin could overcome Hegel only with Hegel's own weapons.[22]

[20] Zavitnevich was especially insistent on this point: "Slavophilism began as Khomiakov's struggle against Hegelianism . . . . the abjuration of Hegelianism was the first condition for becoming a conscious member of the Slavophile circle, in the same way as the abjuration of Satan and his angels is regarded as an essential prerequisite for becoming a Christian." Zavitnevich, *op. cit.*, volume one, pp. III–IV.

[21] Zenkovskii, *op. cit.*, pp. 188–213, especially p. 199, pp. 204–207, and pp. 212–213.

[22] Chizhevskii, *op. cit.*, pp. 179–182.

A study of the romantic sources of Slavophilism demonstrates that the Slavophiles were very well acquainted with the romantic ideology, that they attached an extremely high significance to that ideology, and that they could criticize it only in its own terms. An analysis of the Slavophile doctrines themselves indicates beyond dispute their romantic origin. The romantic concept of organism, organic nation in particular, permeated the entire Slavophile thought. It explained their emphasis on history and tradition, their belief in the gradual growth and the organic evolution of society, their opposition to contracts and written constitutions, and their hatred of revolution. The Slavophile discussions of these topics, indeed, often read like excerpts from Fichte, Schelling, Schlegel, or De Maistre. The romanticists offered their loyalty to the national soul itself rather than to particular governments which were often criticized, especially when they hampered the organic life of the people. This "anti-state" tendency was present in the writings of numerous Western romanticists, and its accentuation in Slavophilism may be a reflection of the relatively greater separation between the government and the romantic intellectuals in Russia than in the other countries.

A number of romantic rhythms and historical dialectics found their reflection in Slavophilism, and although there is much argument concerning the relative influence of particular romanticists, such as Herder, Schelling, and Hegel, on the Slavophile view of history, there is no doubt about the romantic character of this view. The romanticists stressed the basic spiritual principles which activated a nation and determined its role in history. These very principles became the main preoccupation of the Slavophiles. The Slavophiles, as much as the Western romanticists, appealed for an organic society, for a development of social life and varied social activities; they were in dread of the "atomization of the individual," that is, of the breakdown of society into isolated and mutually hostile individuals. Khomiakov's and Ivan Aksakov's warnings against that danger form the Russian counterpart of similar admonitions by Novalis, Baader, Goerres, and other romantic thinkers of the West. The romanticists had an overwhelming sense of mission as a personal calling as well as a national destiny. They denied the ability of a thinker to find the rational pattern of social life, or of an "enlightened despot" to impose this pattern on his people, and they taught that history was moved by mystical, elemental forces, which could not be shaped or successfully opposed by individuals. But they also preached that these mystical forces were revealed in men, that they could move history through the consciousness of such men. The Slavophiles accordingly were determined to represent their ideology as the revelation of the true spirit of Russia.

The Slavophiles proved their skill in adapting the general romantic concepts to their particular needs. Their main desire was to affirm the importance of their own nation, race, and religion, a desire all the more understandable because Russia, Slavdom and Orthodoxy had been wholly neglected in most of the preceding romantic schemes, which were predominantly German in their origin and orientation. Moreover, it has been well pointed out by one critic that Russia borrowed its ideas from the West with a certain lag in time: when the romantic fervor of the Slavophiles reached its height, the West was already abandoning romanticism, and was turning to positivism, materialism, and other ideologies which were totally unacceptable to the Slavophiles. The Slavophiles therefore had to condemn the contemporary West in the name of Western romanticism itself, and they found a haven for their romantic beliefs in their idealized conception of Old Russia.[23] Khomiakov and his friends accepted the basic romantic distinction between the rationalistic, atomistic, analytic, mechanistic, and thoroughly bad Age of Enlightenment on the one hand, and the harmonious, organic, truly intellectual, profoundly religious, and thoroughly good coming era of romantic culture on the other. Then they substituted "the West" for "the Age of Enlightenment," and "Russia" for "romantic culture." Orthodoxy was proclaimed to be the essence of Russia and the only true source of "organic society," "comprehensive knowledge," and other romantic ideals.

[23] F. Steppun, "Nemetskii romantism i russkoe slavianofilstvo," in *Russkaia Mysl*, March 1910, pp. 65–91, pp. 73–75. Steppun's article provides the best discussion of the relation between the Slavophiles and the Western romanticists.

The appeal to Orthodoxy was the making of Slavophilism. In Orthodoxy the Slavophiles found Russian tradition, the binding element of Russian state and society, the basic inspiration of Russian culture, the meaning and the mission of Russia. Orthodoxy was the Russian past, the Russian present, but above all, the Russian future. The Slavophile emphasis on Orthodoxy was not, however, entirely felicitous. The Orthodox ideal was universal, and as such could not be bound to any nation. The Slavophiles indeed had to realize the transcendental nature of Orthodoxy, and they left many express statements of their recognition of this fact, but at the same time they continued their pathetic attempts to monopolize Orthodoxy and truth for Russia.

Byzantium was an obvious obstacle in the way of this identification of the Orthodox social and cultural ideal with the Russian, and Byzantium was either conspicuously absent from the various Slavophile schemes, or it was dismissed on the specious ground that while its religion was true, its social and cultural foundations dated back to the pagan days of the Roman empire, and had never become really Christian.[24] More dangerous than Byzantium was the intrinsic contradiction between the broad, universal, inclusive, Christian concept of the world, and the narrow, particularistic, exclusive views of the romanticists, who often developed a quasi-religious attitude toward their own people, race, or ideology, and found other gods than Christ. This contradiction goes far to explain both much of the confusion in the ideas of the Slavophiles themselves, and the rapid disintegration of their teaching in the hands of their professed followers.

As the Slavophiles turned from the futuristic utopia of German romanticism to the idealization of the Russian past, they placed themselves squarely on the road to exclusiveness and chauvinism, to the denial of the West, and of the very culture which gave birth to their ideology. This in itself was again typically romantic, and the Slavophile treatment of "Russia," and "the West" formed a close parallel to numerous schemes of the German romanticists,

[24] Khomiakov discussed Byzantium at some length, in an interesting and at times brilliant manner in his *History*, but his conclusion was the one stated above.

for instance, Friedrich Schlegel's views on Germany and "the West," or Fichte's contrast between "Deutschland" and "Ausland" in his "Addresses to the German Nation." The German romanticists also began with "the urge for the infinite," and ended in the worship of their Teutonic ancestors.

The Slavophile view of society and history represented a Russian version of the romantic ideology of the age. Their interpretation of the basic human psychological and religious experience was intrinsically connected with romanticism, but it also had other sources, which were Christian, and included in particular the writings of the Eastern Doctors of the Church.

THE SLAVOPHILES AND ORTHODOX RELIGIOUS THOUGHT

The Slavophiles were very well versed in the literature of the Orthodox Church. Whether their interest in Orthodoxy developed steadily and gradually, as in the case of Khomiakov, or whether it came as a result of a drastic change of orientation, as in the case of Ivan Kireevskii, or whether it consisted of periods of great concentration on religious subjects interspersed with work of a totally different nature, as in the life of Samarin, this interest led the Slavophiles to a thorough knowledge and understanding of Orthodox religious thought, while Khomiakov himself became an outstanding theologian. It should be emphasized that the Slavophiles bitterly criticized German idealistic philosophy, whereas they considered the writings of the Orthodox theologians as truth itself. Even Koshelev who has been often treated as the most practical and the least theologically inclined of the Slavophiles, read extensively in the Doctors of the Church, and stated that he found in them "a bounteous source of that for which I had been looking in vain in life, in Schellings, and so on." [25]

The Slavophile emphasis on the Orthodox tradition made many of their followers, and some historians, declare that Slavophilism was nothing, but a development and a further revelation of Orthodox thought, of the specific Russian Orthodoxy, while the influence

[25] Koliupanov, *op. cit.*, volume 1, book II, appendix VIII. (Correspondence between Koshelev and the leading Slavophiles), p. 50.

of Western romanticism was merely a superficial one. This view, quite widespread in Russian historical literature, has been expressed on occasion in English publications as well, for instance in H. Lanz' article on "The Philosophy of Ivan Kireyevsky." [26]

Lanz began by complaining that it was absurd "to identify such a complex spiritual phenomenon as Slavophilism with a provincial branch of Hegelian philosophy." [27] Then he took Ivan Kireevskii's doctrine of the necessity to bring all human faculties together, to integrate them as an organic whole in order to attain true knowledge, and demonstrated that a similar doctrine could be found in the Eastern Doctors of the Church, and in particular in Isaac the Syrian and Maximus the Confessor, with whose writings Ivan Kireevskii had been acquainted. Lanz concluded:

Slavophilism is not a patriotic perversion of German idealism, not even a reaction against modern European rationalism. It is simply and solely a modern continuation of a religious tradition which has been dominating Russian life since the time of Saint Vladimir, and which was temporarily driven into the underworld by the violent reforms of Peter the Great and his successors. [28]

Lanz in his analysis failed to take into account that the Western romantic influences on the Slavophiles had been by no means limited to Hegelianism, least of all in the case of Ivan Kireevskii. He did not mention any of the Western contemporaries of Ivan Kireevskii, who had been searching for the "wholeness of personality," and "integral knowledge," both of which had been favorite romantic concepts. Finally he stated that his particular example was representative of the entire Slavophile ideology, and therefore implied that there was a legitimate connection between Maximus the Confessor's view of knowledge and similar patristic sources on the one hand, and Konstantin Aksakov's glorification of ancient Russia or Ivan Aksakov's Balkan projects on the other.

In considering the influence of the Eastern Doctors of the Church on the Slavophiles, it is necessary to distinguish very sharply among the various aspects of Slavophilism. Patristic litera-

---

[26] H. Lanz, "The Philosophy of Ivan Kireyevsky," in *The Slavonic Review*, volume IV, 1925–1926, pp. 594–604.

[27] Lanz, *op. cit.*, p. 595.   [28] Lanz, *op. cit.*, p. 604.

ture had no appreciable influence on the Slavophile social, political, or historical views which were purely romantic. The Slavophiles themselves had a clear understanding of the fact that the Doctors of the Church gave ready answers only in a certain sphere of knowledge, and Ivan Kireevskii left an excellent description of the nature and the limitations of that sphere. After discussing Byzantium as a state which had never become Christian, and in which the Church and Christian philosophy had remained apart from society, he concluded:

As a result of this state of things, the problems of contemporary enlightenment could not acquire a social character, and philosophy had to limit itself to the development of the inner, contemplative life. But the external life of man, and the laws dealing with the development of the family, the civil, the social, and the state relations were practically absent from its compass.[29]

Patristic influence on Slavophilism was thus effective in the limited, although very important, sphere of the basic religious and psychological problems of man, and in the special field of theology.

It is impossible to disentangle the exact origins of the Slavophile view of human personality. The component elements of this view, such as the aversion to "one-sided rationalism," the demand for the coördination and for "organic union" of the human faculties, the desire for "integral knowledge," for "deep religious understanding," could be derived from the Eastern Doctors of the Church, and from the Christian tradition in general, but they were also prominently present in the writings of numerous Western romanticists. Romanticism itself cannot be understood without its Christian background, and a reaffirmation of Christian values formed one of the most distinctive aspects of the romantic movement. The Slavophile discussions of human personality bore resemblance to similar discussions of various Western romanticists, and their emphasis on the idea of freedom probably had romantic as well as Christian sources.[30] One may note, for instance, the role

[29] I.K., vol. I, p. 256.

[30] For instance, Khomiakov's doctrine of the primacy of the will in man, which is usually regarded as his most original contribution in philosophy, had many Western romantic antecedents. See, e.g., Friedrich Schlegel's treatment of the subject in his *Philosophy of History*, the work in which he described

which "freedom" occupied in Fichte's philosophy, or Hegel's interpretation of history as the development of the consciousness of freedom.

The Slavophiles had a much greater respect for the opinions of the Eastern theologians than for those of the Western philosophers, but in general their knowledge of the West antedated their appreciation of Orthodox thought. This was notably true of Ivan Kireevskii, who turned to Orthodoxy only after he already had a completely formed romantic view of the world. N. Giliarov-Platonov, who was connected with the translation and the editing of Khomiakov's theological works, complained that Khomiakov had originally learned to express himself in French, and that that had exercised a bad influence on his use of Russian theological terms.[31] Vladimir Soloviev and some other specialists criticized the Slavophile attitude toward religion itself as, in a certain sense, romantic rather than Christian.[32]

The Slavophiles were probably more dependent on the more religious of the Western romanticists than has been generally realized. Zenkovskii, who noted a remarkable resemblance between the views of Khomiakov and those of Jacobi, stated that there was no direct evidence that Khomiakov knew Jacobi's works, but because of Khomiakov's excellent acquaintance with Western romanticism, and Jacobi's prominent position as a romanticist, this

---

primitive history as a struggle of two races activated by opposite spiritual principles, and which may have formed the foundation for Khomiakov's views on the Iranians and the Kushites: "Independently of particular traits of national character, and the special destiny of nations, it is philosophically certain, or if we may so speak, it is a truth grounded on psychological principles, that the will and not the understanding is in man the principal organ for the perception of divine truths. . . ." F. Schlegel, *The Philosophy of History*, p. 170.

[31] Zavitnevich, *op. cit.*, volume I, book I, p. 26.

[32] There was, for instance, Ivan Kireevskii's famous description of how he understood the miraculous power of an ikon by considering the fact that for years crowds of people had been worshiping this ikon, and that it must be magnetized with the faith and the prayers of the common folk. Khomiakov observed fasts all his life in order to underscore his unity with millions of Russians who were doing the same thing. In both cases the motivation seems to have come from a romantic admiration of the people, not from the views of the Church on ikon worship or on fasting.

knowledge is very likely.[33] Ivan Kireevskii, furthermore, did mention Jacobi in his writings, and probably was influenced by him.[34]

Berdiaev was mistaken when he remarked that: "The Slavophiles evidently did not know Baader, and he did not exercise any influence on them."[35] The writings of the Slavophiles contain a number of references to Baader: Samarin stated in his correspondence that he had read Baader. Ivan Kireevskii spoke of Baader with great respect as of a thinker whose profound theories had contributed much to the development of modern philosophy, but whose authority was insufficient to change its perverse course, and Petr Kireevskii mentioned in a letter from Munich a lecture of Baader which he had attended, and made a few passing remarks about Baader and his philosophy.[36] De Maistre's influence on Ivan Aksakov has been observed by several scholars, but not analyzed in any detail. In general one may conclude that the Slavophiles in their acquaintance with Western romanticism did not ignore the religious aspect of that movement, the aspect which was particularly dear to them.

The Slavophiles themselves denied any fundamental connection between them and any thinkers of the West, and insisted in a typically romantic manner on their own originality. Konstantin Aksakov, for instance, argued that the Slavophiles bore no resemblance to the German romanticists, and that the Germans tried to resurrect the dead past, whereas the Slavophiles wanted to revive the true principles, not the historical forms, of ancient Russia.[37] Sometimes, however, when in a less bellicose mood, the Slavophiles were willing to admit their kinship with certain thinkers of the West. Ivan Aksakov once described Riehl as "the German Konstantin Aksakov." [38] Samarin left the following curious note in pen-

[33] Zenkovskii, *op. cit.*, p. 194. Zenkovskii himself considered Jacobi's influence on Khomiakov as "more than probable."

[34] I. K., vol. I, p. 258. Dorn, *op. cit.*, p. 166.

[35] Berdiaev, *Khomiakov*, p. 124.

[36] I. K., vol. II, p. 260.
"Pisma bratiev Kireevskikh," in *Russkii Arkhiv*, book III, 1894, pp. 207–224, esp. pp. 220–221.

[37] See especially: Konstantin Aksakov, "O sovremennom literaturnom spore," in *Rus*, 1883. No. 7 (written in 1847).

[38] Ivan Aksakov, *Pisma*, volume III, p. 381.

cil on his copy of de Tocqueville's "L'ancien régime et la révolution":

De Tocqueville, Montalembert, Riehl, Stein are the Western Slavophiles. All of them, in their fundamental convictions and in their ultimate demands, are closer to us than to our Westernizers.[39]

The Slavophile doctrine of man and religion was a mixture of general Christian, specific patristic, and romantic views. The Christian sources were more prominent than in the case of most Western romanticists, and these sources were Orthodox rather than Catholic, but in general this aspect of the Slavophile doctrine, as well as all others, presented a close analogy to various Western systems. The relatively greater emphasis on Christianity may have accounted for the fact that the Slavophile concept of human personality was remarkably sane and democratic, free from "demoniac," "Byronic," and "elitist" tendencies, which pervaded much of Western romanticism.

The Slavophiles were well read in Catholic and in Protestant theologians. Many specialists have noticed some remarkable similarities between Khomiakov's theological views and those of his Catholic contemporary Moehler. Khomiakov knew Moehler's works very well, but the resemblance is generally attributed to common sources rather than borrowing.[40] Vinet was the Protestant theologian most discussed in the Slavophile circles: Khomiakov, Ivan Kireevskii, and Koshelev all held spirited and different opinions about him. None of the Western theologians, with the possible exception of Pascal, have been credited, however, with a strong influence on the Slavophile thought.[41]

[39] S., vol. I, p. 394.

[40] Khomiakov's relation to Moehler was discussed in almost every work dealing with Khomiakov's theology. There are two special studies: a brief article by N. Arseniev, and a book by S. Bolshakoff. N. Arseniev, "Chomjakov und Moehler," in Die Ostkirche, 1927, pp. 89–92. S. Bolshakoff, The Doctrine of the Unity of the Church in the Works of Khomyakov and Moehler. See also: M. Congar, "La pensée de Moehler et l'ecclesiologie orthodox," in Irenicon, July, 1935.

[41] Both Khomiakov and Ivan Kireevskii had a very high regard for Pascal, and Khomiakov even called him his master. Several specialists, particularly Catholics, suggested that Pascal had exercised a profound influence on Kho-

SOME ROMANTIC ASPECTS AND CONTRADICTIONS
OF SLAVOPHILISM

UNIVERSALISM VERSUS EXCLUSIVENESS

Many and varied opinions have been expressed concerning the inherent chauvinism of the Slavophile ideology as contrasted with its claim of world message and mission. Some authorities stressed the nationalist element, and regarded the degeneration of the Slavophile ideals after the death of the Slavophiles as a logical and inevitable process, whereas others emphasized the universalist aspect of Slavophilism, and insisted that the Slavophiles wanted to save the entire world and were free from any particularism. It was discovered in the process of argument that the views of the individual Slavophiles on this subject showed a considerable degree of difference, and also that the Slavophiles often expressed both a bitter hostility to the West and a tender care for its future, a complete denial of the West and a recognition of its great value in history.[42] This paradoxical mixture of universalism and exclusiveness can be understood only in the general framework of romantic ideology.

The Slavophiles felt certain that their mission, the mission of Russia, was of universal significance, and was bound to save the whole world. They buttressed their theory by identifying Russia with Orthodoxy, and by proclaiming that it was the historical destiny of Russia to create a new society based on the true prin-

---

miakov's theology. See, e.g., Abbé Pierre Baron, "Un Theologien laic orthodoxe russe au XIXe siecle: Alexis Stepanovitch Khomiakov," in *Orientalia Christiana Analecta*, no. 127, 1940, p. 59.

[42] As to the individual differences among the Slavophiles, Konstantin Aksakov was the most nationalistic member of the group, whereas Ivan Kireevskii combined his sweeping denunciations of the West with a constant insistence that the West must form an organic part of the renovated world of the future. It is interesting to observe the difference between the two in the various fields of their activity. E.g., Ivan Kireevskii made the following comment to Konstantin Aksakov concerning Aksakov's study of Russian verbs: "If one accepts your opinion without what seems to me to be its exaggeration, then our language appears as richer than the others, but less different from them in its physiological structure. Not an animal of a different breed, but a creature of the same breed, only with a better developed organism." I.K., vol. I, p. 77.

ciples of faith. The message was obviously of a universal import, and the Slavophiles were careful to describe the national and all the other interests as subordinate to the religious principles. Thus they definitely considered themselves to be thinking in terms of humanity rather than of a single nation, an opinion also cherished by most Western romanticists. But this "universalism" was romantic: it meant not a recognition of the common traits of humankind and the equal value of all as the basis for unity, but rather an accentuation of the differences among the nations, and the claim of a certain chosen people to impose its true principles and redeem the world.

Of the romantic analogies, that of the seed was perhaps the most important. As a tree grew out of its seed, so a nation developed organically from its basic principles. In the last analysis a fruitful intercourse, or a union of nations, was no more possible than a fruitful intercourse or a union of trees. The exclusiveness was complete. The Slavophiles never quite realized the full force of this drastic conclusion, but the inherent romantic contradiction between the self-determined and self-contained nature of national organisms and the need to bring these organisms together permeated their entire outlook. It was especially conspicuous in the Slavophile vacillations on the subject of Western culture: on the one hand this culture was praised as a most valuable achievement of human genius, on the other it could find no place in the Slavophile scheme of things, because all the significant elements of the universal Russian culture of the future had to be derived organically from the Russian past, and from no other source.

The Slavophile bitterness against the West was also influenced by another principle of Western romanticism: romantic doctrines of history provided roles for several nations, but only one at a time; in every given period of history the absolute spirit was revealing itself in only one organism. Therefore, in order to assert the significance of Russia the Slavophiles had to deny the significance of the West. This they did by treating the entire West as a single organism activated by false principles.

The Slavophiles believed in the intrinsic superiority of their ideal, and its inevitable eventual triumph. Truth was by its very nature stronger than falsehood, and knowledge was bound to convert ignorance. Like many other romanticists, the Slavophiles were convinced that some day all nations would eagerly accept their message. Their Christian faith and their strong opposition to all violence made them emphasize peaceful conversion as the only true road of progress, and made them denounce force and conquest. But the facts were against them. The West may have been spiritually dead, but it still dominated the political scene. Instead of repenting and accepting the true faith of the East, it made war on Russia and on Orthodoxy. Faced with this turn of events, the Slavophiles remembered that wars had a providential significance, proclaimed the Crimean War to be "holy," and decided that the force of arms could be very effective in the solution of some historical problems. Khomiakov's writings contained a pronounced martial strain, and this strain became almost an obsession in Ivan Aksakov, who regarded a decisive war against the West as inevitable, and who became famous as an ardent advocate of a "strong," and "forward" Russian policy in Europe and in Asia.[43]

THE ROLE OF "THE GREAT MEN"

The Slavophiles remained faithful to the romantic tradition in their discussion of the respective roles of the masses and of the individuals in history. They regarded history as the story of nations, not of rulers, and they emphatically denied the ability of political leaders to plan or alter in any fundamental sense the life of society, but at the same time they bestowed such gifts on certain select individuals as only romanticism could bestow.

Peter the Great was the most important man of all for the Slavophiles, who attributed to him a much greater power than did the Westernizers: the Westernizers believed that Peter the Great had turned Russia sharply to its logical and historically determined course, a participation in European culture; the Slavophiles maintained that Peter the Great's momentous reforms had been contrary to logic and opposed to history. All Slavophile efforts to fit

[43] Professor Ustrialov made a penetrating analysis of the Slavophile views on national mission and war. N. Ustrialov, "Natsionalnaia problema u pervykh slavianofilov," in *Russkaia Mysl*, October, 1916, pp. 1–22.

Peter the Great into their idealized version of Russian history proved to be singularly unsuccessful, and their rationalizations concerning the significance of the St. Petersburg period of Russian history carried little conviction.[44] In the last analysis the Slavophiles had little more than Peter the Great himself to explain Peter's reforms, which they regarded as a most significant turning point of Russian history. Deprived of its background, Peter the Great's figure acquired a truly gigantic stature as an incarnation of the odious, yet mighty, principles of rationalism, legalism, and brute force.

The Slavophiles knew of no man who embodied the true Russian principles as effectively as Peter the Great embodied their antithesis, but they considered several persons, notably the writers Pushkin and Gogol, the painter Ivanov, and the composer Glinka, as profoundly expressive of the spirit of Russia. Later Ivan Aksakov added several more figures, in particular Dostoevskii and, much less judiciously, General Skobelev, to that select circle.[45]

THE SLAVOPHILE ARGUMENTATION

The Slavophiles represented a typical group of men with a fanatical faith in their ideal. They preached rather than talked, demanded rather than suggested, exposed rather than criticized, and they constantly repeated themselves. Their views could not be shaken. They usually knew the answer before they began a discussion or a study, and therefore they were often careless with facts and heedless of their opponents. In their passion to denounce their enemies they sometimes forgot to use their critical faculties. This was the case of Samarin, when in his study of the Jesuits he relied extensively on what proved to be a forged document. Ivan Aksakov repeated the same unintentional error in a more striking

---

[44] These efforts and rationalizations were described in Chapter Three.

[45] I have already made a number of references to Khomiakov's article on Ivanov, Konstantin Aksakov's study of Gogol, Ivan Kireevskii's analysis of Pushkin's works and Ivan Aksakov's speech about Pushkin. Additional material can be found in the general commentaries on Russian letters written by several of the Slavophiles. Khomiakov also wrote an article on Glinka's opera "A Life for the Tsar" (Kh., III, pp. 98–103). For Ivan Aksakov's evaluations of Skobelev and several other "truly Russian" figures see I. A., V, pp. 654–675.

fashion, when he gave in his periodical immediate credence and prominence to a forged account of the aims and principles of the Jewish World Alliance. When he was forced to recognize his mistake, he made the typical comment that the document gave a correct version of the Jews and could have been true, and that therefore it did not really matter whether or not it actually was true.

Romanticism provided a number of very valuable elements for the Slavophile argumentation. Khomiakov followed Church tradition, when he wrote that:

> All the notes of the Church, whether inward or outward, are recognized only by herself, and by those whom grace calls to be members of her.[46]

But he, as well as the other Slavophiles, went further and transferred in a characteristically romantic fashion this religious concept of inner comprehension to such entities as nation, race, and peasant commune. One had to be a part of an organism in order to comprehend it. The Slavophiles then claimed that they and they alone could understand Russia.

They developed this important point at some length:

> Society, as well as man, is conscious of itself not according to the ways of logic. Its consciousness is its very life; it lies in the unity of customs, in the identity of moral and intellectual motives, in the living and uninterrupted intellectual intercourse, in that entire ceaseless motion which creates a people and its inner history. It belongs only to the personality of the people, just as the living, inner consciousness of man belongs only to his proper personality. It is inaccessible to a foreigner and to those members of society who had willingly or unwillingly alienated themselves from it.[47]

The opinions of foreigners about Russia, as well as the opinions of the Westernizers and the other critics of Slavophilism, could be thus written off. The Slavophiles, on the other hand, had the plenitude of national life and consciousness. They were conscious of Russia in the way in which "a man feels and knows the events of his own life, or a member is conscious of the life of the organism of which he forms a part."[48]

---

[46] A. S. Khomiakov, *The Church is One*, p. 15.
[47] Kh., vol. I, p. 20.　　　　　　　　[48] Kh., vol. III, p. 265.

The knowledge of the West, however, was a different thing. The Slavophiles were convinced that they and only they could comprehend the West, describe it, and foretell its future because they were objective and because they based their thought on the true principles. The West could not understand itself because it was blinded by its own interests and passions, and therefore could not conceivably attain detachment, which was the first prerequisite of intelligent judgment.[49]

Some admirers of the Slavophiles in an effort to understand the nature and the significance of their teaching stressed the "prophetic element" of the movement.[50] Berdiaev, on the contrary, criticized Khomiakov and the Slavophiles because they did not develop sufficiently this aspect of their doctrine. According to Berdiaev, the Slavophiles made a mistake and ran into a contradiction when they tried to prove their view of history and proclaim the mission of Russia on the basis of ancient documents, philology, and similar scholarly studies. They failed to realize that the idea of national mission was a profound spiritual and religious truth, which did not depend on material evidence.[51]

Slavophilism was above all an expression of a certain feeling, a particular outlook on the world. The Slavophiles interpreted their basic psychological experience in Christian and romantic terms, then they used romanticism to project their psychological likes and dislikes onto the social plane, and create a romantic doctrine of history, society, and life. The Slavophiles showed considerable ability and originality within the general romantic framework, both in adapting romanticism to the Russian background and in developing some of its aspects, such as the theory of "integrated personality," which was the center of Ivan Kireevskii's interest; or

[49] See, e.g., Kh., vol. I, pp. 197–198. Khomiakov's letters to Palmer present an interesting combination of flat assertions about the West, about the "essence" of contemporary Western attitudes and policies, and of complaints to the effect that it is impossible for Khomiakov to follow Western life from his distant residence in Russia.

[50] Gratieux, for instance, noted carefully "the prophetic tendencies" of Khomiakov throughout his abovementioned admirable study. N. Zernov spoke of *Three Russian Prophets. Khomiakov. Dostoevsky. Soloviev.*

[51] Berdiaev, *The Russian Idea*, pp. 48–49. *Khomiakov*, p. 29, pp. 146–151.

the concept of the will, with which Khomiakov was especially concerned. The Slavophiles were indeed guilty of the vices of the Western romanticists, but they also shared their virtues and with them, offered a permanent contribution to our civilization.

CHAPTER VI

ESTIMATES AND INFLUENCE
OF SLAVOPHILISM

The Slavophiles were always conscious of the fact that they represented only a small minority of the Russian educated class, the bulk of which either admired the West or subscribed to the doctrine of Official Nationality promulgated by Nicholas I. They were a partisan, sectarian group convinced of the unique truth of their message, and devoted to their "great mission" of developing, defending, and spreading this message. They preferred to stress the differences rather than the similarities between their ideology and other contemporary currents of thought; to contrast, not to compare. The bitter partisan nature of Slavophilism was intensified by a similar attitude on the part of many of its opponents: Belinskii was a match for Konstantin Aksakov in fanatical devotion to his own doctrine, while the historian Soloviev not only refused to recognize the validity of any of the Slavophile criticism of his writings, but also denied the right of "the anti-historical school" to make such criticism.

The Slavophile world was thus divided into a small, closely knit group of faithful followers, and the hostile masses outside. The followers had a thorough knowledge of the Slavophile teaching, but, once Khomiakov, Ivan Kireevskii, and Konstantin Aksakov had laid the foundations, they showed very little creative or even critical ability. The numerous critics on the outside cared little about Slavophilism, except for polemical purposes, and usually knew even less. This situation had already established itself by the late forties, and was maintained after the Slavophiles themselves had died: but for a few exceptions, the writers on Slavophilism can be divided into a small, but relatively productive, group of uncritical admirers, and a large number of historians, who had little interest in the Slavophile ideology and who wrote on the Slavophiles no more than was necessary to dispense with them. This second, dominant group of Russian historians was directly connected with the opponents of the Slavophiles, the Westernizers, and inherited from them many of their basic principles, as well as some of their particular views, and notably their estimate of the Slavophiles. The opinions of Herzen and Chernyshevskii proved to be especially influential in the evaluation of the Slavophiles by the historians.

Although Herzen and Chernyshevskii belonged to different generations, and although their knowledge and interest in Slavophilism, as well as their personal acquaintance with the Slavophiles, were by no means identical, their verdicts on the Slavophiles showed a remarkable similarity and became the basis of most of the subsequent estimates of that movement.[1] Both Herzen and Chernyshevskii had a very high personal regard for the Slavophiles, whom they described as some of the "most cultured, noble, and gifted," members of Russian society. They appreciated the fact that Slavophilism formed a part of the general Russian intellectual awakening of the forties and discussed its beneficial effect in stimulating thought, introducing Western theories into Russia, and formulating important problems of Russian life and culture. Chernyshevskii in particular emphasized that doctrines which had already been outmoded and "surpassed" in the West could still be of considerable utility in the more backward Russia.[2] Moreover, both Herzen and Chernyshevskii valued highly the Slavophile concentration on the Russian people: Herzen praised their pioneer attempt to reach to the basic elements of Russia, while Chernyshevskii stated that everything might be pardoned the Slavophiles considering their view of the peasant commune.

[1] Most studies of Herzen and Chernyshevskii deal with their relation to the Slavophiles. The latest on Chernyshevskii is Sladkevich's article, which emphasizes the hostility between Chernyshevskii and the Slavophiles. N. Sladkevich, "K voprosu o polemike N. G. Chernyshevskogo so slavianofilskoi publitsistikoi," in *Voprosy Istorii*, June, 1948, no. 6, pp. 71–79.

[2] N. Chernyshevskii, *Ocherki gogolevskogo perioda russkoi literatury*, pp. 103–105.

But notwithstanding the above qualifications, Herzen and Chernyshevskii were uncompromisingly opposed to Slavophilism, which they regarded as a series of abominations. They found the Slavophile emphasis on religion particularly detestable: it meant to them an appeal to superstition and authority against reason, science, and intellectual freedom. The Slavophile stress on nationalism was equally objectionable, especially because it was combined with a thorough denunciation of the West.[3] And so were the Slavophile political views which justified autocracy, although in an original and curious manner, and stressed the "nonpolitical" nature of the Russian people. Slavophilism was therefore classified as a reactionary ideology, antagonistic to the nineteenth-century idea of scientific progress. It was, in the words of Herzen: "a new holy oil anointing the tsar, new fetters binding thought, a new subjugation of conscience to the servile Byzantine church."[4]

The radical and revolutionary Russian intelligentsia which followed in the footsteps of Herzen and Chernyshevskii showed disregard or contempt for the Slavophile teaching, but some of its own doctrines were connected with certain aspects of this teaching. The *narodniks* in particular, who based their ideology on the peasant masses of Russia, preached agrarian socialism, and formed for a long time the main force of the revolutionary movement in Russia, were linked with the Slavophiles by their conception of the Russian people and notably of the peasant commune.

To the Slavophiles the people meant the peasants. They considered the peasant commune to be the most important, even the only important Russian institution: the nation was nothing but "the great commune of all-Russia," and the church itself was the same commune, only on a higher plane. The whole of Russian history and tradition was mystically linked with the peasants and their

[3] Herzen was among the first to expose the chauvinistic tendency in Slavophilism. He linked the Slavophiles in this respect with all the other Russians, who, in his opinion, also believed in national superiority and exclusiveness: "All the Old Believers are Slavophiles. The entire secular clergy and all the monks are Slavophiles of a different kind. The soldiers who demanded the dismissal of Barclay de Tolly because of his German name were forerunners of Khomiakov and his friends." Herzen, *op. cit.*, p. 270.

[4] Herzen, *op. cit.*, p. 267.

commune, and the future was also theirs. In that future all classes, the separate existence of which testified to social split and disease, would be organically absorbed by the commune, and although the Slavophiles did not describe the details of that process, they were certain that it was both desirable and inevitable. They even made some pathetic attempts to "approach" the people by wearing "native" dress and observing popular traditions. Many students of the Slavophiles have noted their *narodnik* character. Gershenzon concluded his essay on Petr Kireevskii by declaring him to be "the founder of our modern *narodnik* movement." [5] Berdiaev's statement was brief and very much to the point: "The Slavophiles were the first *narodniks* among us; they were *narodniks* on a religious basis." [6]

The *narodniks* proper dropped the religious basis, and their teaching also differed from Slavophilism in numerous other aspects, but they were closely allied to it in their fundamental emphasis on the peasant commune as the essence and the salvation of Russia, and in their contrast between youthful Russia and the decrepit West. The basic principles of the *narodnik* ideology were formulated largely by Herzen and Chernyshevskii, who were very well acquainted with and had the highest regard for the Slavophile view of the peasant commune. A historian of the *narodnik* movement, V. Bogucharskii, even exaggerated the case and concluded that Slavophilism formed the main source of the social and economic ideas and ideals of the *narodniks*. Bogucharskii also emphasized the fact that the Slavophiles themselves felt a certain connection with the *narodniks*, and that Ivan Aksakov used to refer to them as "the Slavophiles who have lost their way." [7]

While the Russian radicals as a group turned away from Slavophilism, there was the curious incident of one of them, E. Dmitriev-Mamonov, claiming that he remained a true disciple of his friend and teacher, Khomiakov, and accusing the later Slavophiles of perverting their master's teaching.

[5] Gershenzon, *op. cit.*, p. 118.

[6] Berdiaev, *The Russian Idea*, p. 41.

[7] V. Bogucharskii, *Aktivnoe narodnichestvo semidesiatykh godov*, pp. 10–24.

For us, who knew Khomiakov well, it is indisputable that a true follower of Khomiakov is the man who seeks knowledge freely, even if he
arrives at conclusions which are directly opposed to those, which Khomiakov *had the time* to write down, not the man who regards Khomiakov as the Pope of Rome, the phenomenon which Khomiakov hated
most.[8]

Dmitriev-Mamonov declared that freedom of investigation had
been the cardinal principle of Slavophilism and that tradition had
been accepted only in as much as it had been found compatible
with that freedom: "Freedom was considered to be the most fundamental thing of all."[9] Slavophilism had been a protest against
the lethargy of Russian society, and an attempt to spur this society
to freedom and knowledge.

In an angry answer to Dmitriev-Mamonov, Ivan Aksakov argued convincingly that Slavophilism was much more than a mere
declaration of freedom, and that it had a positive content, which
Khomiakov had considered to be its true value.[10] Ivan Aksakov
was essentially correct, but Dmitriev-Mamonov's strange opinion
was not a wholly unbecoming tribute to the passion for knowledge
and the spirit of freedom which had been characteristic of early
Slavophilism.[11]

Numerous historians, who were usually linked with Herzen and
Chernyshevskii by common positivist and materialist assumptions
combined with liberalism or radicalism, repeated in a variety of
ways Herzen's and Chernyshevskii's estimate of Slavophilism. The
Slavophiles were dismissed as religious mystics, confused romanticists, and political reactionaries, although the "liberal" elements
of their program, such as freedom of the press, were often mentioned as a mitigating circumstance. Following Chernyshevskii,
this group of historians declared that Slavophilism had been en-

[8] E. Dmitriev-Mamonov, "Slavinofily, Istoriko-kriticheskii ocherk," in
Russkii Arkhiv, 1873, columns 2488–2508, esp. column 2491.

[9] E. Dmitriev-Mamonov, "Nauka i predanie, Pismo k N.," in *Otechestvennye Zapiski*, 1875, no. 8, August, pp. 245–265, esp. p. 246.

[10] *Pismo k izdateliu Russkogo Arkhiva po povodu stati E. Mamonova Slavianofily.* I. A., vol. VII, pp. 766–784 (written in 1873).

[11] It is interesting to note that such an important member of the group as
Koshelev also accused Ivan Aksakov of betraying the Slavophile spirit of freedom. See: Koshelev, *op. cit.*, pp. 249–251.

tirely borrowed from the West, but they did very little to unravel its precise sources, with the result that the Slavophiles were for a long time erroneously classified simply as Hegelians or as disciples of Schelling. Herzen and Chernyshevskii had recognized very clearly the difference between the Slavophiles on the one hand and the proponents of Official Nationality on the other, but some of the later critics, who had no personal knowledge of the Slavophiles, were misled by certain apparent similarities between the Slavophile views and those of the government, and tended to confuse the two doctrines, a tendency which has not yet been entirely overcome.[12]

The prevailing estimate of the Slavophiles found its best expression in a number of general studies, notably those of A. Pypin and P. Miliukov, as well as in a few monographs, such as V. Smirnov's analysis of the lives and the work of the Aksakovs. In addition to describing the "backward" nature of Slavophilism itself, the historians of this group often established direct and precise connections between the Slavophiles and various later Russian nationalists and obscurantists, who were treated as products of certain elements or contradictions within Slavophilism. Miliukov's outline became especially well known and popular.[13]

Miliukov defined the fundamental contradiction of Slavophilism as the struggle between chauvinism and the Christian idea of universal mission. Chauvinism proved to be the stronger element of the two and produced first Danilevskii as the expression of extreme nationalism divorced from all religious foundations, and then Leontiev as the further accentuation of this tendency of particularism and exclusiveness, when it had lost faith in itself and wanted to check all historical development. The universal, Chris-

[12] For Herzen's and Chernyshevskii's opinions see in particular: Herzen, *op. cit.*, p. 272; Chernyshevskii, *op. cit.*, pp. 93–108.

The confusion persists, e.g., in Dorn, *op. cit.*, p. 18, and in some Soviet historians.

[13] P. Miliukov, "Razlozhenie slavianofilstva," in *Voprosy Filosofii i Psikhologii*, year IV, 1893, May, pp. 46–96. And: P. Miliukov, "Slavianofilstvo," in *Entsiklopedicheskii Slovar*, volume XXX, pp. 307–314 (edited by F. Brockhaus and I. Efron).

tian aspect of Slavophilism was taken up by Vladimir Soloviev, but his efforts to give it new life failed.[14]

Since the Revolution, the Soviet historians have continued the extreme Westernizer tradition. The Slavophiles have been treated as a "reactionary" group and have been given little consideration compared to "the progressive thinkers" of nineteenth-century Russia. Several attempts, however, have been made to analyze Slavophilism from the Marxist standpoint, and to give it a comprehensive interpretation as a class teaching.

The Soviet evaluations of the Slavophile ideology had been foreshadowed by some earlier writers, notably by V. Smirnov, who was one of the first to state in unmistakable terms the class character of Slavophilism, and Plekhanov, who also stressed the class element, as well as the reactionary nature of the Slavophile teaching and its links with the *narodiks*.[15] Among the Soviet historians, M. Pokrovskii presented his well-known rough and ready outline of the nature and fortunes of Slavophilism, which he explained in terms of the fluctuation of agricultural prices.[16] The problem was considered much more thoroughly by N. Rubinstein, who gave what has been so far the most comprehensive Marxist interpretation of the Slavophile movement.[17]

To account for Slavophilism, Rubinstein emphasized, in addition to the corn prices, the deepening of the class conflict in Russia and the rise of the revolutionary tide in the West. The vision of revolution had had a very great and terrifying effect on the Slavophiles, and had determined the general character as well as many particular points of their ideology. Slavophilism had been

[14] Miliukov in his lecture on "The Decomposition of Slavophilism" spoke vaguely of the nationalist Slavophile Right and the universalist Slavophile Left. Soloviev, in an answer to Miliukov in the same number of the review in which the lecture was published, stated that he was, as far as he could tell, the only member of "the Slavophile Left," and begged to be dismissed from that office. V. Soloviev, "Zamechaniia na lektsiiu P. N. Miliukova," in *Voprosy Filosofii i Psikhologii*, year IV, 1893, May, pp. 149–154.

[15] V. Smirnov, *op. cit.*, pp. 19–20.

[16] M. Pokrovskii, *Brief History of Russia*, vol. I, pp. 244–246.

[17] N. Rubinstein, "Istoricheskaia teoriia slavianofilov i ee klassovye korni," in *Trudy Instituta Krasnoi Professury. Russkaia istoricheskaia literatura v klassovom osveshchenii. Sbornik statei*, volume I, pp. 53–118.

an assertion of the unique nature of Russia, which had nothing in common with the revolutionary West. The Slavophiles' passion for old Russia, their bitter arguments concerning the particular form of ancient Russian society, their devotion to Russian folklore, and their studies in philology had all been a part of a frenzied effort to utilize the past as a defense against the future and prove that revolution could not happen in Russia.

The same awareness of the danger of revolution had guided the Slavophiles in their reliance on and criticism of Western thought. They had preferred Schelling to Hegel because Schelling was conveniently mystical and vague, whereas Hegel's clear affirmation of logic in history could sanction revolution as much as gradual growth, and Hegel's dialectic was well suited to provide for sudden breaks and leaps.

The Slavophiles' theory of the boundless attachment of the people to their unique head, the tsar, had been a reflection of their views concerning their own estates: *"The devotion of the people to the monarchy in the Slavophile system was nothing but a projection into history of their own 'monarchy' as landlords."* [18] Rubinstein insisted that the significant element of the Slavophile political theory had been certainly not its "anarchism," but its determined demand for a complete separation of the functions of the people from those of the state, a separation in which the state retained the absolute political power. By their emphatic affirmation of the "nonpolitical" nature of the Russian people, the Slavophiles had tried to convince themselves and others that this people could not rise against either its tsar or its landlords.

Rubinstein classified the Slavophiles as representatives of the middle layer of the landowning class. They had been much more progressive than the large landowners, but they had shared the latter's fear and hatred of the proletariat and of the growing class struggle. They had had a good reason to detest Peter the Great, because he had put Russia on the road to becoming an industrial Western society. The conflict between them and the government of Nicholas I had arisen from the fact that Slavophilism had been an ideology of the middle layer of the gentry, whereas the govern-

[18] Rubinstein, *op. cit.,* p. 92.

ment at the time had reflected primarily the interests of the upper layer. The basic assumptions of the two sides had been the same, but the Slavophiles had been more progressive and had demanded a faster development of Russian economy. In particular, they had advocated the emancipation of the serfs, because they had found hired labor to be cheaper than serf labor. When Alexander II had decided in favor of emancipation and had based his policy on the interests of the broad mass of the gentry, the Slavophiles had been loud in their support of the government, but had proved to be, according to Rubinstein, more conservative and cautious than the government. The Slavophile protests against "formalism," "legalism," and bureaucracy had stemmed from their desire for a greater measure of liberty in their economic pursuits, which had been hampered by various government restrictions.

The Slavophile theory of the peasant commune had demonstrated its value in buttressing their views of the unique, "nonpolitical" nature of the Russian people, but it had contained also an element of shrewd calculation based on extensive experience. The Slavophiles had been quick to discover in their capacity of landlords that the commune, because of its tight organization and common responsibility, offered the best guarantee of the performance of all their obligations by the peasants. Similarly, they had objected to government interference with the commune because they had realized that the commune operated better and produced more profit when it was left alone.

The ambivalent Slavophile attitude toward the West, which they had hated, but with which they had not been able to dispense, had been a perfect reflection of the position of their class. The progressive landowners had been bitterly opposed to the rising industrial society, but they had been forced to borrow from this society for the sake of their agriculture, which had been undergoing a rapid change from feudalism to capitalism. This had been quite clear, for instance, in the case of agricultural machinery, and it had been no less compelling in such things as the increase of popular education, for otherwise the people could not operate the machines. The unavoidable contradiction in the relations with the West had been therefore fundamental both in the

Slavophile ideology and in the life of the class which it had represented: the Slavophiles had desired social development, but not
class struggle, Western machines, but not Western ideas, factory
goods, but not the proletariat; in short, they had wanted capitalism, but not its consequences.

In describing the connection of the Slavophiles with subsequent Russian thinkers, Rubinstein took Miliukov's main line of
exposition, from the Slavophiles to Danilevskii to Leontiev, but
gave it a Marxist content. Danilevskii had to modify Slavophilism:

*Because that theory was not suitable in its original form for the justifica-
tion of the aggressive policy of Russian merchant capital in the East.*[19]

He appealed to the state because the power of the state was
necessary to seize Constantinople. Leontiev had to make further
changes in the Slavophile doctrines because he saw the imminent
danger of revolution. His entire ideology was nothing but "a warning to the landlords about the red peril."[20]

The positivists and the Marxists could readily dismiss Slavophilism as utterly incompatible with their view of the world, but
their understanding and interpretation of that movement suffered
from the fact that they had very little in common with it. The
criticism of the philosopher Vladimir Soloviev was of a totally different nature. Soloviev himself had experienced a very powerful
influence of Slavophile ideas, which dominated the first period of
his creative life and left a profound imprint on his entire ideology.
When he came to denounce Slavophilism, he based his views not
on positivism, but on his allegiance to the same Orthodox Church
and even to the same romantic conception of nation and national
mission which had inspired the Slavophiles.

Soloviev's main charge against the Slavophiles was their identification of the Orthodox Church with the Russian people. He became convinced that in spite of their professions to the contrary,
Orthodoxy was for them merely "an attribute of the Russian peo-

[19] Rubinstein, *op. cit.*, p. 109.
[20] Rubinstein, *op. cit.*, p. 114. Rubinstein's analysis has been challenged by
several other Soviet historians. See, e.g., L. Piper, *Mirovozzrenie Gertsena*,
which contains not only an account of Herzen's relations with the Slavophiles,
but also a section on Slavophilism as such (pp. 66–87).

ple; it is the true religion, in the last analysis, only because it is the religion of the Russian people."[21] Because of their worship of the people, the Slavophiles based their teaching not on the objective, universally applicable principles of truth and justice, but on the subjective concept of "the Russian ideal." In fact, they idealized the same Russian life in the past which they so forcibly denounced in the present. The Slavophile criticism of the West proved to be trickery rather than honest argument. They emphasized all the atheistic, destructive elements of the West, but they overlooked or summarily dismissed its entire religious culture and spiritual heritage. They noticed Buechner, but failed to discern Dante or Saint Francis of Assisi. They were especially unjust towards Catholicism, which they arbitrarily refused to regard as a form of Christianity. Their favorite artifice was to contrast the historical expression of Catholicism and all its mistakes and shortcomings with their own abstract and idealized version of Orthodoxy.

Vladimir Soloviev considered chauvinism as the logical outcome of Slavophilism, and included all the extreme nationalists, even Katkov, who had stronger connections with the Westernizers than with the Slavophiles, among the Slavophile progeny. The process had three stages:

The worship of one's own people as the preëminent bearer of universal truth; then the worship of this people as an elemental force, irrespective of universal truth; finally the worship of those national limitations and anomalies which separate the people from civilized mankind, that is, the worship of one's own people with a direct negation of the very idea of universal truth — these are the three consecutive phases of our nationalism represented by the Slavophiles, Katkov, and the new obscurantists, respectively. The first were purely fantastic in their doctrine, the second was a realist with fantasy, the last finally are realists without any fantasy, but also without any shame.[22]

[21] V. Soloviev, *Sobranie sochinenii*, volume V, p. 185. Soloviev's writings against the Slavophiles were collected in the fifth volume of his *Works*. Some of them were written as a polemic against Ivan Aksakov. For Aksakov's side of the argument see his articles "Against the National Self-Renouncement and the Papal Tendencies Revealed in the Articles of V. S. Soloviev." I.A., vol. IV, pp. 218–237, pp. 237–258 (written in 1884).

[22] V. Soloviev, *op. cit.*, p. 228.

Soloviev concluded:

The worship of the virtue of the people, the worship of the might of the people, the worship of the savagery of the people — these are the three descending steps of our pseudo-patriotic thought.[23]

While most specialists proclaimed Slavophilism to be an aberration in Russian intellectual history, a group of devoted followers accepted many of its basic ideas. First among these followers were the members of the families, and the immediate friends of the Slavophiles, for instance the Slavic scholar A. Hilferding and the historian I. Beliaev. Some later scholars, in particular, V. Zavitnevich, who published a monumental study of Khomiakov, V. Liaskovskii, who wrote a brief monograph on Khomiakov and another one on the Kireevskiis, and a few others, were in essential agreement with Slavophilism, and considered it the true Russian ideology.

The admirers of the Slavophiles emphasized the fact that Slavophilism had been a rebellion against the slavish imitation of the West and a triumphant assertion of the ability of Russia to think in her own right. [24] Most of them, however, went much further and sanctioned the claim of Slavophilism to be regarded as a profound revelation of Russia, or of Orthodoxy, and preferably of both at the same time. They spoke of the spirit of Russia, which had finally found its voice after it had been stunned and pushed underground by Peter the Great's reforms, or of the mystical essence of Orthodoxy, which had chosen Khomiakov and Ivan Kireevskii to be its champions. They stressed the influence of the Eastern Doctors of the Church on Slavophilism, and denied or minimized all the Western connections of the movement. They were uncertain about the role of mysticism in the Slavophile doctrine because they wanted to emphasize both the deep religious nature of that doctrine and its manifestly rational and

---

[23] V. Soloviev, op. cit., p. 241.

[24] E.g., K. Bestuzhev-Riumin considered this to be the most significant aspect of Slavophilism. K. Bestuzhev-Riumin, "Slavianofilskoe uchenie i ego sudby v russkoi literature," in Otechestvennye Zapiski, 1862, February, pp. 679–719; March, pp. 26–58; May, pp. 1–23; esp. May, p. 22.

reasonable character.[25] They were willing to praise the Slavophiles for everything, but they had little critical judgment to offer in addition to their praise.

A. Kireev's *Brief Summary of Slavophilism*, published in 1896, was both typical of this school of Slavophile admirers and distinguished by its extreme faithfulness to the original Slavophile ideals. Russian nationality was indissolubly connected by the author with Orthodoxy, and there was an added emphasis on autocracy as the political expression of the same nationality. The primacy of the religious element was again affirmed, and it was emphasized that "a Russian is more, and in the first place a Christian, and a son of the Orthodox Church and only after that a citizen of the Russian state." [26] "The blind conservatives" were declared to be as pernicious to Russia and as distant from the Slavophile ideal as the radicals. The Russian people were described as profoundly "nonpolitical," but the advantage of Russia over Byzantium was discovered in the fact that Russia had the zemskii sobor, whereas Byzantium had not. The relations between the church and the state in ancient Russia were extolled. The West was once more presented as in the throes of dissolution and death, and there was an increased awareness and fear of socialism. The world crisis was depicted as the struggle between the ancient principle of morality, ethics, and its perennial opponent legalism. Russia was the incarnation of the former, and Dostoevskii and Tolstoi were adduced as further proof of the validity of the Slavophile concept of the Russian spirit. The impending victory of the Russian principles in the entire world was proclaimed, and a "positive" Russian policy towards the Slavs was urged.

[25] The problem of mysticism in the Slavophile movement cannot be properly considered apart from the romantic background. Whether one is to regard Konstantin Aksakov's view of Russian history or Khomiakov's concept of society as mystical depends on one's opinion concerning the nature of romantic knowledge. The Slavophiles themselves, Khomiakov in particular, objected strongly to any implication of mysticism in their doctrine and stressed its alleged rational and reasonable character. On one occasion Khomiakov compared this accusation against the Slavophile ideology to an illiterate woman's view of the electric telegraph: in both cases the resort to "mysticism" covered one's own ignorance of the subject. Kh., vol. III, pp. 321–322.

[26] A. Kireev, *Kratkoe izlozhenie slavianofilskogo ucheniia*, p. 5.

The Slavophiles received further and usually indiscriminate praise from such groups as the Pan-Slavs and the extreme Right, who were connected with Slavophilism only in certain aspects of their doctrines.

Since panslavism was in general not so much an organized policy or even a creed, but rather an attitude of mind and feeling, it was at the time correspondingly difficult to gauge its power, just as it is now to analyze its different elements.[27]

Some of these elements were linked with Slavophilism. The question of Slavdom came early to occupy an important place in the Slavophile ideology, and it was developed especially by Khomiakov and later by Ivan Aksakov.

Khomiakov's love for the Balkan Slavs dated from his youthful travels and campaigns in the Balkans, or even earlier, if one is to believe the story of his childhood admiration for "Black George" of Serbia, and it lasted until his death. It found its most powerful expression in a number of Khomiakov's poems, of which "The Eagle," written as early as 1832, was the most famous, and which kept repeating the theme of Slavic unity.[28] Sometimes the appeal to the Slavs was a very direct one: "Rise, Slavic brothers, the Bulgarian, and the Serb, and the Croatian! Quickly embrace one another, quickly draw the sword of your fathers! "[29] It was natural for Khomiakov to attach a very great significance to Slavdom in his history of the world, and occasionally he used "Slavdom" in his varied writings as a synonym of "Russia," or of "Orthodoxy," and as an antonym of "the West." In the last year of his life Khomiakov composed his "Letter to the Serbs: a Message from Moscow," which Gratieux called "the true testament of Slavophilism," and which admonished the Serbs to preserve their Slavic

[27] B. H. Sumner, *Russia and the Balkans, 1870–1880*. The section on "Panslavism" occupies pp. 56–80, esp. p. 57.

[28] "The Eagle" was published in a Slavic periodical in the Austrian Empire before it appeared in print in Russia, and the periodical was promptly confiscated. Zavitnevich, *op. cit.*, volume I, p. 54.

[29] Kh., vol. IV, p. 63.

See O. Miller's above-mentioned article on "Khomiakov — the Poet of Slavdom."

traits of character and of social life and avoid the seduction of the West.[30]

Ivan Aksakov developed extensively Khomiakov's views on Slavdom. The basic outline remained the same, but the relative emphasis given to the Slavic problem increased in a very marked manner.

Aksakov insisted that:

The connection of the Slavic peoples with Russia, the feeling which attracts them to Russia, is a natural, organic, free feeling, which flows from the deepest depths of their popular essence.[31]

The other Slavs had to unite under the leadership of Russia, for apart from such a union they meant nothing:

Because they are called to a universal role, not as Czechs, Slovaks, Slovenes, and so on, separately, but *as Slavs and through Slavdom*: only by this aspect of their existence, only as parts of the universally significant Slavic tribe can they attain importance in the history of the world. When they are outside this common Slavic bond, or when they betray the idea of Slavdom they are nothing.[32]

The Slavophile interest in Slavdom led to practical results. Most Slavophile publications were distinguished by the amount of attention paid to the Slavs: special articles were written by the leading Slavophiles themselves and by their followers, such as A. Hilferding, A. Popov, and V. Panov. Later Pan-Slavs of the professorial type, for instance V. Lamanskii, owed a debt of gratitude, professional and often personal, to Khomiakov and his friends. In 1858 the Slavophiles were active in the formation of the Moscow Slavonic Benevolent Committee, the purpose of which was to assist the cultural development of the Southern Slavs and enable some Balkan students to study in Russia. Branches were opened in the larger Russian cities. In 1867 the Slavonic Ethnographic Exhibition was held in Moscow, and the representatives of various Slavic countries had an opportunity to meet and exchange ideas. There was much disagreement, espe-

---

[30] Gratieux, *op. cit.*, volume II, p. 201.
The "Letter" was published in Kh., vol. I, pp. 371–404.
[31] I. A., vol. I, p. 364.   [32] I. A., vol. I, p. 555.

cially because many of the visitors were Catholics, but the Exhibition was nevertheless a landmark in the growth of Pan-Slav sentiment in Russia. It is worth noting that long before 1867 the Slavophiles had shown a great interest in such leaders of the Slavic revival as Hanka and Safarik, and had met many of them personally.

The Moscow Benevolent Committee, headed by Ivan Aksakov, became very prominent during the Balkan Crisis of 1875–1878, when it sent thousands of volunteers to fight in Serbia under General Cherniaev, and when Ivan Aksakov was recognized as the tribune of the millions who wanted war against Turkey and the liberation of the Balkan Slavs. The Congress of Berlin and the dissolution of the Committee came as hard blows to Aksakov, but he continued his tireless Pan-Slav agitation and activity until his death in 1886. Ivan Aksakov managed to combine a broad religious and cultural interest in Slavdom with narrow, political motives. In this respect he marked a transition from the "purely fantastic" early Slavophiles to the Pan-Slavs of the type of R. Fadeev, who were "without any fantasy, but also without any shame."

There was a direct succession, in particular through Ivan Aksakov, from Slavophilism to Pan-Slavism. But the Pan-Slavs developed only certain aspects of the Slavophile teaching and abandoned many of its fundamental tenets, such as its emphasis on religion and its doctrine of human personality. Moreover, the Pan-Slav ideology borrowed from many sources other than Slavophilism. Its first nineteenth-century forerunner was Admiral Shishkov rather than Khomiakov.[33] Some Slavophile contemporaries of the Right, for instance Tiutchev, and especially Pogodin, contributed their share.[34] The Western sources of Pan-Slavism were also varied, and Danilevskii's reading in Western literature had little in common with Ivan Kireevskii's.

While Pan-Slavism may be regarded as the development of a

[33] On Shishkov's significance as a forerunner of the Pan-Slavs see Koliupanov, *op. cit.*, volume I, book I, pp. 242–244.

[34] On Pogodin and Pan-Slavism see: A. Pypin, *Panslavism v proshlom i nastoiashchem*, pp. 86–104.

certain aspect of the Slavophile ideology to the detriment of all others, the use of Slavophilism in defense of extreme monarchism and conservatism had no logical justification whatever. The Slavophiles believed in autocracy, but their emphasis was on the people, who had called in the Varangians and who had elected the first Romanov to rule Russia, and autocracy had no religious or metaphysical sanction in their eyes. An appeal to Slavophilism on behalf of extremely conservative views and measures was still more incongruous: the Slavophiles had indeed expressed an unqualified opposition to any kind of constitution, but they had objected in equally strong terms to the "reactionary" policies of the government, to the stifling of the life and thought of society, to the absence of freedom in Russia. On matters of practical policy, such as the emancipation of the serfs, the Slavophiles had usually argued against the Right as much as against the Left.[35]

Some penetrating representatives of the extreme Right, for instance P. Florenskii, understood the Slavophile political theory and warned against its dangers, but many were willing to forget logic, praise the Slavophiles, and twist their teaching to their own advantage. The ideology of the Right, based on the defense of the status quo and possessing Western sources as well as numerous Russian predecessors of its own, was essentially independent of Slavophilism, but the latter was used to bolster some of the doctrines of the Right. In particular the extreme nationalists made use of the detailed Slavophile analysis of the unique nature of Russia and her superiority over the West, as well as of the Slavophile criticism of Western political systems. Slavophile "mysticism" was also found to be helpful. Khomiakov's emphasis on the immemorial origins of the basic principles of Russian life and society and his constant references to the spirit of Holy Russia had a stronger emotional appeal than Danilevskii's naturalistic doctrines. Ustrialov even suggested that:

Perhaps the tragedy of St. Petersburg Russia consisted in the fact that the government itself was excessively dominated by the refracted echoes of certain kinds of "Slavophile" prejudices.[36]

[35] See Chapter IV for an exposition of the Slavophile political theory.
[36] Ustrialov, *Politicheskaia doktrina slavianofilstva*, p. 71.

These prejudices were evident in the determined effort of the government to preserve "the ancient foundations of autocracy" in all their purity, and in the pronounced archaistic tendencies in the lives and the entourage of the last Romanovs.

Sometimes individual Slavophiles went beyond their doctrine in the direction of nationalism and conservatism. In the last, obsessed years of his life, Ivan Kireevskii continued to subscribe to the Slavophile ideals, but his attitude towards contemporary Russia became as drastic as that of Leontiev or any other extreme opponent of all social and political change.[37] Ivan Aksakov marked in a certain way a transition from the early Slavophiles to the nationalists of the end of the century. He remained faithful to the Slavophile teaching, but he paid much more attention to its political, nationalist aspect than to its religious or philosophical side. Some articles in *The Day* and especially in Aksakov's last publication, *Rus*, bear a closer resemblance to the Black Hundreds than to Khomiakov.[38] Even during the lifetime of the early Slavophiles some members of the extreme Right used Slavophile arguments and tried to associate themselves with certain aspects of Slavophilism, foreshadowing their subsequent utilization of this doctrine to their own ends.[39]

[37] See in particular Ivan Kireevskii's letters during the last years of his life. E.g., in 1851 he wrote to Koshelev in connection with Koshelev's desire to see the emancipation of the serfs: "Thank God that you consider the present time unsuitable to do anything about your favorite question. God grant us, God grant us that it does not develop until the time when opinions change in our land and the Western spirit no longer dominates our thought and our life, for now only that which stands still continues to be Russian, whereas everything that moves, moves towards Germanization." I.K., vol. II, p. 253. For other examples, see the discussion of Ivan Kireevskii in Chapter II.

[38] This was notably true of Aksakov's lengthy treatment of the Jewish question. Ivan Aksakov's contradictions with the early Slavophiles were implicit, not explicit: he always proclaimed his allegiance to all their principles in their hierarchical order. E.g., Aksakov would describe the coronation of Alexander III in almost religious terms, but would at the same time maintain the Slavophile doctrine of political power as a necessary evil and of autocracy as a historical arrangement made by the Russian people rather than as a divine institution. For the description see: I.A., vol. V, pp. 118–126, p. 131.

[39] This was especially true of Pogodin and Shevyrev, who in turn exercised some influence on the Slavophiles. See also F. Vigel's letter to Khomiakov in which Vigel professed himself to be Khomiakov's associate. In "Pisma k A. S. Khomiakovu," in *Russkii Arkhiv*, 1884, book III, pp. 225–228.

The measure of the degeneration of Slavophilism in the hands of some of its self-professed followers of the Right is provided by M. F. Taube's book which appeared in 1912, entitled *The Science of Knowledge of the Eastern Conciliar Enlightenment Following the Philosophy of the Slavophiles.* Taube insisted on a direct connection between Khomiakov and the Black Hundreds:

Nobody doubts the existence of the Black Hundreds, but few realize that the Black Hundreds enlightened by philosophic teaching have become the White Hundreds. The principle of the White Hundreds is the universal, highly spiritual *Eastern enlightenment.* Contemporary Slavophilism is precisely this enlightening White Hundred movement in the realm of thought and intellectual generalizations.[40]

The Slavophile analysis of the West was further simplified by Taube:

It is indisputable that the West is being engulfed by the swamp of rationalism, by the torrent of evolutionism, by the nirvana of nihilism, by the magic of spiritualism, by the charmed circle of mysticism and occultism, and by the abyss of the other cunning "isms" of theosophy and necromancy.[41]

Russia had been seduced by the West and had been struggling for two hundred years in its snake-like coils. "Russia was in love with the beauty, Europe, and, confident of finding in her a friend and an ally, she found a painted venal debauchee, a crafty huckstress, and a spiteful intriguer."[42] Salvation lay solely in the return to the true principles of Eastern enlightenment, which had been suggested, but not developed by Khomiakov. Taube proceeded to unfold these principles in a most fantastic manner.[43]

In contrast to the Pan-Slavs, whose attention was centered exclusively on Slavdom, and to the members of the extreme Right, who made an illicit use of some of the political and historical

[40] M. F. Taube, *Poznanievedenie sobornogo vostochnogo prosveshcheniia po liubomudriiu slavianofilov,* p. 5.

[41] Taube, *op. cit.,* p. 7.

[42] Taube, *op. cit.,* p. 18.

[43] Taube's "system" was "*a construction based on coördinates (relations) or an arrangement according to the points of the compass: North-South, East-West, the zenith–the nadir, that is, a construction which is spatial, geometrical, and in addition, spherical.*" Taube, *op. cit.,* p. 12.

doctrines of the Slavophiles, certain Russian thinkers were linked with Khomiakov and his friends by the fundamental similarity of interest and approach in the study of man, religion, and culture. In the nineteenth century this was especially true of Vladimir Soloviev and of Dostoevskii. Soloviev finally abandoned Slavophilism as incompatible with the Christian ideal, but Dostoevskii continued to develop some basic Slavophile themes.

Dostoevskii was a religious thinker and his attitude toward life was similar to that of the Slavophiles. Like Khomiakov and his friends, he proclaimed the supreme value of man's soul, defended ardently the freedom of the human spirit, and believed that in the future the true Christian ideals would triumph on earth. His passion for freedom was equal to Khomiakov's, and his conviction that the state would eventually be transformed by true faith and become the church, went beyond the views of the Slavophiles, although comparable ideas had been suggested by Ivan Kireevskii and Kireevskii's associates. The supreme importance of belief in God for man and nation alike formed one of the cardinal points of Dostoevskii's philosophy, and his discussion of this problem in *The Possessed* or in *The Brothers Karamazov* was much more moving than Samarin's clever arguments or Ivan Aksakov's vituperations.

Dostoevskii's treatment of Russia and the West also closely resembled the Slavophile teaching. His sweeping criticism of the West and his ambivalent emotional attitude toward it — an attitude which expressed hatred, and deep interest, and a certain kind of love — were almost identical with the Slavophile approach, and so were some particular points of his outline, such as his discussion of the Catholic and the Protestant principles of the West, and his emphasis on the connected, organic nature of Western history, notably on the derivation of socialism from Catholicism. Dostoevskii was aware even more than Khomiakov of the vices and the defects of the Russians, but he shared the Slavophile belief that Russia, and Slavdom in general, contained the true principles which would lead to the attainment of happiness and harmony for all the nations. His doctrine of Russian

Messiahship was essentially a continuation of the Slavophile attempt to reconcile the universal and the national element through an appeal to the special spiritual gifts of the Russian people, Russian spirit, "Russian Christ": Dostoevskii stressed in particular the all-inclusive nature of the Russians, which enabled them to understand, help, and lead all the nations of the world. Ivan Aksakov, who was in general very bitter to his contemporaries, hailed Dostoevskii as a revelation of the Christian soul of Russia.[44]

The revival of interest in religion and speculative philosophy in Russia in the first two decades of the twentieth century gave a powerful new impetus to the study of the Slavophiles. Khomiakov came to be recognized as an extremely important theologian and religious thinker, and the entire Slavophile ideology was reexamined by some students in relation to its religious and philosophical assumptions. That there was much disagreement and confusion was attested by the fact that a leading Orthodox theologian, Father P. Florenskii, denounced Khomiakov with utmost bitterness, while a Jewish scholar, M. Gershenzon, proclaimed the great significance of Ivan Kireevskii's intuitions in religion and psychology.[45] On the whole the reëxamination led to a much better appreciation of the nature of Slavophilism and of the problems which it involved. Several of the new "admirers" showed remarkable critical ability, and the most outstanding one of them, N. Berdiaev, became famous as an original thinker.

The First World War served to emphasize the contrast between Russia and the West, and between Orthodox religious thought and German philosophy, which had formed a basic motif of

[44] Dostoevskii's ideology is to be found not only in his critical commentaries such as *The Diary of a Writer*, but also in his great novels. Dostoevskii stated his theory of Russian Messiahship most strikingly and completely in his famous "Pushkin Address."

[45] Florenskii argued that Khomiakov's religion was immanent and humanitarian, not transcendent and Christian. See: Florenskii, *op. cit.* Berdiaev's attack on Florenskii was just as violent as Florenskii's denunciation of Khomiakov. Berdiaev concluded that Florenskii's "secret" was the same as that of Dostoevskii's Grand Inquisitor: "We are not with Thee, but with *him*." N. Berdiaev, "Khomiakov i sviashch. P. A. Florenskii," in *Russkaia Mysl.*, 1917, February, pp. 72–81, esp. p. 81.

the Slavophile ideology, and which was revived by such "neo-Slavophiles" as V. Ern. The Revolution sent most students of Slavophilism into exile, where many of them continued their former interests and studies. The Orthodox Theological Institute in Paris, with such specialists as professors S. Bulgakov, G. Florovskii, and V. Zenkovskii, became the foremost center of critical appreciation of the Slavophiles.

In reëxamining Slavophilism, the new critics were especially concerned with determining its fundamental meaning and permanent value, as distinct from all transient aspects and specific points of doctrine. Berdiaev, Zenkovskii, and some others found this meaning in its affirmation of the Orthodox Church, and its call to build a new culture on the foundations of Orthodoxy. A very different opinion was given by M. Gershenzon, who studied the Slavophiles with much understanding and sympathy, but whose own point of view was not Christian.

Gershenzon reached the conclusion that Slavophilism resulted from an incorrect application on the social plane of Ivan Kireevskii's metaphysical and psychological intuitions. Because of his background, Ivan Kireevskii came naturally to exalt Orthodoxy and Russia, and the other Slavophiles, who did not possess Kireevskii's fundamental prophetic insight, were only too willing to develop his ideas along the conventional romantic and nationalistic lines. But this basic insight had nothing to do with any religious denomination, nation, or race: it was, according to Gershenzon, a vision of the true nature of human personality. In his investigation into the nature of man, human motivation, the limitations of reason, and the depth as well as the organic unity of the ego, Kireevskii had gradually recognized and described the subconscious mind and the complex psychological structure of man which the psychologists discovered only fifty years later. This, Gershenzon emphasized, had indeed been the work of a genius.[46]

[46] Gershenzon's views on Ivan Kireevskii's insights into the human character are interesting and useful because they stress a very important aspect of Kireevskii's ideology, but they are open to many criticisms. Gershenzon

Just as the critics hostile to the Slavophiles connected Danilevskii and all the other nationalists with Slavophilism, so some of
the scholars who argued from the Orthodox point of view established direct and precise connections between Khomiakov and
his friends on the one hand and the subsequent Russian religious
thinkers on the other. For instance, A. Volzhskii described the
evolution of Slavophilism as a triple development of its basic
religious idea, the three aspects of which resulted in Leontiev,
Soloviev, and Dostoevskii.[47] Berdiaev declared that, "Among us
only the Slavophile philosophy is original and full of creative
spirit," and claimed that all those who contributed to the religious development of Russian society and culture were the successors of the Slavophiles: the members of the group ranged from the
leading theologians of the Church to such unique figures as L.
Tolstoi and N. Fedorov.[48]

Slavophilism was a typically romantic ideology characterized
by the peculiar traits, the aspirations, and the contradictions of

---

admitted that Kireevskii had left only brief remarks, hints, and allusions concerning the psychological truths which he had discovered. The system, as
reconstructed by Gershenzon, was more logical, clear, and comprehensive
than the original, and also markedly more scientific. For instance, Gershenzon
paid particular attention to the fact that Kireevskii had regarded dreams as a
revelation of the basic personality of man, as distinct from the mere conscious
side of it, but he did not take sufficient notice of Kireevskii's view of dreams
as prophetic warnings of the future, as messages from the outside. It is not at
all clear what Gershenzon meant by modern psychology, of which Ivan
Kireevskii was the alleged forerunner, and his mention of such thinkers as
Nietzsche, Maeterlinck, and William James confuses rather than clarifies the
issue. The analysis also suffered from the fact that Kireevskii was studied
apart from Western romanticism: using Gershenzon's approach, there is no
reason why such romanticists as Baader and Novalis, and perhaps romanticism
in general, should not also qualify as forerunners of modern psychology.
Finally, it may be noted that Ivan Kireevskii himself would have never agreed
with Gershenzon's interpretation of his doctrine: he had been convinced that
his view of man formed the very essence of Orthodoxy, whereas Gershenzon
claimed that there was no connection between the two. See the essay on
Ivan Kireevskii in Gershenzon, *op. cit.*, pp. 7–43.

[47] A. Volzhskii, "Sviataia Rus i russkoe prizvanie," in *Voina i Kultura.*

[48] Berdiaev, *Khomiakov*, p. 123. For another very high evaluation of the
Slavophile philosophy see: E. Radlov, *Ocherk istorii russkoi filosofii*, pp. 30–42.

romanticism. It was also a nationalist teaching. Nationalism formed an essential element of romanticism, but it played a greater role in Slavophilism than in many Western romantic doctrines. Slavophilism may be regarded as a part of the general Slavic national revival of the nineteenth century, and the Slavophiles emphasized their connection with similar groups of intellectuals in other Slavic lands.[49] Their ideology was primarily inspired by the strikingly nationalist doctrines of rising Germany rather than by the forms which romanticism took in the more firmly established societies of England and France.

Numerous admirers of the Slavophiles made futile efforts to present their teaching as different in kind from anything produced by the West, as a true revelation of Holy Russia. A few critics fell into the opposite error and depicted Slavophilism as a peculiarly Russian perversion. The correct view should include the European context of Slavophile thought, and treat the Slavophiles as one of the groups of romantic intellectuals who flourished in the nineteenth century in various European countries.

Some considered the time of Liubusa, Przemysl, or Zaboi as the Heroic Age; another group — the time of Sviatoslav and Vladimir; a third — the period of the ancient German knighthood; finally, the fourth group found the Heroic Age in the days of the mighty warriors glorified in the tales of the Eddas or in the songs of the Niebelungs. The religious foundation also changes: the poetry of ancient Catholicism can be found here next to Protestant piety, just as in the Russian nationalist-romantic school the advantage lies with Orthodoxy. Then . . . . each school understands in its own manner the dogma which is common to them all and which proclaims the solemn erecting of the new idea which is destined to liberate the whole of humanity and heal the wounds of civilization. Some affirm that this idea lies at the foundation of the Polish national character, others see it in the Czech tribal principle,

[49] On Slavophilism and the national revivals in the other Slavic lands see: M. Ursin (M. Zdekhovskii), *Ocherki iz psikhologii slavianskogo plemeni.* Chapter IV deals with the Slavophiles and contains a comparison between the Slavophiles and the proponents of Polish Messiahship. See also: P. Lavrov, "Filosofiia istorii slavian," in *Otechestvennye Zapiski,* 1870, no. 6, pp. 347–420; no. 7, pp. 65–126.

still others expect the Messiah from Germany, while yet another group points to the "far North" and successively to Denmark, Sweden, Norway.[50]

In line with the fate of most romantic teachings, little has been left of the Slavophile doctrines a hundred years after their formulation. The Slavophile views on history, which had been opposed from their very inception by the leading Russian scholars, can no longer be seriously entertained. A century of scholarship has also exposed the fantastic nature of the Slavophile concepts of Russian government and society much more clearly than could be done by Herzen or Granovskii. The philology of the Slavophiles lost its attraction, and their contribution to the study of Russian folklore was absorbed by the modern discipline, which denies the romantic premises on which the Slavophile work had been based. Khomiakov and his friends proved to be very bad prophets: the Russian people, in particular, showed its ability to stage a revolution.

And yet Slavophilism is not entirely dated. Its permanent value lies in its emphasis on the fundamental problems of human faith, motivation, and life, and in its attempt to find the basis for a true Christian society. The attempt was thoroughly romantic, the principles of faith were strangely combined or rather confused with the peasant commune, the Russian people, or the Slavic traits of character, but the main argument could be detected in spite of all these defects and additions. The controversy on human faith, life, and freedom, between Samarin and Herzen, between the Slavophiles and the Westernizers has not been resolved by our society, and few thinkers have given it as much consideration as Khomiakov and his friends.

In tracing the influence of the Slavophiles in the history of ideas it is necessary to beware of all rough and ready schemes which derive various Russian thinkers and schools of thought from the component elements or the contradictions of Slavophilism. Whether, as in the case of Miliukov, they emphasize the transformation of Slavophilism into chauvinism, or, as in the case of

[50] A. Veselovskii, *Zapadnoe vliianie v novoi russkoi literature*, p. 228.

Volzhskii, read into various religious thinkers the influence of different aspects of the Slavophile teaching, they are invariably extremely artificial, and reflect the romantic concept of history with its immanent dialectic and its rhythms. Their artificiality is especially evident in their treatment of a thinker like Leontiev, who is sometimes defined as "the antithesis," or "the nemesis" of Slavophilism, 'ut it is also present in all other cases.[51] It is useless, for instance, to describe Danilevskii, as Rubinstein does, as the Slavophile exactly opposed to Slavophilism. In fact, with the possible exception of such very minor figures as Khomiakov's son Dimitrii or A. Kireev, Ivan Aksakov was the last of the Slavophiles. None of the leading Russian thinkers of the second half of the nineteenth century can be intrinsically connected with Slavophilism or intelligently interpreted as a part of its development.

But, in many less overwhelming ways, the Slavophiles did influence these thinkers and the numerous and diverse intellectual, social, and political movements in Russia. The members of the extreme Right exaggerated their relation to the Slavophiles, while the *narodniks* ignored it, the Pan-Slavs utilized Khomiakov's and Ivan Aksakov's treatment of Slavdom, and the scholars profited from the Slavophile study of Russian history and folklore. The Slavophiles exercised their most important influence in the discussion of the basic problems of man's life and culture. This aspect of their teaching was primarily responsible for the connection of Vladimir Soloviev and Dostoevskii with Slavophile thought, and in the twentieth century it affected in a fundamental manner Russian theology and Russian philosophy, while Slavophile political and historical theories dwindled into insignificance.

Slavophilism occupies an important place in the history of Russian culture. Its varied background included such elements as the ancient national exclusiveness, and xenophobia, the tradi-

---

[51] In addition to Leontiev's role in the systems mentioned in this chapter, see an interesting interpretation of Leontiev as "the disappointed Slavophile" in: S. Trubetskoi, "Razocharovannyi slavianofil," in *Vestnik Evropy*, 1892, October, pp. 772–810.

tional teaching of the Orthodox church, a new enthusiasm for German idealistic philosophy, and the first attempts to plot the course of Russian history. Its ideology consisted of many different and even contradictory doctrines, and its influence ranged from the Black Hundreds to the Social Revolutionaries, and from theologians to the Pan-Slavs. It expressed Russian romanticism and Russian nationalism, and above all it explored some of the fundamental problems of human life and thought which form the very basis of the history of culture.

APPENDIX: Khomiakov's *History* and Friedrich Schlegel's *Philosophy of History*

Khomiakov's *History* was a typical product of the Romantic Age, and it presents interesting parallels to various writings of Western romanticists. It bears a particularly striking and fundamental resemblance to Friedrich Schlegel's *Philosophy of History*.[1]

Both Schlegel and Khomiakov defined the basic idea of history as a struggle between two races representing conflicting religious principles. Schlegel wrote:

So is the race of Cain and Cain's sons represented from its origin, as one attached to the arts, versed in the use of metals, disinclined to peace, and addicted to habits of warfare and violence, as again, at a later period, it appears in Scripture as a haughty and wicked race of giants (p. 96).

On the other hand, the peaceful race of Patriarchs, who lived in a docile reverence of God and with a holy simplicity of manners, was descended from Seth (p. 96).

Under these two different forms, therefore, doth tradition reveal to us the primitive world, or, in other words, these are the grand conditions of humanity which fill the record of primitive history. On the one hand, we see a race, lovers of peace, revering God, blessed with long life, which they spend in patriarchal simplicity and innocence, and still no strangers to deeper science, especially in all that relates to sacred tradition and inward contemplation, and translating their science to posterity in the old or symbolical writing, not in fragile volumes, but on durable monuments of stone. On the other hand, we behold a giant race of pretended demigods, proud, wicked, and violent, or, as they are called in the later Sagas of the heroic times, the heaven-storming Titans (p. 97).

For the hostility of two rival races in the primitive world, considered in itself, and independently of adventitious circumstances, must be looked upon as a positive and well authenticated fact (p. 100).

Schlegel and Khomiakov agreed that the division of the world had been based on the difference in principles rather than on blood. Schlegel expressed it as follows:

The struggle which divided the primitive world into two great parties, arose far more from the opposition of feelings and of principles, than from difference of extraction (p. 97).

[1] Friedrich von Schlegel, *Philosophie der Geschichte*, in achtzehn Verlesungen gehalten zu Wien im Jahre 1828, erster Band, Wien, 1829, zweiter Band, Wien, 1829.

The Philosophy of History in a Course of Lectures. Delivered at Vienna by Frederick von Schlegel, translated from the German, with a Memoir of the author by James Burton Robertson, Esq., fifth edition, revised, London, 1847.

It was, in one word, a contest between religion and impiety, conducted, however, on the mighty scale of the primitive world, and with all those gigantic powers which, according to ancient tradition, the first men possessed (p. 99).

Schlegel's and Khomiakov's definitions of the two warring principles were identical. Schlegel stated:

This opposition and this discord — this hostile struggle between the two great divisions of the human race, forms the whole tenure of primitive history. When the moral harmony of man had once been deranged, and two opposite wills had sprung up within him, a divine will or a will-seeking God, and a natural will or a will bent on sensible objects, passionate and ambitious, it is easy to conceive how mankind from their very origin must have diverged into two opposite paths (p. 97).

And:

this original contest and opposition among men according to the two-fold direction of the will, a will conformable to that of God, and a will carnal, ambitious, and enslaved to Nature. . . . (p. 101).

Khomiakov described the Iranian principle as that of freedom and of accord with the divine, and the Kushite as that of necessity and of enslavement to nature.[2]

Schlegel discussed the two basic principles which activated humanity as an introduction to the history of the world, whereas Khomiakov worked them into specific historical events and into the development of various historical nations. But Khomiakov's line of exposition was foreshadowed by Schlegel, who wrote:

The pre-eminence of the Sethites, chosen by God, and entirely devoted to his service, must be received as an undoubted historical fact, to which we find many pointed allusions even in the traditions of the other Asiatic nations. Nay, the hostility between the Sethites and Cainites, and the mutual relations of these two races form the chief clue to the history of the primitive world, and even of many particular nations of antiquity. That, after the violent but transient interruption occasioned by the deluge, the remembrance of many things might revive, and the same or a similar hostility between the two races which had existed in the ante-diluvian world, might be a second time displayed, is a matter which it is unnecessary to examine any further (p. 152).

The same struggle continued even in the modern world:

This leading subject of primitive history — the struggle between two races, as it is the first great event in universal history, is also of the utmost impor-

---

[2] Khomiakov in his *History* made over a hundred specific references to the Iranians and the Kushites, but he never gave an exhaustive discussion of these two basic terms. Some of the most important references are to be found on the following pages: Kh., vol. V, p. 217, p. 235, p. 363, pp. 530–532; vol. VI, p. 22.

tance in the investigation of the subsequent progress of nations; for this original contest . . . often recurs, though on a lesser scale, in later history; or at least we can perceive something like a feeble reflection or a distant echo of this primal discord. And even at the present period which is certainly much nearer to the last than to the first ages of the world, it would appear sometimes as if humanity were again destined, as at its origin, to be more and more separated into two parties, or two hostile divisions (p. 101).

In addition to the identity of the basic motif, Schlegel's *Philosophy of History* and Khomiakov's *History* resembled each other in some other special points. Both Schlegel and Khomiakov linked their accounts of the two races with the biblical narrative, and Schlegel emphasized the connection between the wicked race and Cain, while Khomiakov stressed the relation between the Kushites and Ham. Both believed in the especially great energy and might of the peoples before or at the dawn of history, and Khomiakov ascribed it to their more homogeneous nature. There were striking similarities between the two in the treatment of certain peoples. Khomiakov stated that the most bitter struggle of the Iranians and the Kushites took place in India. Schlegel wrote: "In the Indian Sagas the two races of the primitive world are represented in a state of continual or perpetually-renewed warfare. . . ." (p. 99). The following comparison of Egypt and Israel, drawn by Schlegel, may just as well have been produced by Khomiakov, to whom Egypt and the Egyptian science were the essence of Kushitism, whereas Israel represented the free spirit of the Iranians.

Completely opposed to the Egyptian science — to the Egyptian understanding, that dived and penetrated by magical power into the profoundest secrets and mysteries of nature, the ruling element of the Hebrew spirit was the *will* — a will that sought with sincerity, earnestness and ardour, its God and its Maker, far exalted above all nature, went after his light when perceived and followed with faith, with resignation, and with unshaken courage, his commands, and the slightest suggestions of his paternal guidance, whether through the stormy sea, or across the savage desert (p. 169).[3]

Khomiakov and the other Slavophiles certainly knew the general ideas of Friedrich Schlegel, but I could not determine the extent of this knowledge. The Slavophile writings contain only a few scattered insignificant references to Friedrich Schlegel, and Khomiakov did not give the sources for his *History*.

Two aspects stand out in the comparison between Schlegel's *Philosophy of History* and Khomiakov's *History*: the identity of the fundamental view of history, and the great difference in the expression of

[3] For Khomiakov's account of India, Egypt, and Israel see the index made by the editors to the fifth, sixth, and seventh volumes of his *Works*, and in particular to the first two. This index is especially valuable because the manuscript itself had no subdivisions of any kind.

this view. Schlegel's description of the struggle of the two races activated by the opposite spiritual principles occupied several pages and
was in the nature of an introduction to a conventional account of human history. Khomiakov depicted the same struggle in the course of
some fifteen hundred pages, and in doing so treated history in an
original and fantastic manner. It seems highly probable that Khomiakov borrowed the main idea from Schlegel and then developed it with
his characteristic ingenuity and diffusiveness.

BIBLIOGRAPHY

(Journals, books, essays, articles, and monographs given English titles in the text are usually available only in Russian, as they are listed in the footnotes and in the Bibliography. Throughout the Bibliography M denotes Moscow and P St. Petersburg or Petrograd.)

THE WRITINGS OF THE SIX LEADING SLAVOPHILES

Only the editions used in this book are listed.

IVAN AKSAKOV

Sochineniia. Seven volumes. M: 1886–1891. The references to Ivan Aksakov's *Works* were made to this edition, except for all the references to volume II, which was more readily available in the edition: *Slaviano-filstvo i zapadnichestvo, 1860–1886,* volume II, M: 1886.
Pisma. Three volumes. M: 1888–1892.
Biografiia F. I. Tiutcheva. M: 1886.
Biograficheskii ocherk poeta s prilozheniem ego stikhotvorenii. M: 1902.
Sbornik stikhotvorenii. M: 1886.
"Perepiska dvukh slavianofilov" (The correspondence of Ivan Aksakov and V. Lamanskii), in *Russkaia Mysl.* Year XXXVIII. February, 1917, pp. 82–89.

KONSTANTIN AKSAKOV

Polnoe sobranie sochinenii. Three volumes. M: 1861–1880. The references to volume I were made to the more readily available edition: *Sochineniia istoricheskie.* M: 1861. The projected complete edition of Konstantin Aksakov's works has never advanced beyond the first three volumes which cover Aksakov's historical and linguistic studies.
Kniaz Lupovitskii ili priezd v derevniu. Leipzig: 1857.
"Literatory naturalisty," in *Russkaia Beseda.* 1856. Book II, pp. 58–60.
"O povesti g-zhi Kokhanovskoi: 'Posle obeda v gostiakh,'" in *Russkaia Beseda.* 1858. Book IV, pp. 141–144.
"O russkom vozzrenii," and "Esche neskolko slov o russkom vozzrenii," in *Russkaia Beseda.* 1856. Book I, pp. 84–86; Book II, pp. 139–147.
"O sovremennom cheloveke," in *Rus.* 1883. Nos. 8, 12, 13.
"O sovremennom literaturnom spore," in *Rus.* 1883. No. 7.
"Obozrenie sovremennoi russkoi literatury," in *Russkaia Beseda.* 1857. Book I, pp. 1–39.
Oleg pod Konstantinopolem. P: 1858.
Sobranie stikhotvorenii. M: 1909.

"Vospominaniia studenchestva," in *Den.* 1862. Nos. 39 and 40.
"Zamechaniia na novoe administrativnoe ustroistvo krestian v Rossii," in *Rus.* 1883. Nos. 3, 4, 5.

Konstantin Aksakov's memorandum *O vnutrennem sostoianii Rossii* and some of his editorials in *Molva* were published in their complete form in L. Brodskii, *Rannie slavianofily.* M: 1910, pp. 69–122.

ALEKSEI KHOMIAKOV

Polnoe sobranie sochinenii. Eight volumes. M: 1900–1914. This edition contains all of Khomiakov's works, and material is very well arranged.

Russia and the English Church during the Last Fifty Years, Volume I, Containing a Correspondence between Mr. William Palmer, Fellow of Magdalen College, Oxford, and M. Khomiakoff, in the Years 1844–1854. Edited by W. Birkbeck, London: 1895.

The Church Is One. London: 1948.

IVAN KIREEVSKII

Polnoe sobranie sochinenii. Edited by M. Gershenzon. Two volumes. M: 1911. This is an excellent and a complete edition of Ivan Kireevskii's writings.

PETR KIREEVSKII

"Ob otmene krepostnogo prava. Pismo Petra Vasilievicha Kireevskogo k A. I. Koshelevu," in *Russkii Arkhiv.* 1873. Book II. Columns 1345–1360.

"Pisma bratiev Kireevskikh," in *Russkii Arkhiv.* 1894. Book III, pp. 207–224.

"Petr Vasilievich Kireevskii, Ego pisma," in *Russkii Arkhiv.* 1905. Book II, pp. 113–173.

Byliny-pesni, sobrannye P. V. Kireevskim. M: 1868. Kireevskii's brief introduction to this collection of songs is on pp. IV–VI.

IURII SAMARIN

Sobranie sochinenii. Edited by D. Samarin, F. Samarin, and P. Samarin. M: 1877–1911. Volumes I–X, and XII. Volume XI, as well as the projected volumes XIII and XIV have not appeared. I used the second edition of the first volume, Moscow: 1900. The *Works* lack Samarin's correspondence after 1853, many of his speeches and articles in connection with the zemstvo, as well as several of his political articles published abroad.

Correspondence de G. Samarine avec la Baronne de Rahden. 1861–1876. Edited by D. Samarin. M: 1894.

"Dva slova v otvet na statiu Sovremennoi Letopisi (iiun, no. 22) po voprosu: polezno li bylo by dlia Rossii, esli by russkie, prozhivaiushchie za granitseiu, vozvratilis v svoe otechestvo?" in *Den*. 1863. No. 31.

"Iz Samary," in *Den*. 1862. No. 27.

"Iz Vladimira," in *Den*. 1861. No. 24.

"Perepiska Samarina s Gertsenom," in *Rus*. 1883. Nos. 1 and 2.

Predislovie, primechaniia i poseslovie k knige: Russkii administrator noveishei shkoly, Zapiska Pskovskogo Gubernatora V. Obukhova i otvet na nee. Berlin: 1868.

With Dmitriev, F. *Revolutsionnyi konservatism*. Berlin: 1875.

Poslednee slovo o polskom voprose v Rossii. Berlin: 1869. This unsigned work is not included in Nolde's exhaustive list of Samarin's writings, but it is attributed to Samarin in *Volnaia Russkaia Pechat v Rossiiskoi Publichnoi Biblioteke*, edited by V. Anderson, P: 1920, p. 102. Because of the style and the language used in the pamphlet, I doubt strongly that Samarin was its author.

NOTE: I was unable to obtain Petr Kireevskii's only article (his debate with Pogodin in *Moskvitianin*, 1845), and a number of articles and essays by Konstantin Aksakov and by Samarin.

BIBLIOGRAPHIES

The best bibliography of Khomiakov and the Slavophile movement is provided in Gratieux (A. Gratieux, *A. Khomiakov et le Mouvement Slavophile*. Volume I. *Les hommes*. Volume II. *Les doctrines*, Paris: 1939). Volume I, pp. XIII–XXXII. Zavitnevich's list is very detailed, but out of date. (V. Zavitnevich, *Aleksei Stepanovich Khomiakov*. Two volumes. Kiev: 1902.) For Samarin an excellent bibliography was compiled by Nolde: Nolde (B. Nolde, *Iurii Samarin i ego vremia*. Paris: 1926), pp. 234–241. See also Kolubovskii's bibliographies of Samarin, Khomiakov, and Ivan Kireevskii in *Voprosy Filosofii i Psikhologii*, 1891.

LITERATURE ON SLAVOPHILISM

The following list is intended as a working bibliography of the Slavophile movement as presented in the foregoing study. It is not exhaustive, especially in its biographical aspect. Care had to be exercised to include only the material which had specific importance for this study because otherwise the bibliography could have become an enormous and extremely diffuse collection of titles from the history of Russian thought. Works which I have reason to believe are directly relevant to Slavophilism, but which I was unable to consult, are marked by an asterisk. No works of or about Western romanticism are listed, nor are the writings of such authors as Zhukovskii, Gogol, and Dostoevskii. Political and other histories of the period which served only as a general background for this study are also omitted. The notes are meant to provide some additional information on the books listed, and do not repeat the evaluations made in the text.

*Aksakov, N. "O starom i novom slavianofilstve," in *Blagovest*, Nos. 22–23.

Aksakov, V. *Dnevnik Very Sergeevny Aksakovoi.* P: 1913. This diary of a sister of Konstantin and of Ivan Aksakov throws interesting light on the Aksakov family and the genesis of Slavophilism.

Anichkov, E. "Ocherk Pushkinskogo perioda," in *Istoriia Rosii v XIX v, izd. t-va Granat.* P: volume II, pp. 403–443.

Annenkov, P. *Literaturnye vospominaniia.* P: 1909. Especially the article, "Zamechatelnoe desiatiletie."

Arseniev, N. "Chomjakow und Moehler," in *Die Ostkirche.* 1927, pp. 89–92.

—— *La Sainte Moscou. Tableau de la vie religieuse et intellectuelle russe au XIXe siecle.* Paris: 1948. Originally published in English, in London, in 1940. This popular work includes an outline of the religious and social background of the Slavophiles. Pages 65–79 deal with Ivan Kireevskii, pages 80–90 with Khomiakov.

Baron, P. "Un Theologien laic orthodoxe russe au XIXe siecle: Alexis Stepanovitch Khomiakov," in *Orientalia Christiana Analecta.* No. 127. Rome: 1940. The best Catholic answer to Khomiakov. Baron interpreted Khomiakov's charge that Catholicism represented rationalism to mean that Khomiakov had to argue against reason and logic whenever he differed from the Roman Catholic teaching.

Belinskii, V. *Sobranie sochinenii.* Edited by Noskov. P: 1913. In particular, the article, "Vzgliad na russkuiu literaturu 1846 goda."

Berdiaev, N. *A. S. Khomiakov.* M: 1912.

—— *Dostoevskii.* Prague: 1923.

—— "Khomiakov i sviashch. P. A. Florenskii," in *Russkaia Mysl.* February, 1917, pp. 72–81.

—— *Leontiev.* Paris: 1926.

—— *The Origin of Russian Communism.* London: 1937.

—— *The Russian Idea.* London: 1947.

Berdiaev's studies in philosophy which do not mention the Slavophiles and which are not listed here are nevertheless of interest because of Berdiaev's relation to Khomiakov and Slavophile thought in general.

Bestuzhev-Riumin, K. "Slavianofilskoe uchenie i ego sudby v russkoi literature," in *Otechestvennye Zapiski.* February, 1862, pp. 679–719; March, 1862, pp. 26–58; May, 1862, pp. 1–23. Verbose and confused, but interesting as an attempt to combine admiration and criticism of the Slavophiles.

Bogucharskii, V. *Aktivnoe narodnichestvo semidesiatykh godov*. M: 1912.

Bolshakoff, S. *The Doctrine of the Unity of the Church in the Works of Khomyakov and Moehler*. London: 1946.

Brianchaninov, A. *Ideological Foundations of Russian Slavonism*. London: 1916. A political pamphlet.

Brodskii, L. *Rannie slavianofily*. M: 1910. Popular, interesting, and able, but tends to make the Slavophiles too liberal.

Chaadaev, P. "Pisma k A. S. Khomiakovu," in *Vestnik Evropy*. Year VI. 1871, pp. 340–342.

—— *Sochineniia i pisma*. Edited by M. Gershenzon, two volumes. M: 1913.

Chernyshevskii, N. *Ocherki gogolevskogo perioda*. Second edition. P: 1893. Chapter III deals with the Slavophiles.

Chizhevskii, D. *Gegel v Rossii*. Paris: 1939. The original version was in German: *Hegel in Russland*, Prague: 1934.

Congar, M. "La pensée de Moehler et l'ecclesiologie orthodox," in *Irenicon*. July, 1935. Very brief.

Dmitriev-Mamonov, E. "Nauka i predanie," in *Otechestvennye Zapiski*. 1875. No. 8, pp. 245–265.

—— "Slavianofily," in *Russkii Arkhiv*. 1873. No. 12. Columns 2488–2508.

Dorn, N. *Kireevskii, Opyt charakteristiki ucheniia i lichnosti*. Paris: 1938.

Dovnar-Zapolskii, M. *Idealy dekabristov*. M: 1907.

*Ern, V. *Vremia slavianofilstvuet*. Ern was one of the most noted "neo-Slavophiles" as evidenced by his various works, but I could not find this one article dealing directly with Slavophilism.

Every, E. "Khomiakoff and the Encyclical of the Eastern Patriarchs in 1848," in *Sobornost*. Series 3, No. 3. Summer, 1948, pp. 102–104.

Fischel, A. *Der Panslavismus bis zum Weltkrieg*. Stuttgart: 1919.

Florenskii, P. *Okolo Khomiakova*. M: 1916. Also published in *Bogoslovskii Vestnik*. 1916, Nos. 7 and 8. The appendices include the genealogical table showing the relationship of the Slavophile families and biographical material about Khomiakov.

Florovskii, G. *Puti russkogo bogosloviia*, Paris: 1937. One of the most important and thorough studies in the field of Russian intellectual history. Much broader than the title might suggest. The discussion of the literature of the subject is especially valuable.

Fonvizin, D. *Pervoe polnoe sobranie sochinenii*. P–M: 1888.

Gershenzon, M. *Istoricheskie zapiski*. Berlin: 1923. (First published in M: 1909). Four essays, one each on Ivan Kireevskii, Petr Kireevskii, Samarin, and Gogol. Several other books by Gershenzon deal in a stimulating manner with the same period.

Giliarov-Platonov, N. *Voprosy very i tserkvi. Sbornik statei 1868–1886*. Volume II. M: 1900. In particular the following articles: "O bogoslovskikh sochineniiakh Khomiakova," pp. 206–208; "Bogoslovskie sochineniia Khomiakova," pp. 209–213. Giliarov-Platonov stood very close to Khomiakov and the Slavophiles and gave a very high evaluation of Khomiakov's theology.

*Gorskii, A. "Zamechaniia. . .," in *Bogoslovskii Vestnik*. November, 1900. A strong criticism of Khomiakov's theology.

Gradovskii, A. *Natsionalnyi vopros v istorii i v literature*. P: 1873. Pages 217–309 provide an appreciative analysis of Slavophilism from the nationalist standpoint.

Granovskii, T. *Sobranie sochinenii*. M: 1892. Granovskii's polemic against Khomiakov was published in Kh., vol. III as follows: *Pismo iz Moskvy T. N. Granovskogo*, pp. 140–143; *Otvet Granovskogo Khomiakovu*, pp. 152–156.

Gratieux, A. *A. Khomiakov et le Mouvement Slavophile*, volume I: *Les hommes*; volume II: *Les doctrines*. Paris: 1939. One of the best books written on the Slavophiles. The point of view is that of an admirer, although a Roman Catholic one.

Herzen, A. I used mostly the ten-volume edition of Herzen's *Works* published in Geneva in 1875–1880. Whenever the Lemke edition was used (twenty-two volumes, P: 1919–1925), this was specified in the footnotes.

Hilferding, A. *Predislovie*. Hilferding's introduction to the first edition of Khomiakov's *History*. In Kh., vol. V, pp. XI–XXIII. A first-hand account of the composition of the work.

Iakovenko, B. *Geschichte des Hegelianismus in Russland*. Prague: 1938. There is a chapter on the Slavophiles, a special chapter on Konstantin Aksakov, and a chapter on such thinkers as A. Popov, Chizhov, Giliarov-Platonov, and Grigoriev, who were closely associated with the Slavophiles.

Iazykov, D. "Literaturnaia deiatelnost I. S. Aksakova," in *Istoricheskii Vestnik*. Volume XXIV. April, 1886, pp. 134–139.

Ivantsov-Platonov, A. "Neskolko slov o bogosloyskikh sochineniiakh A. S. Khomiakova," in *Pravoslavnoe Obozrenie*. 1869. The first half year, pp. 97–119. A panegyric of Khomiakov's theology occasioned by the appearance of the first edition of Khomiakov's collected theological writings.

Ivantsov-Platonov, A. *Predislovie.* An introduction to Samarin's theological works. In S., vol. V, pp. VII–XXXIV. An important essay.

* Kapustin, K *voprosu ob ekonomicheskoi storone slavianofilskogo ucheniia.* Mentioned only in Koliupanov, *op. cit.*, volume I, book II, pp. 167–168.

Karamzin, N. *Istoriia gosudarstva rossiiskogo.* Twelve volumes. Sixth edition. Published by A. Smirdin. P: 1851–1853 (in six books). *Primechaniia k Istorii gosudarstva rossiiskogo.* Twelve volumes. Published by A. Smirdin. P: 1852, etc. (in four books).

—— "O drevnei i novoi Rusi v ee politicheskom i grazhdanskom otnosheniiakh," in *Russkii Arkhiv.* Year VIII. 1871. Columns 2225–2350.

Katkov, M. "Vopros o narodnosti v nauke," in *Russkii Vestnik.* June, 1856. Book II, pp. 312–319. A penetrating criticism of Samarin's article *O narodnom obrazovanii.*

Kavelin, K. *Sochineniia.* Four volumes. P: 1897–1900. Volume II: obituaries of Petr Kireevskii (columns 1219–1222), and of Samarin (columns 1228–1233). Volume III: *Zadachi psikhologii: soobrazheniia o metodakh i programme psikhologicheskikh issledovanii,* and the discussion of it including the debate with Samarin (columns 375–874); *Avdotia Petrovna Elagina* (columns 1115–1132), an interesting biographical and character sketch of the mother of the Kireevskiis.

* Khomiakov, D. *Samoderzhavie.* Fourth edition, Kharkov: 1907.

* —— *Pravoslavie.* M: 1907.

* —— *Narodnost.* Kharkov: 1908. Only the first of these three booklets is generally known. All three are listed in Gratieux, *op. cit.*, volume I, p. XXIX. Dimitrii Khomiakov was a son of the famous Slavophile, and proved himself to be a faithful follower of the Slavophile ideals.

—— *O zamechaniiakh A. V. Gorskogo na bogoslovskie sochineniia A. S. Khomiakova.* In Kh., vol. II, pp. 515–540.

—— "Po povodu istoricheskikh oshibok otkrytykh g. Solovievym v bogoslovskikh sochineniiakh Khomiakova," in *Pravoslavnoe Obozrenie.* 1888. The first six months, pp. 611–615.

Khomiakov, F. "Pisma k A. S. Khomiakovu," in *Russkii Arkhiv.* 1884. Book III, pp. 221–225. Concerning the Decembrist rebellion and various literary topics. Fedor Khomiakov, who died young, was an elder brother of the Slavophile.

Kireev, A. *Kratkoe izlozhenie slavianofilskogo ucheniia.* P: 1896.

—— *Slavianofilstvo i natsionalism.* P: 1890. A booklet written in defense of the Slavophiles against Vladimir Soloviev.

*Kizewetter, A. "Zapiski po istorii politicheskikh idei v Rossii. Slaviano-filstvo i anarkhism," in *Traveaux scientifiques de l'Universite populaire russe de Prague*. Volume I. Prague: 1928.

Kniazev, G. "Kireevskii, Ivan Vasilievich," in *Russkii biograficheskii slovar*. Volume VIII, P: 1897, pp. 672–695. This dictionary provides excellent outlines of the lives and work of the leading Slavophiles.

—— "Kireevskii, Petr Vasilievich," in the same volume, pp. 695–700.

Koialovich, M. *Istoriia russkogo samosoznaniia*. P: 1884. The Slavophiles form the subject of Chapter XIV. Written from the standpoint of an admirer, and rather badly.

Koliupanov, N. "Ocherk filosofskoi sistemy slavianofilov," in *Russkoe Obozrenie*. 1894. Volume XXVIII, pp. 6–22, 489–504; Volume XXIX, pp. 85–104, 547–565; Volume XXX, pp. 48–71. A detailed study.

—— *Biografiia A. I. Kosheleva*. Two volumes, M: 1889–1892. (The first volume is divided into two books). Most disorganized, and pays little attention to Koshelev, but contains a wealth of valuable information on various aspects of Russian intellectual life and culture in the second half of the eighteenth and the first half of the nineteenth centuries. Valuable appendices, especially appendix VIII, which consists of the correspondence between Koshelev and the leading Slavophiles.

Koshelev, A. "Moi vospominaniia ob A. S. Khomiakove," in *Russkii Arkhiv*. 1897. Book II, pp. 265–276.

——*Zapiski Aleksandra Ivanovicha Kosheleva (1812–1883 gody)*. Edited by O. Kosheleva, Berlin: 1884. One of the most important works for the study of Slavophilism. Seven appendices contain Koshelev's views on various subjects. Koshelev's numerous writings on the social, economic, and political problems of the day are also important because Koshelev belonged to the Slavophile circle.

Kostomarov, N. *O znachenii kriticheskikh trudov K. Aksakova po russkoi istorii*. P: 1861. An important evaluation.

Kotliarevskii, N. "A. S. Khomiakov, kak poet," in *Russkaia Mysl*. 1910, No. 10.

Kovalevskii, M. "Borba nemetskogo vliianiia s frantsuzskim v kontse XVIII i v pervoi polovine XIX stoletiia," in *Vestnik Evropy*. October, 1915, pp. 123–163.

—— "Filosofskoe ponimanie sudeb russkogo proshlogo mysliteliami i pisateliami 30kh i 40 kh godov," in *Vestnik Evropy*. December, 1915, pp. 163–201. The article deals principally with Chaadaev.

—— "Rannie revniteli filosofii Shellinga v Rossii, Chaadaev i Ivan Kireevskii," in *Russkaia Mysl*. 1916, no. 12.

—— "Shellingianstvo i gegelianstvo v Rossii," in *Vestnik Evropy*. November, 1915, pp. 133–170.

Koyré, A. "La jeunesse d'Ivan Kireevski," in *Le Monde Slave*. Year V. February, 1928, pp. 213–238.

—— *La philosophie et le problème national en Russie au début du XIX siècle*. Paris: 1929. The best study of the Russian intellectual life in the period just preceding that of the Slavophiles.

—— "Russia's Place in the World. Peter Chaadaev and the Slavophiles," in *The Slavonic Review*. Volume V. 1927, pp. 594–608.

Kozmin, N. *Ocherki po istorii russkogo romantisma. (N.A. Polevoi, kak vyrazitel literaturnykh napravlenii sovremennoi emu epokhi)*. P: 1903. Some valuable material on Western romantic, especially French romantic influences in Russia. Pages 235–237 give the evaluations of Khomiakov's *Ermak* and *Dimitrii Samozvanets* in *Moskovskii Telegraf*.

Lanz, H. "The Philosophy of Ivan Kireyevsky," in *The Slavonic Review*. Volume IV. 1925–1926, pp. 594–604.

*Laskeev, P. "Dva proekta pravoslavno-khristianskoi filosofii," in *Khristianskoe Chtenie*. May, 1898. About Karpov and Ivan Kireevskii.

Lavrov, P. "Filosofiia istorii slavian," in *Otechestvennye Zapiski*, 1870, no. 6, pp. 347–420; no. 7, pp. 65–126.

*Lebedev, M. *Vzaimnoe otnoshenie Tserkvi i gosudarstva po vozzreniiu slavianofilov*. Kazan: 1907.

Lemke, M. *Nikolaevskie zhandarmy i literatura 1826–1855 gg*. P: 1908. Pages 67–78 are concerned with the closing down of Ivan Kireevskii's *Evropeets* in 1832; pages 214–220 with the censorship difficulties of the Slavophiles in 1852–1854.

Liaskovskii, V. *Aleksei Stepanovich Khomiakov. Ego biografiia i uchenie*. M: 1897. A brief popular biography written by an admirer. Also a selection from Khomiakov's writings, pp. 67–166.

—— *Bratia Kireevskie, zhizn i trudy ikh*. P: 1899. Similar biographies of the Kireevskiis.

*Linitskii, P. "Po povodu zashchity slavianofilov v 'Pravoslavnom Obozrenii'," in *Trudy Kievskoi Dukhovnoi Akademii*. January, 1884.

Loviagin, A. "Khomiakov, Aleksei Stepanovich," in *Russkii biograficheskii slovar*. Volume XXI. P: 1901, pp. 397–411.

*Lushnikov, A. I. V. *Kireevskii, ocherk zhizni i religioznofilosofskogo mirovozzreniia*. Kazan: 1918.

Maksimovich, G. *Uchenie pervykh slavianofilov*. Kiev: 1907. A good brief summary and discussion.

Masaryk, Th. *The Spirit of Russia*. Two volumes. London: 1919.

M-ev, "Zhozef de-Mestr i ego politicheskaia doktrina," in *Russkii Vestnik*. May, 1889, pp. 220–238; June, 1889, pp. 74–95. Mentions de Maistre's influence in Russia, in particular on Ivan Aksakov.

Miliukov, P. *Glavnye techeniia russkoi istoricheskoi mysli.* P: 1913. Pages 320–323 are devoted to Ivan Kireevskii's article "The Nineteenth Century."
—— *Iz istorii russkoi intelligentsii.* P: 1902. Contains a discussion of S. T. Aksakov and the Aksakov family.
—— *Ocherki po istorii russkoi kultury.* Three volumes. Paris: 1930–1937.
—— "Razlozhenie slavianofilstva," in *Voprosy filosofii i psikhologii.* Year IV. May, 1893, pp. 46–96.
—— "Slavianofilstvo," in *Entsiklopedicheskii Slovar.* Volume XXX, 1900, pp. 307–314 (edited by F. Brockhaus and I. Efron).
*Miller, O. "Osnovy ucheniia pervonachalnykh slavianofilov," in *Russkaia Mysl.* January and March, 1880.
—— *Slavianstvo i Evropa.* P: 1877. A collection of Miller's articles for the years 1865–1877. The following are especially relevant to Slavophilism: "Khomiakov – poet slavianstva," pp. 114–130; "Iu. F. Samarin. Opyt kharakteristiki," pp. 131–192.
Mirsky, D. S. *A History of Russian Literature,* New York: 1949. The book contains incisive and very favorable evaluations of the contributions of several Slavophiles to Russian literature.
Moskoff, E. *The Russian Philosopher Chaadayev, His Ideas and His Epoch,* New York: 1937. Emphasizes the connection between Chaadaev's concept of "freedom" and that of the Slavophiles.

Nifontov, A. *1848 god v Rossii.* M–Leningrad: 1931.
*Nikolskii, A. "Russkaia dukhovno-akademicheskaia filosofiia, kak predshestvennitsa slavianofilstva i universitetskoi filosofii v Rossii," in *Vera i Razum.* 1907.
Nolde, B. *Iurii Samarin i ego vremia.* Paris: 1926. An excellent study of Samarin.

Odoevskii, V. *Russkie nochi.* Edited by Tsvetaev. M: 1913.
"Pamiati Iu. F. Samarina," in *Pravoslavnoe Obozrenie.* 1876. No. 4, pp. 673–729. A collection of appreciations, obituary notices, and of extracts from various speeches and articles brought about by Samarin's death.
Panov, N. "Slavianofilstvo, kak filosofskoe uchenie," in *Zhurnal Ministerstva Narodnogo Prosveshcheniia.* 1880. Book II, pp. 1–67.
Piper, L. *Mirovozzrenie Gertsena,* Leningrad: 1935.
Pokrovskii, M. *Brief History of Russia.* Volume I. London: 1933.
Pypin, A. *Belinskii, Ego zhizn i perepiska.* P: 1876.
—— *Kharakteristiki literaturnykh mnenii ot 20ykh do 50ykh godov.* P: 1890.

BIBLIOGRAPHY 229

—— "Konstantin Aksakov," in *Vestnik Evropy.* Year XIX. March, 1884, pp. 145–177; April, 1884, pp. 589–618. Valuable bibliographical material, in particular in the notes to pages 146 and 151.
—— *Panslavism v proshlom i nastoiashchem.* P: 1913.
—— *Russkoe masonstvo XVIII i pervoi chetverti XIX v.* Edited by G. Vernadsky. P: 1916.

Quenet, C. *Tchaadaev et les Lettres Philosophiques.* Paris: 1931. An important detailed study of Chaadaev and of the Russian intellectual life at the time of Chaadaev, but the treatment of the Slavophiles is confused and unsatisfactory.
—— *Tchaadaev et les Lettres Philosophiques. Sources et recherches.* Paris: 1931. The bibliography to the foregoing.

Radlov, E. *Ocherk istorii russkoi filosofii.* Second edition. P: 1920. The Slavophiles are discussed on pp. 30–42.
Riasanovsky, V. *Obzor russkoi kultury. Istoricheskii ocherk.* New York: 1947–48. The Slavophiles are discussed in Part II, issue I, pp. 310–322.
Rozanov, V. "Pamiati A. S. Khomiakova (loe maia 1804 g.-loe maia 1904 g.)," in *Novyi Put.* Year II. June, 1904, pp. 1–16.
—— "Zametki o vazhneishikh techeniiakh russkoi filosofskoi mysli v sviazi s nashei perevodnoi literaturoi po filosofii," in *Voprosy Filosofii i Psikhologii,* 1890. Year I. No. 3, pp. 1–36. Rozanov's list of translations of Western philosophers into Russian is incomplete.
Rubinstein, N. "Istoricheskaia teoriia slavianofilov i ee klassovye korni," in *Trudy Instituta Krasnoi Professury. Russkaia istoricheskaia literatura v klassovom osveshchenii. Sbornik statei.* Edited by M. Pokrovskii. M: 1927. Volume I, pp. 53–118.
"Russkii bogoslov iz svetskikh liudei sorokovykh godov," in *Pravoslavnoe Obozrenie.* 1880. No. 5, pp. 42–98. A very favorable appreciation of Samarin as a theologian occasioned by the appearance of the fifth volume of Samarin's *Works.* The article is composed mostly of extracts from A. Ivantsov-Platonov's and D. Samarin's introductions to the volume, and from the volume itself.
Sakulin, P. *Iz istorii russkogo idealisma. Kniaz V. Odoevskii.* M: 1913.
—— "Russkaia literatura do Pushkina," in *Istoriia Rossii v XIX v, izd. t-va Granat.* P: Volume II, pp. 379–402.
—— "Russkaia literatura vo vtoroi chetverti veka," pp. 443–508 of the same volume as the foregoing. The essay includes a discussion of Official Nationality in literature (pp. 444–453), of the influence of Western ideologies on the Russian literature and thought of the thirties (pp. 453–460), of the Slavophiles (pp. 460–472), of the Westernizers and the early Russian socialism (pp. 473–489), and

a section on "Social Motives in the Artistic Literature of the For-ties," which devotes much space to the Slavophiles (pp. 489–508).

Samarin, D. Dimitrii Samarin, a brother of the Slavophile, edited Vol-umes I, II, III, V, VI, VII, VIII, IX and X of Iu. Samarin's Works, and contributed long and valuable introductions to several of these volumes.

—— "Samarin, Iurii Fedorovich," in *Russkii biograficheskii slovar.* P: 1904, volume XVIII, pp. 133–146.

°—— *Pobornik vselenskoi pravdy.* P: 1890. A booklet in defense of the Slavophiles against Vladimir Soloviev. Also published in *Novoe Vremia.* 1890, nos. 5015, 5021, and 5029.

°Shakhovski, N. "N. P. Giliarov-Platonov i Khomiakov," in *Russkoe Obozrenie.* October, 1895.

Schelting, A. *Russland und Europa im Russischen Geschichtsdenken.* Bern: 1948. The author is primarily concerned with Chaadaev, but he also discusses the Slavophiles, as well as numerous other Russian thinkers. The interpretation of Russian thought is interest-ing, but highly questionable, and in particular it suffers from the fact that the author does not pay sufficient attention to the Euro-pean context of Russian intellectual development, and tends to regard nationalism and exclusiveness, whether those of the Slavo-philes or those of various other Russian thinkers, as a peculiarly Russian perversion.

Schenrok, V. "S. T. Aksakov i ego semia," in *Zhurnal Ministerstva Narodnogo Prosveshcheniia.* 1904, nos. 10–12.

Schmurlo, E. "From Krizanic to the Slavophiles," in *The Slavonic Re-view.* 1927–1928, volume VI, pp. 321–335. The author concludes that there was no connection between Krizanic and the early Pan-Slav feeling in Russia on the one hand and the Slavophiles on the other.

Schulze, B. "A. S. Chomjakow und das Halb-jahrtausend Jubilaeum des Einigungskonzils von Florenz," in *Orientalia Christiana Periodica.* Volume IV. 1938. Nos. 3–4, pp. 473–496. One of the more impor-tant Catholic discussions of Khomiakov.

Sechkarev, W. *Schellings Einfluss in der russischen Literatur der 20er und 30er Jahre des XIX Jahrhunderts.* Berlin: 1939. The only monograph on Schelling's influence in Russia.

Semevskii, V. *Krestianskii vopros v Rossii.* P: 1888. Especially Chapter XIII, "Otnoshenie slavianofilov k krestianskomu voprosu." Semev-skii is in general hostile to the Slavophiles.

—— *Politicheskie i obshchestvennye idei dekabristov.* P: 1909.

°Shcheglov, B. *Rannie slavianofily, kak religioznye mysliteli i publit-sisty. Chast Iaia. K voprosu o sushchnosti ucheniia Khomiakova.* Kazan: 1917.

Shpet, G. *Ocherk razvitiia russkoi filosofii.* P: 1922. Generally regarded as the best book on the subject.

Sidonskii, O. "Rech pri otpevanii Iv. V. Kireevskogo," in *Russkaia Beseda.* 1856. Book II, pp. 1–4.

Simmons, E. *English Literature and Culture in Russia (1553–1840).* Cambridge, Mass.: 1935. Discusses the influence of the English romanticists in Russia; special chapters are devoted to Walter Scott and to Byron.

Skobtsova, E. A. *Khomiakov.* Paris: 1929. A very good brief, popular account of Khomiakov's teaching from the standpoint of an Orthodox admirer, with a fine selection of quotations from Khomiakov.

Sladkevich, N. "K voprosu o polemike N. G. Chernyshevskogo so slavianofilskoi publitsistikoi," in *Voprosy Istorii.* No. 6, June, 1948, pp. 71–79.

*Smirnov, E. "Slavianofily i ikh uchenie v otnoshenii k bogoslovskoi nauke," in *Strannik.* 1877, nos. 2 and 3.

*Smirnov, F. "Bogoslovskoe uchenie slavianofilov," in *Pravoslavnoe Obozrenie.* October, 1883.

—— "Vopros o protestanstve v vozzreniiakh Khomiakova," in *Pravoslavnoe Obozrenie.* March, 1884, pp. 533–552. An ardent defense of Khomiakov's theology against Linitskii's accusation of Protestant tendencies.

Smirnov, V. *Aksakovy, ikh zhisn i literaturnaia deiatelnost.* P: 1895. Extremely hostile to the Slavophiles, sketchy, and superficial, but very intelligent and interesting. One of the first to draw attention to the psychological content and to the class nature of the Slavophile ideology.

*Smolich, I. "I. V. Kireevskii. Leben und Weltanschauung," in *Jahrbücher für Kultur und Geschichte der Slaven.* 1933. No. 9.

Soloviev, S. *Istoriia otnoshenii mezhdu russkimi kniaziami Riurikova doma.* M: 1847.

—— *Istoriia Rossii s drevneishikh vremen.* Third edition. P: 1911.

—— "Schloetzer i anti-istoricheskoe napravlenie," in *Russkii Vestnik.* 1857. Volume VIII, pp. 431–480.

—— "Moi zapiski dlia detei moikh, a esli mozhno, i dlia drugikh," in *Vestnik Evropy.* April, May, June, 1907 (nos. 4, 5, 6). Also published separately. Soloviev's monumental history of Russia and his study of the princes of the house of Riurik formed the main target of the Slavophile historical criticism. Soloviev's article about the "antihistorical" school was aimed at the Slavophiles, and his *Memoirs* describe the Slavophiles, and in particular Khomiakov.

Soloviev, V. *Sobranie Sochinenii. Tom piatyi.* Edited by E. Radlov. P: 1901, etc. Soloviev's polemic against the Slavophiles and other Russian nationalists was published in a collected form in the fifth

volume of his works, but because of Soloviev's connection with the
Slavophiles, as well as of his fundamental criticism of that movement, all Soloviev's *Works* were important for the purpose of this
study.

Steppun, F. "Nemetskii romantism i russkoe slavianofilstvo," in *Russkaia Mysl.* March, 1910, pp. 65–91. The best discussion of that
subject.

°——— "Proshloe i budushchee slavianofilstva," in *Severnye Zapiski.* November, 1913.

Stojanovic, J. "The First Slavophiles: Khomyakov and Kireyevsky," in
The Slavonic Review. Volume VI. March, 1928, pp. 561–578.
Written from the standpoint of an admirer, and poorly.

Strakhovskii, L. *L'Empereur Nicholas Ier et l'Esprit national russe.*
Louvain: 1928.

Struve, P. "S. P. Shevyrev i zapadnye vnusheniia i istochniki teorii-
aforizma o 'gnilom' ili 'gniiushchem' Zapade," in *Zapiski Russkogo
Nauchnogo Instituta v Belgrade.* Belgrade: 1940. The analysis of
Shevyrev's attitude towards the West throws much light on some
Western sources of the Russian criticism of the West.

Sukhomlinov, M. "I. S. Aksakov v sorokovykh godakh," in *Istoricheskii
Vestnik.* Year IX. February, 1888, pp. 324–348. Contains valuable
source material on Ivan Aksakov's arrest in 1849.

Sumner, B. H. *Russia and the Balkans, 1870–1880.* Oxford: 1937, pp.
56–80 provide a good account of the Pan-Slavs.

Taube, M. *Poznanievedenie sobornogo vostochnogo prosveshcheniia po
liubomudriiu slavianofilstva.* P: 1912.

°Troitskii, V. "A. S. Khomiakov i drevne-tserkovnye polemisty," in
Vera i Razum, 1911. No. 18, pp. 731–748.

Trubachev, S. "Aksakov, Ivan Sergeevich," in *Russkii bibliograficheskii
slovar.* P: 1896, volume I, pp. 97–100.

——— "Aksakov, Konstantin Sergeevich," in the same volume, pp.
100–103.

Trubetskoi, S. "Razocharovannyi slavianofil," in *Vestnik Evropy.* No. 10.
October, 1892, pp. 772–810. About Leontiev.

Turgenev, I. "Iz perepiski I. S. Turgeneva s semei Aksakovykh," in
Vestnik Evropy. February, 1894, pp. 469–499. Mostly Turgenev's
letters to S. T. Aksakov.

°Ursin, M. (Zdekhovskii, M.), *Ocherki iz psikhologii slavianskogo
plemeni.* P: 1887. Contains a comparison between the Slavophiles
and the proponents of Polish Messiahship. Discussed in Koliupanov, *op. cit.,* volume I, book I, p. 581.

Ustrialov, N. "Natsionalnaia problema u pervykh slavianofilov," in
Russkaia Mysl. October, 1916, pp. 1–22.

—— "Politicheskaia doktrina slavianofilstva (Ideia samoderzhaviia v slavianofilskoi postanovke)," in *Izvestiia Iuridischeskogo Fakulteta* (Harbin). Year I, 1925, pp. 47–74.

V.E.K., "Chto umerlo? Slavianofilstvo ili zapadnichestvo?" in *Russkoe Obozrenie*. Year VIII. February, 1897, pp. 617–645. Slavophilism admiringly interpreted by an extreme nationalist.

*Vasiliev, A. *Khomiakov i slavianskoe delo*. P: 1877. Two additional articles by Vasiliev are listed in Gratieux's bibliography.

Veselovskii, A. *Zapadnoe vliianie v novoi russkoi literature*. Fifth edition. M: 1916.

Vengerov, S. *Ocherki po istorii russkoi literatury*. P: 1907. Includes a valuable study of *Peredovoi boets slavianofilstva* (Konstantin Aksakov), pp. 379–492.

Vetrinskii, T. (Cheshikhin, V.), *V sorokovykh godakh. Istoriko-literaturnye ocherki i kharakteristiki*. M: 1899. Contains an essay on Ivan Aksakov and Nikitenko, taken as two representative Russian intellectuals, and this essay provides valuable information on the relationship between Ivan Aksakov and Belinskii.

Vigel, F. "Pismo k A. S. Khomiakovu," in *Russkii Arkhiv*. 1884. Book III, pp. 225–228.

Vinogradov, P. *I. V. Kireevskii i nachalo moskovskogo slavianofilstva*. In *Voprosy Filosofii i Psikhologii*. 1892, book II, pp. 98–126. A conventional interpretation of the Herzen-Pypin-Miliukov school.

Vinogradov, V. "Russkaia nauka o russkom literaturnom iazyke," in *Uchenye Zapiski*. Volume III, Book I. M: 1946, pp. 22–147.

Vladimirov, L. *Aleksei Stepanovich Khomiakov i ego etiko-sotsialnoe uchenie*. M: 1904. Valuable as the only special study of Khomiakov's views on law and justice, but poorly written.

Volzhskii, A. "Sviataia Rus i russkoe prizvanie," in *Voina i Kultura*. M: 1915.

Zamotin, I. *Russkii romantism dvadtsatykh godov*. Warsaw: 1903–1907. Book I tells in detail about the struggle between "the classicists" and "the romanticists" in Russian literature.

Zavitnevich, V. *Aleksei Stepanovich Khomiakov. Tom pervyi. Kniga I. Molodye gody, obshchestvennaia i nauchnoistoricheskaia deiatelnost Khomiakova. Kniga II. Trudy Khomiakova v oblasti bogosloviia*. Kiev: 1902. A monumental study of some fifteen hundred pages of Khomiakov and the Slavophiles. The point of view is that of an Orthodox and strongly nationalist admirer. The book contains a wealth of factual data, and is indispensable to the student of Slavophilism.

—— "Znachenie pervykh slavianofilov v dele uiasneniia idei narodnosti i samobytnosti," in *Trudy Kievskoi Dukhovnoi Akademii*. 1891.

234   BIBLIOGRAPHY

No. 11. Also published as a separate booklet in Kiev in 1891. Danilevskii considered as a true Slavophile.

Zenkovskii, V. *Istoriia russkoi filosofii.* Paris: 1948. Volume I, pp. 188–244 are devoted to the Slavophile thinkers and deal successively with Khomiakov (pp. 188–213), Ivan Kireevskii (pp. 215–235), Samarin (pp. 235–242), and Konstantin Aksakov (pp. 242–244). Volume 11, Paris: 1950. The two volumes constitute a very important and complete history of Russian philosophy.

—— *Russkie mysliteli i Evropa.* Paris: 1929.

—— "The Slavophil Idea Restated," in *The Slavonic Review.* 1927–1928, volume VI, pp. 302–310. Berdiaev and Zenkovskii did more than anybody else to reinterpret Slavophilism and affirm its value in terms of the twentieth-century historical and intellectual development.

Zernov, N. *Three Russian Prophets. Khomiakov. Dostoevsky. Soloviev.* London: 1944. Popular and interesting.

—— *Introduction* to Khomiakov, *The Church Is One.* London: 1948, pp. 5–13.

INDEX

HARVARD HISTORICAL STUDIES

4. *Frederick William Dallinger.* Nominations for Elective Office in the United States. 1903.
12. *Clyde Augustus Duniway.* The Development of Freedom of the Press in Massachusetts. 1906.
13. *William Bennett Munro.* The Seignorial System in Canada: A Study in French Colonial Policy. 1907.
14. *William Alfred Morris.* The Frankpledge System. 1910.
15. *Everett Kimball.* The Public Life of Joseph Dudley: A Study of the Colonial Policy of the Stuarts in New England, 1660–1715. 1911.
16. *Robert Matteson Johnston.* Mémoire de Marie Caroline, Reine de Naples, Intitulé de la Révolution du Royaume de Sicile, par un Témoin Oculaire, Publié pour la premiere fois, avec Introduction, Notes critiques, et deux Facsimiles. 1912.
17. *Edward Channing.* The Barrington-Bernard Correspondence. 1912.
18. *Albert Howe Lybyer.* The Government of the Ottoman Empire in the Time of Suleiman the Magnificent. 1913.
19. *Solon Justus Buck.* The Granger Movement in the United States: A Study of Agricultural Organization and Its Political, Economic, and Social Manifestations, 1870–1880. 1913.
20. *Morley de Wolf Hemmeon.* Burgage Tenure in Mediaeval England. 1914.
21. *Charles Howard McIlwain.* Wraxall's Abridgment of the New York Indian Records, 1678–1751. 1915.

22. *Howard Levi Gray.* English Field Systems. 1915.
23. *Robert Howard Lord.* The Second Partition of Poland: A Study in Diplomatic History. 1915.
24. *Charles Homer Haskins.* Norman Institutions. 1918.
25. *Charles Wendell David.* Robert Curthose, Duke of Normandy. 1920.
26. *Joseph Vincent Fuller.* Bismarck's Diplomacy at its Zenith. 1922.
27. *Charles Homer Haskins.* Studies in the History of Mediaeval Science. Second edition, 1927.
28. *Robert Howard Lord.* Origins of the War of 1870. 1924.
29. *Dexter Perkins.* The Monroe Doctrine, 1823–1826. 1927.
30. *William Leonard Langer.* The Franco-Russian Alliance, 1890–1894. 1929.
31. *Frederick Merk.* Fur Trade and Empire: George Simpson's Journal, 1824–1825, together with Accompanying Documents. 1932.
32. *Lawrence D. Steefel.* The Schleswig-Holstein Question. 1932.
33. *Lewis George Vander Velde.* The Presbyterian Churches and the Federal Union, 1861–1869. 1932.
34. *Howard Levi Gray.* The Influence of the Commons on Early Legislation. 1932.
35. *Donald Cope McKay.* The National Workshops: A Study in the French Revolution of 1848. 1933.
36. *Chester Wells Clark.* Franz Joseph and Bismarck before 1866. 1934.

37. *Roland Dennis Hussey.* The Caracas Company, 1728–1784: A Study in the History of Spanish Monopolistic Trade. 1934.
38. *Dwight Erwin Lee.* Great Britain and the Cyprus Convention Policy of 1878. 1934.
39. *Paul Rice Doolin.* The Fronde. 1935.
40. *Arthur McCandless Wilson.* French Foreign Policy during the Administration of Cardinal Fleury, 1726–1743. 1936.
41. *Harold Charles Deutsch.* The Genesis of Napoleonic Imperialism. 1938.
42. *Ernst Christian Helmreich.* The Diplomacy of the Balkan Wars, 1912–1913. 1938.
43. *Albert Henry Imlah.* Lord Ellenborough: A Biography of Edward Law, Earl of Ellenborough, Governor-General of India. 1939.
44. *Vincent Mary Scramuzza.* The Emperor Claudius. 1940.
45. *Richard William Leopold.* Robert Dale Owen. 1940.
46. *Gerald Sandford Graham.* Sea Power and British North America, 1773–1820. 1941.
47. *William Farr Church.* Constitutional Thought in Sixteenth-Century France. 1941.
48. *Jack H. Hexter.* The Reign of King Pym. 1941.
49. *George Hoover Rupp.* A Wavering Friendship: Russia and Austria, 1876–1878. 1941.
50. *Oscar Handlin.* Boston's Immigrants, 1790–1865. 1941.
51. *Frank Edgar Bailey.* British Policy and the Turkish Reform Movement. 1942.
52. *John Black Sirich.* The Revolutionary Committees in the Departments of France. 1943.
53. *Henry Frederick Schwarz.* The Imperial Privy Council in the Seventeenth Century. 1943.
54. *Aaron Ignatius Abell.* Urban Impact on American Protestantism. 1943.
55. *Holden Furber.* John Company at Work. 1948.
56. *Walter Howe.* The Mining Guild of New Spain and Its Tribunal General. 1949.
57. *John Howes Gleason.* The Genesis of Russophobia in Great Britain. 1950.
58. *Charles Coulston Gillispie.* Genesis and Geology. 1951.
59. *Richard Humphrey.* Georges Sorel: Prophet Without Honor. 1951.